RALLY YEARBOOK
1998–99

© 1998, Chronosports Editeur, Jordils Park, Chemin des Jordils 40, CH-1025 St-Sulpice, Switzerland.

This is a Dempsey Parr Book

Dempsey Parr
13 Whiteladies Road,
Clifton,
Bristol BS8 1PB,
United Kingdom
ISBN 1-84084-389-6
Printed in France

RALLY YEARBOOK
1998–99

Pictures
Pascal Huit

Written by
Stefan L'Hermitte
Philippe Joubin

Translated by
Eric Silbermann

Statistics and results
Séverine Huit

DP
DEMPSEY
PARR

THANKS

The authors would like to thank everyone who has helped them in the production of this book. A special thanks to Tiina Lehmonen, the press offices at Ford, Mitsubishi, Peugeot, Seat, Subaru and Toyota, to Monique Demont of Castrol France, Chantal Rodon and Pierre Sodano of the FIA, to Ayme Chatard and Andy Pope of Michelin, Bertil Grandet of Peugeot, Jean-Pierre Colly at Canon, Guy Dassonville and all the Pro Canon service team at the La Comete (Paris) laboratories and Picto (Lyon,) as well as Richard Studient of Photo Lyon Optique. Thanks also to Tommi Makinen for agreeing to write the preface to this work.

FOREWORD

Hyvä lukija,

Kausai 1988 oli minulle vaikeampi kuin kaksi edellista mestaruuskauttani.

Välillä tulin jo ajatelleeski, ettei tästä mitään tule. Kaikki näytti ennen kilpailuja hyvältä, mutta liian usein jäimme seisomaan reitin varelle joko jonki pienen technisen tai oman virheen vuoksi.

Kotokilpailussa Jyväskylässä onni vihdoin kääntyi, mutta Sanremo oli varsinainen taitekohta. Saimme auton toimimaan juuri niin kuin halusimme, ja voitto entoi uuta voimaa mestaruunden tavoitteluun.

Myös onnetar voi puuttua peliin täysin odottamatta; sen osoittivitat kauden lopussa Ison Britannian rallin uskomattomat vaiheet, jotka tulevat jäämään historiaan. Täytyy kuitenkin tunnustaa, että olisin mieluummin voittanut mestaruuteni tailstelemalla siitä loppuun saakka.

Tämän kirjan kautta voitte elää kanssani uudestaan niin alkukauden pettymykset kuin sitäkin makeammat voitot loppuvuodesta.

Kolmas perättäinen mestaruus on upea saavutus minulle henkilökohtaisesti. Se on sitä myös koko Mitsubishin tiimille, joka nyt ensimmäistä kertaa saa samalla juhlia autonvalmistajien maailmanmestaruutta.

Se on sitä varmasti myös suomalaisille, jotka nyt -ensimmäisenä kansana- saivat historiallisen tuplan: rallin ja formula 1 : n maailmanmestaruuden samana vuonna.

Toivottavasti olette mukana reitin varrella myös ensi kaudella !

The 1998 season was harder for me than the two previous ones. There were even a few moments when I almost lost my confidence. Everything seemed perfect before the rallies, but too often we were forced to retire with small mechanical problems or because of my own driving errors.

My luck finally changed in the Rally of Finland, "my rally," which we won for the fifth time. But the real turning point in the season was actually the San Remo. The car worked perfectly and this win gave us some extra strength to tackle the rest of the championship.

Finally, the incredible events of the Rally of Great Britain showed that you must always count on luck. It was a strange way to make it into the history books. Of course, I would rather have fought for the title rather than win the championship in this way.

I invite you to relive the disappointments and the joyful victorious moments of the season, through the pages of "Rally Yearbook."

A third consecutive title is a splendid result for me personally and for all the team who are celebrating their first constructors' world championship. It is also very special for the Finns, who can enjoy this historic double - winning the F1 world championship and the rallying one in the same year.

I hope to meet you somewhere along the road next year.

See you soon,

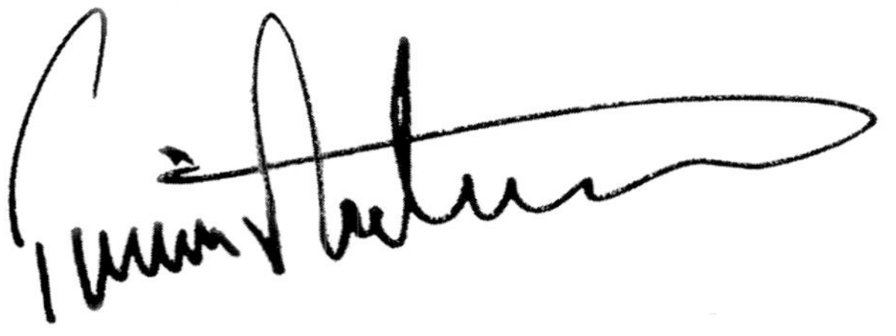

Tommi Makinen

A true motor sport fan, over the course of the years, Pascal Huit is recognised as the rally photography specialist. His photographs are published in several magazines around the world. Agence Presse Sports/L'Equipe is responsible for the distribution of his work. He chose to specialise in this sport a little over 15 years ago, because he liked the atmosphere on rallies and the down to earth nature of the people involved.

Since 1991, he puts his faith in the Canon EOS Pro system, working with EOS-1N bodies which give maximum reliability from the wet conditions in Sweden to the dust of Australia. On the lens front, the auto-focus Ultrasonic telephoto 300 mm f:2.8L and the Ultra wide angle 14 mm f:2.8L are his favourites and they really make the difference. Today, it is the only equipment that allows for rapid and precise set up, even when dealing with cars moving at high speed.

PHOTO VIDEO FRANCE S.A.

102, AVENUE DU GÉNÉRAL DE GAULLE - 92257 LA GARENNE COLOMBES
TÉLÉPHONE : 01 41 30 15 15 - TÉLÉCOPIEUR : 01 41 30 15 05

CONTENTS

ANALYSIS
1998

Tommi Makinen set a new record this year by winning his third consecutive championship. He was crowned, literally in the dying seconds of the season, which also saw Mitsubishi take the constructors' title for the very first time.

The season's strange finale was spookily incongruous. To start with, the sun was shining over Margam Park in Wales, a setting more suitable to contemplative meditation than contemporary motor cars. In the park stands a manor and next to the manor there is an orangery. Oranges growing in Wales? There is no sense to that and there was no sense to the way the championship was tipped on its head. Because it was in sight of the flag of the final stage of the final rally that it was all decided. Thirteen rounds had not been enough, after the fourteenth in Indonesia was scrubbed, when it was wisely decided that rallying in a dictatorship was not a good idea. Can you recall any championship as thrilling as this? Have you witnessed any stranger end than the one this year served up? "Rally is magic!" as Tommi Makinen, Champion Tommi Makinen likes to declare.

And three rounds of applause for the triple crown, which was richly deserved. Makinen did not steal this title. He fought back with panache after notching up some noughts on the points sheet just as surely as he would go on to collect those nice ten point placings. Just as in 1997, rarely would a world champion be as fickle. But fickle does not mean feckless. Makinen's year was a roller-coaster with a big off on the Monte, followed by a win in Sweden; a timing belt let go on the Safari, he went off again in Portugal. Then came wins in Argentina and Finland and yet another two in San Remo and Australia. That is Makinen for you, with an amazing ability to bounce back and to fight his way up from the bottom of the time sheet to the top of the podium over one leg of a rally. It is a skill which has shown that only Carlos Sainz is capable of whipping the crown off his blonde locks. Makinen is also a constantly hard worker, who can really get his team motivated, asking them to work at test after test

after test in order for his car to be perfectly suited to his needs and his small frame. With his record, he could be out on the town, but instead, he is always out on the track testing. Mitsubishi completed around 10,000 kilometres this season and no other team even got close. The Evolution V was a good car straight from the crate, but Cowan, Short and Lindauer made it into a stage crunching winning machine. Mitsubishi has a lot to thank Makinen for. Legend has it that several years ago, Andrew Cowan said to his Japanese bosses: "give me Makinen and I will give you the world title." The Scotsman does not look like a wily old horse trader for nothing. He can sniff out a thoroughbred a mile away, which is how, at the end of 1994, without a drive, Makinen ended up in the team. Four years later and there are three drivers' championships in the bag as well as this first constructors' prize. Richard Burns played his part in this success story which totalled seven wins from thirteen rallies in 1998. So what if Makinen only took the title by two points. Who dares to say that Makinen and Mitsubishi had stolen anything?

Not even Carlos Sainz would dare. Even though he performed magnificently all year, as he has done for the past ten actually. No one has been as consistent as him as he makes the most of his experience. Maybe he is no longer the quickest and is dominated in this area by Makinen, McRae and Auriol. He is certainly the most consistent. All in all he finished eleven rallies and scored points nine times. By comparison, Makinen only finished seven times, while Sainz' two retirements were both caused by mechanical failures. Makinen cannot make that claim. While banging on about the excellence of his Eminence, let us not forget he led the championship for the longest time. Only McRae, on two occasions, after Corsica and the Acropolis and Makinen after Australia of course, ever headed him. The 1998 season was extremely close fought as Sainz' title lead was never bigger than nine points, so maybe he deserved the title because of that. But with ten points on offer, winning quite rightly carries an advantage. All the same, Sainz in tears, with the end of the Rally of Great Britain in sight, where he lost it all with 800 metres to go as his Corolla's engine inexplicably expired, will always remain one

of the saddest images in the sport. Sainz is a rock, a workaholic with a surplus of talent, self sufficiency and self control. He is a king and the fact that, at the age of 36, he can break down in tears when his silly little car has broken down in flames in the Welsh countryside only serves to make him more human. His last championship came in 1992 and since then he has always been near the head of the field. He had an erratic season in 93 at the wheel of a dodgy Lancia, but apart from that he has always given his best. Nobody, but nobody has done the same. Even when looking down from the record of 22 wins in the world championship, a figure he reached this year, if he chokes on his bad luck, then one should feel nothing but sympathy.

On the subject of bad luck, it seemed keen to stick with Didier Auriol for most of the year. It set fire to his dash in Sweden, it sent oil drums flying around the boot of his car in Kenya, it subtly stole wins from him at the very last moment, ending up with a wrecked clutch in England. In fact, as things turned out, we discovered it was not just Didier who was cursed, but the entire Toyota Team Europe. Lady luck titillated the team with a win in the Monte Carlo Rally. It was a convincing display from the Japanese manufacturer, returning after its one year ban from the world stage because of the turbo saga. Ove Andersson and his boys were defi-

nitely there to win but he issued a timely reminder after the Monte, that their plan was still to take the title in 1999. But it is hard to resist the siren call of success and having allowed themselves a lucky win, it set them dreaming. And why not leave realism behind for a moment, especially when Auriol did the business in Catalunya and Sainz finally did it again in New Zealand. With these two and with the budget, the experience, the engineers and the car, they seemed to be set fair for further success, but it was not to be. Try again in 1999. Next year with a well sorted car and these tough and talented drivers, Toyota will have to be taken very seriously indeed.

In contrast, what happened to Subaru? Once again this season, just as in 1997, the superb dark blue racers robbed Colin McRae of a double crown, despite three convincing wins. Ever since he buried the McCrash tag and had Nicky Grist at his side to cool his ardour and to channel his aggression and to make good use of his fiery temperament, McRae has learnt how to win. In the end it was his ironically sweet sounding engine which let him down and was not up to the constructor's desire to defend its 1995, 1996 and 1997 titles. It would be too unkind to list the numerous mechanical failures posted by this car over the last two years. We will not stick the knife in further. All the same, it is worth pointing out that a turbo failure was the cause of the Scotsman's demise in Australia which pushed him out of the championship and it did the same on his home turf in the Rally of Great Britain, robbing him of any chance of winning in front of his fans. It was too painful to deal with, even for a seasoned campaigner. Team mate Liatti was overwhelmed by McRae, just as he was by the whole Subaru team, with whom the Italian did not enjoy the best of relationships. This was McRae's last year at Subaru under the fatherly wing of David Richards. It is hard to think of the pale faced

Scot slipping into a pair of overalls bearing the Ford badge. For Subaru-Prodrive, deprived of a fourth consecutive constructors' title by Mitsubishi, an era is ending. Preparations are well underway for 2000 and Burns, Kankkunen and Thiry must be anxiously awaiting the arrival of the new Impreza.

Juha Kankkunen and Bruno Thiry looked after that rheumatic old lady, the Escort, all the way to the retirement home. The Ford was never going to let them shine unless the stars in the other cars ran into trouble and eliminated themselves. Mr. K's fourth place in the championship owes as much to miracles as to the experience of the man with the cigarillo. Kankkunen was never very motivated in 1998 and will try and rejuvenate himself in 1999. We must wait and see if he still has the means, when confronted by this new wave which does not give a damn for the past and shows scant respect for reputations - Makinen, McRae, Burns- now he has finally taken his first two well deserved wins and Loix, who will surely soon do the same and maybe Gronholm and Panizzi.

What about Panizzi then? Four appearances on the World stage and as many great moments. To start with, there was his incredible time, dragged up from inside him as he rushed down the Turini. It was the only fastest time for the two wheel drive 306 on the Monte and it was a great one on snow and ice which set new records. You also need to take your hat off to the Corsican determination of Delecour, the stunning arrival of the Citroen Xsara in Catalunya with Bugalski in flamboyant form. The French Kit Cars were the terrors of the tarmac and just as in '97, they arrived to upset the order of the world championship. They swept through the hierarchy and challenged the establishment. It

was magnificent but meaningless as there were no wins. It seems the big boys had made too much progress for one of the little ones to win. They had come close, but, barring miracles, the chance will not come again and that is a shame.

The Kit Cars are not good enough anymore. So Peugeot selects top gear and the much awaited 206 WRC. Also planning their arrival, Seat hope the Cordoba WRC will be competitive as soon as possible and there are similar if more modest aspirations for Skoda and even Hyundai as they all prepare to cross the Rubicon. In 1999, the number of works teams in WRC form or Group A guise will on occasion be double what it is now. From four, the number will increase to eight on some events and there will be eight teams on every event in 2000. Such wonders have never been seen before and they are eagerly awaited.

A Peugeot driver through and through, Gilles Panizzi too

...he 306 Maxi to the top, as the sun turns to orange over Rosans.

In the past he drove on far too few rallies, but this year, Richard Burn

ook two great wins to make a major contribution to Mitsubishi's title.

ANOTHER WINNING
206
NUMBER

A French constructor back in the world championship is an event. And when it turns out to be Peugeot, then memories of the great days of the twice champion 205 T16 come flooding back. Will the 206 be as successful? We will have to wait and see, but in the meantime, a quick trawl through Peugeot's rallying history.

14.1

14.1

Jean-Pierre Nicolas, the man in charge of the rally department, with Francois Delecour and Herve Panizzi are eagerly awaiting the 1999 Tour of Corsica.

15.1

Francois Delecour and his faithful co-driver Daniel Grataloup will be the only team to tackle all six rallies on the 1999 programme.

15.2

Michel Nandan, former Toyota Team Europe engineer, is in charge of development for the new beast.

15.1

15.2

16.1

16.1

1000 Lakes 1984: First win for the Peugeot 205 Turbo 16 (Vatanen-Harryman)

16.2

1978: That year, Jean-Pierre Nicolas won both the Safari and the Ivory Coast rallies with a Peugeot 504 V6 coupe.

16.3

Africa was the scene of Peugeot's first rally successes with the 404 (1966, 1967, 1968.)

16.4

1985: Timo Salonen and Peugeot are crowned as world champions for the first time.

16.2

16.3

17.1

There he is with his Marseille street urchin look. His Rabelaisian physique born of a love of life has kitted him out with fine love handles and a greedy man's outline which earned him the nickname Jumbo. But Jean-Pierre Nicolas is above all part of the furniture when it comes to going back over Peugeot's lifelong marriage to rallying. He is everywhere in the story and usually centre stage, at the wheel of a 504 V6, as test driver of the 205 T16, as project leader of a modest 106 followed by a more serious programme with the 306 Maxi and finally the 206 WRC. Peugeot's history lives comfortably in his shadow and the company which has been sorely missed is now making a comeback in 1999 with the aim of taking the title in 2000. Rallying without Peugeot is Smith without Wesson, Harley without Davidson, Richards without his smile, Auriol without his shades, Delecour without his sharp tongue. As the Peugeot Lion prepares to sharpen its claws on another rallying challenge, we look back on the highlights of a saga with Jean-Pierre Nicolas as the ever-present central character.

On close inspection of his face, there are many who would swear that on his forehead, wrinkled from a hectic existence, Jean-Pierre Nicolas bears the mark of the Renault logo and indeed he was a Renault man through and through for many a long year. In those days, you did not change your allegiance the way one does today, especially when it came to cars. His father ran a big Renault dealership not far from the old port of Marseilles, he served his apprenticeship at the wheel of a Renault 8 Gordini and most important of all, he squeezed his large frame into the tiny seat of an Alpine, the company whose life would be linked to Renault for so many years. This golden age, the Sixties and Seventies, is still alive in black and white on the walls of the Italian inn, above the San Remo mountain, where last October, Jean-Pierre Nicolas drank a final tearful vino rosso toast to the 306 Maxi which was being put out to grass to make way for the 206 WRC. Nicolas is there in the photos, a jovial, jolly man although slightly slimmer. Also pinned up on the wall are Bernard Darniche and Jean-Luc Therier. Missing is Jean-Claude Andruet, who always had to do just that little bit more in the way of practice. There are also a gaggle of co-drivers, stripped to the waist, bent over what were probably pace notes, but not looking too serious about it. They look happy and relaxed, during a break in their recce for the San Remo rally. The innkeeper is also there, although he has long since gone to serve wine to the angels. He used to rustle them up some hearty meals, while closing the restaurant to the tourists, so that the Alpine team could have the place to themselves. Then, one day, Jacques Cheinisse, the legendary boss of this

16.4

17.2

17.1

The 306 Maxi makes its debut on the Alsace-Vosges rally in 1995, when it also set its first fastest stage time. (Two national championships in 1996 and 1997.)

17.2

October 1983: First public appearance for the 205 Turbo 16 in an event held at Sarlat, in memory of Jean Todt's driver and friend, Jean-Francois Piot. It carried the Number 13!

merry bunch was kicked out and his successor, Gerard Larrousse wanted to change the personnel. Exit Jean-Pierre Nicolas, thanked for his win in the 1973 Tour de Corse, as well as for helping to grab the world championship for Alpine. He would have to ply his trade elsewhere. It was then that the Renault lozenge.

In a 504 Peugeot, saloon and then coupe V6, Jean-Pierre Nicolas made the lion roar, particularly in Africa where he won three demanding "Safaris;" in Morocco in 1976, in Kenya and the Ivory Coast in 1978. His win on the Monte that same year was at the wheel of a Porsche.

"Jean-Pierre might not have been the quickest of the bunch," recalls Vincent Laverne, who was occasionally his co-driver, "but he was great at getting a car to the finish." It was a much needed skill. In the Seventies, a Safari would go on for 5,500 kilometres, with only a couple of three hour breaks in an otherwise non-stop day and night event with little outside assistance. It was an adventure that also required a tactical mind. "Sometimes you could not afford to stop, because stopping would let someone by and then you would be choking on their dust for hours," recalls Nicolas. You had to stick at it and never give up.

Peugeot forged an image of an indestructible car, which lasted for a long time in Africa, until the mantle was taken off them by the Japanese constructors. But the strong image remains to this day. In the long caravans of fourth and fifth hand cars which cross Algeria to start a new life as taxis in Ouagadougou, or runabouts in Bamako, there are still a lot of Peugeots.

Back in 1982, a battered light alloy wheel sits bent and twisted as a trophy on Jean-Pierre Nicolas' desk at his Renault dealership. It came off a Ford Escort and it is a joke trophy which was so nearly the real thing for winning the 1978 FIA Cup, the equivalent of today's world championship. That year, Nicolas won three rallies and was fighting the great Markku Alen for the title, until that ruddy wheel let him down. Never mind, that was all in the past and Nicolas no longer rallies cars, he sells them. Then suddenly, the phone rings. It is Jean Todt, former co-driver, now the man in charge of motor sport for Peugeot, with a reputation for being dry and authoritarian.

"Jumbo, I absolutely have to see you here in Paris as soon as possible."

"But, I was going out with friends in Marseille this evening."

"Cancel it. Call me back and let me know what flight you are on. I'll be waiting for you."

A new career was underway. Jean-Pierre Nicolas is taken on as test driver for the M24 project, the code which hides the true identity of the 205 T16. Two months later, on the Mortefontaine test track it turns a wheel for the first time. Actually, this is more of a publicity stunt as the 205 must run for a film to be shown at the car's official launch. The car, which will revolutionise the next era of rallying with its turbo and its centrally mounted engine is not ready. The clutch is not yet operational. It starts with a little push and runs on the end of a tow cable. Over a year later, the 205 sets its first fastest time on the second stage of the Tour de Corse. The rest is history: two world championships in 1985 and 1986, driven in the main by Kankkunen, Vatanen, Salonen. But the first to get this Peugeot up and running was Jean-Pierre Nicolas. With fourth place in the Tour de Corse, Nicolas learnt a lot about the best way to run a project. The knowledge would come in useful again.

Jean-Pierre Nicolas was under no illusions. He knew that all he had invested as a test driver would bring victories to other drivers. Jean Todt had been clear on this point: no rallies. Then the surprise present. He did get to drive after all, in Corsica (4th,) in Greece (retired) and in the San Remo (5th.) It was a reward for the work done. He also began to feel that Peugeot was his real home. He stayed on, to run the promotions department and gradually worked his way up the ladder. In 1994, a few modest little 106 were trying to get themselves noticed in the French championship, a long way behind the powerful machines of guys like Beguin and Bernardini. For the Rouergue rally, a 306 appeared, the prize for the best drivers in the one make series. Gilles Panizzi managed to close in on the leading group and Jean-Pierre Nicolas swore he had never considered going further than the base 106. "The appetite came while I was eating!"

In Nicolas' Velizy office, next to a glass screen a few models are piled up on a table, still in their boxes. The 306 is indeed the story of a model, albeit a life-sized one. In the summer of 1994, reading between the lines of the new FIA regulations, Jean-Pierre Nicolas sees that there is room for a new breed of car which is aggressive and far enough removed from a production car to fire a few dreams. The breed is the kit car. Nicolas says nothing to his bosses, but pursues his idea in the Garenne Colombes, where he goes to see a real racing nut called Gerard Welter. Welter is the man who spent his every waking hour developing the WM

206 WRC

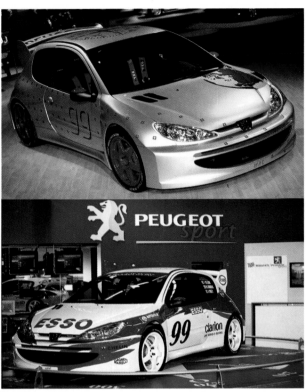

18.1-2

car which hit the 400 km/h mark on the Hunaudieres straight at Le Mans. Welter came up with a good looking drawing. "It gave us all a hard on," said the colourful Xavier Carlotti, Nicolas' right hand man. They want more and Welter is charged with building a full scale model. The next step was for the men in power to be ecstatic about the surprise creation and it is one of the Peugeot sons, in charge of marketing, who does what he can to find room for the beast on the motor show stand. The car is too good looking. It has not turned a wheel, but it will have to run one day. That day came on the 1995 Rally of Alsace, with a first fastest time for Panizzi. Chatriot and then Delecour would also get the most out of it. After two French championships, it was time to hand the reins to its "cousin" Citroen. In extremis, Nicolas salvages a limited world championship programme: Monte Carlo, Corsica, Catalunya, San Remo. And everywhere, the little two wheel drive car shines against the bigger four wheel drive models. Panizzi and Delecour steal fastest times, fight for victory, get on the podium and most of all, build up a solid reputation which surrounds the team. Jean-Pierre Nicolas therefore has some solid arguments when, mid-1997, he makes a case for the car which is yet to be named the 206.

Difficult to keep a secret when one knows already. At Loheac in early December 1997, it is time to celebrate the end of the year with a few rides round the Breton circuit. Nicolas, Delecour and Panizzi have known for several hours. It's Yes! Peugeot is back in the world championship with a WRC. Officially, they will have to keep it a secret for the six months, until the 206 is unveiled at Mulhouse in June. But at Velizy, they have not waited. Right from the beginning of the year, big white sheets have covered a top secret workshop, where the 206 rally car takes shape. Nicolas, Carlotti, Nandan (ex-Toyota), Delfosse, Rossman and Loisy are the deep thinkers of this project. By mid-May work has begun on a full size model. Mid-June and the first body shell is delivered, which by mid-October is built into the first prototype. The 206 is small - 40 cms. shorter than a Subaru - which naturally creates a few problems. There will need to be a few brainstorming sessions to work out how to fit the wiper motor. More fundamentally, the engine and gearbox cannot both be fitted transversely and so the gearbox is longitudinal, which is a challenge.

On Tuesday, 3rd November, with darkness and a barbed wire fence providing camouflage, the

18.1

Presentation of a silver coloured first model when the road going version of the 206 was unveiled at Mulhouse in June 1998.

18.2

A new model in colours similar to those of the 306 Maxi is shown on the Peugeot stand at the Paris Motor Show.

18.3

November 1998: Its first outing on the Pau Arnos circuit ended with a broken engine.

18.3

PEUGEOT

10/98

The transmission, gearbox and all wheel drive system has been developed in conjunction with X-Trac and the 206 body has undergone very evolved aerodynamic testing.

206 turns a wheel for the first time on the tarmac roads of the military base at Velizy, with Gronholm at the wheel. "It was an emotional moment," admitted Delecour.

Two weeks later on 16th November, the world's press turn up at the Pau Arnos circuit for the official presentation of the car. It would not go quite according to plan, as in the morning, after just a few metres with Francois Delecour at the wheel, the engine breaks. "We must be understanding and patient," says motor sport and press boss Corrado Provera, by way of excuse. The more cynical hacks recall the AP01, the Formula 1 car fitted with a Peugeot engine, which did not do much better on the day of its launch. "Lourdes isn't far away," was the ironic remark from a Spanish journalist. "This type of thing is normal," replied Xavier Carlotti. The fried foie gras and the magret served for lunch are good and that is some consolation. The temporarily unemployed co-driver Daniel Grataloup summed it all up during the desert: "Icarus also got it wrong at first."

The failed marriage between Auriol and Peugeot.

It was a done deal or almost. When Didier Auriol turned up at Velizy one afternoon, it was nearly all in place, having been sorted by phone and fax. The top of the fountain pen was off. Surely it was but a formality, a rubber stamping in front of civic dignitaries. Didier Auriol, the first and only French world rally champion, winner of 17 rallies, a remarkable test driver who turned the Toyota Corolla into a rally winner, is about to embark on a three year drive in the 206. But as the clock ticks on, Auriol is still at Velizy, hanging onto his mobile phone. He is supposed to tell Cologne what is happening. The answer he gives them is that he has said no to Peugeot and will stay with Toyota for another two years.

What happened in Jean-Pierre Nicolas' office? Everything ground to a halt "over a detail," to use the phrase put forward by both parties. Was it a financial detail? Apparently not. It was a detail added to the bottom of the contract. Auriol was demanding three years. Corrado Provera, the Peugeot boss, preferred three years but with a get-out clause after two. "It showed a lack of confidence," Auriol would say later. Negotiations broke off there and then and Jean-Pierre Nicolas missed out on his most fervent wish, namely to have a world champion on the squad. He had rejected Kankkunen, not comfortable enough on tarmac and had chased after the other four: Sainz, McRae and most of all, Auriol and Makinen. But it ended in a cul de sac. The answer given to explain the impasse was that "the major problem was the fact we would only be contesting six events in 1999." Francois Delecour, Gilles Panizzi and Marcus Gronholm will settle for that.

Delecour was the first to be called. "He will be our lynchpin," said Nicolas. "He knows the world championship and he is a winner."

Panizzi thought he had missed out. Around the time of the Catalunya rally, he got in a state when he thought Peugeot preferred Delecour to him. He therefore stepped up discussions with the opposition and Ford and Subaru showed a lot of interest. However, the refusal of Auriol and the other world champions guaranteed him his future, that he had dreamed of, as the company's favourite son.

Then Gronholm was called up as the obligatory sideways specialist. A Finn of course, he has a blank result sheet in world championship events, but on the rare occasions when he had a good car under him, he always put on an impressive performance.

The three lads have a common objective: to bring the title home to Peugeot in 2000. In so doing, one of the three might also be crowned, giving Peugeot the champion driver they could not get at the start of the project.

The 1998 RAC was the last rally he would drive, sat in the welcoming seat of his royal blue, 555 liveried Subaru Impreza. Colin McRae has turned a page. It is actually more than a page. It is a whole book made up of all the traditional elements of a good read; suspense, victory, defeat, drama and even romance. Let us not forget that McRae got married to childhood sweetheart Allison under these colours and this union might have signalled something of an evolution as well as a marriage.

Because today, McRae is still the most controversial driver. At the wheel he is pure diamond, with the speed and artistry to dominate all surfaces. He has a rare talent, but once out of the cockpit, he is cold and not very pleasant - at least that is the opinion of many. He is haughty and has little to say and can occasionally lose control as when he knocked over a spectator in a service area. But it is no doubt these qualities which contribute to his astonishing driving.

It was back in 1992, that he put his destiny in the hands of Subaru with a view to tackling the world championship. Then aged 24 and a former Peugeot man, he took part in five rounds of the championship and finished second in Sweden. The son in spirit of Prodrive boss David Richards would have to wait another year to take his first world championship win, in New Zealand. But at the same time, he was developing a reputation as a crasher and a car breaker, which earned him the nickname Colin McCrash.
In 1994, when Carlos Sainz was tackling his first season for Subaru and was fighting for the title, McRae was classified fifth, winning

New Zealand once again. In 1995, he finally became the first British driver to take the world championship title, at the end of a season which brought two wins - New Zealand and the RAC, while Subaru also won its first constructors' championship.

Since then, McRae has always been involved in the title fight, finishing second in 1996 and '97, but always behind his bete noire, Makinen. In the Finn, he found a constant opponent and their duels were often more than heated. As for David Richards, he backed his driver through thick and thin.

There was a big change at the end of 1996, when Nicky Grist replaced Derek Ringer in the hot seat. Despite all his talent, this co-driver could not control McCrash's temperament. Grist and no doubt the effect of marriage, made for a calmer, more even tempered driver. Like a good guard dog, the Welshman barks loudest when the Scotsman goes off the rails. The duo began to win more often than in the past, with no less than five victories in 1997, including amazingly, the Safari, where patience is an essential virtue and then in Corsica.

In 1998, McRae was yet again at the sharp end, but the Impreza was too inconsistent and did not allow him to fight to the end. Nevertheless, his reputation is still at the highest level, as proved by his transfer from Subaru to Ford, starting in 1999, which netted him a colossal ten million dollars; the biggest transfer in the history of the sport. It took some strong arguments for Richards to let his favourite driver, a son almost, move on. What is the betting he will not stay far or for too long away from his family?

Colin McRAE

"McRae has turned a page"

Do not mention Colin McCrash any more: it is indeed Colin McRae who is switching to Ford. 1998 sees the conclusion of a partnership with Subaru which was very often unbeatable.

1991 RAC RALLY
For his first works drive in a world championship event for Subaru, Colin has the third car. His team mates are Markku Alen and Ari Vatanen. He crashes out of the event.

1992 SWEDISH RALLY
Intégré à l'équipe officielle Subaru, il termine deuxième et égale la performance de Michèle Mouton: le meilleur résultat jamais réalisé par un pilote non-scandinave.

1992 1000 LAKES RALLY
Colin spends more time off the road than on it, but still manages to finish eighth.

1993 NEW ZEALAND RALLY
First victory for Colin McRae in the world championship. He is also the first British driver to finish on the podium outside the UK and it is the first British win since Roger Clark won the RAC in 1976.

1994 RAC RALLY
18 years after Roger Clark won the event, Colin wins the British rally by over three minutes from Juha Kankkunen.

1995 RAC RALLY
By winning "his" rally, Colin becomes the youngest world champion in the history of rallying.

1996 AUSTRALIAN RALLY
His father and former rally ace has become a course opener for his son. During the crossing of the boggy Bunnings stage, McRae did not hesitate to help his son out of this sticky situation.

1997 SAFARI RALLY
Famous for crashing and having little mechanical sympathy, Colin astounds everyone by winning the African classic.

Carlos Sainz

"I always thought next year would be better..."

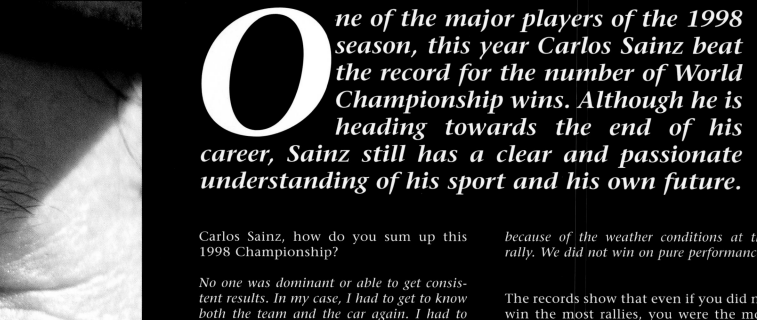

One of the major players of the 1998 season, this year Carlos Sainz beat the record for the number of World Championship wins. Although he is heading towards the end of his career, Sainz still has a clear and passionate understanding of his sport and his own future.

Carlos Sainz, how do you sum up this 1998 Championship?

No one was dominant or able to get consistent results. In my case, I had to get to know both the team and the car again. I had to learn all about it. The Corolla had never been used in Africa and had little tarmac or loose experience. I knew the first part of the season would be difficult for us and would get progressively easier. In general, we were incapable of being quick all the time, especially on tarmac.

Despite that, you won the Monte Carlo...

That was pretty much down to tyre choice. This year the Monte Carlo, in these conditions with the snow and ice was critical. I think that experience was therefore very, very important. But it is true that we kicked off the season better than expected, mainly

because of the weather conditions at this rally. We did not win on pure performance.

The records show that even if you did not win the most rallies, you were the most consistent driver.

That is true. But what is more, if you look at Corsica, Catalunya and the San Remo, we had expected better results. I am a bit disappointed with our tarmac performances. In Catalunya we got the settings wrong. In Corsica it was better, especially in the rain, but we took a decision to run without the ATS foam and we punctured when we were lying second. And it was important to finish second. There were the Peugeots behind. As we could not follow them we decided to run without the foam. We knew it was a bit dangerous. But I had not had a puncture in Corsica since '87, in my first Tour. I was not very lucky! (laughs)

24.1-2 Portugal 1987: his first entry on a world championship rally at the wheel of a private Ford Sierra Cosworth.

24.3 RAC 1988: Part of the works Ford team, Carlos finished a surprising seventh place.

25.1 1000 Lakes 1990: The first non-Scandinavian to win the Finnish event and the first world championship title.

25.2 Greece 1990: First Spanish driver to win a world championship rally and first win for the Toyota Celica GT-4.

24.2

You seem a bit surprised that you were involved in the fight for the title...

I always thought next year would be better. 1999 will be the year we are stronger, from start to finish. We will be competitive everywhere. Before the start of 1998, I thought it would be difficult and that maybe, during the season, things would get better. But we got off to a strong start, too strong perhaps as everyone then thought it would be an easy year for us. Becoming the 98 champion became one hell of a challenge.

Nevertheless, the car has progressed a lot...

Especially on the loose. But first we had to adjust it to suit my driving style and my feeling. That always takes a bit of time. Then I also had to relearn how to work with the guys from TTE. But I think the car still has a lot of untapped potential. It will progress a lot more. Sadly, with all these rallies, you don't have a lot or enough time to test. All you can do is do a lot of miles before the Monte and up to February. Then you can do nothing until June.

Do you already know what improvements are coming on the Corolla?

There will be some for Monte Carlo of course, but after a couple of months there will be a big improvement. It still has a lot of potential. We will have a new engine, probably in March. Some small changes to the transmission and a lot of things I cannot tell you about (smiles.) I am very confident.

It must be very important to have a really good team mate like Auriol, when you are developing a new car?

It is essential. We can exchange and check information. Even when the settings are different, you can always compare. It is always good for a team to have two top drivers, for the motivation of the drivers and also for the team.

And how do you get on?

A lot of people said we would not and that we would be unable to work together. We

proved that was not the case. The proof of that is that Toyota has always been in the running for the constructors' title. Of course we are both trying to beat one another. Above all, we proved we can work together, that we could have fun and that we could both win. We are two professionals who thought about the good of the team.

Is Auriol therefore the best possible team mate for you?

I think so, yes. Didier has a lot of experience. He is quick everywhere. He is one of the best drivers in the world. The combination of Sainz-Auriol; Auriol-Sainz makes for a very solid team.

You quit Toyota Team Europe a while ago. Have you rediscovered the same team?

The team is bigger. It also has other objectives like the Le Mans 24 Hours. I think in the past, TTE was a bit more focussed on the world rally championship. But all the same, I rediscovered a very good team, the

best in my opinion. They have the best facilities and a good way of problem solving with excellent technicians and engineers. Of course there are some other very good team like Subaru and Ford with Malcolm. They are all very good, but they do not have the same approach as TTE.

Were you in touch with any other teams for '99?

Not really. I think everyone knew I was under contract. Anyway, as Toyota is putting all its effort into winning, I am very happy to stay with them.

But with other constructors coming in, it will get even tougher...

There will be more cars, more good drivers and it will be harder to win. That is for certain. But at the same time, that means more indecision, more fights and a more interesting championship. It will be good for everyone. This does not bother me. In fact I am very happy to see other constructors coming in. It is very good, especially

for 2000, when we should see the best championship in the history of rallying. As long as Toyota puts 100% effort into it, I will not be worried by this situation!

You still have two years of your contract to run. Then what?

It is too early to say. We must wait and see. A lot of things can happen. Then, there is also the possibility I can do something other than drive. I will take the decision on my own and at some point in these two years. I am 36 years old. I am fit and I still like driving. I am still motivated and I feel I can still be very competitive. As long as all these factors are in place, I can see no reason for retiring. If one day, just one of these elements is missing, then I think that pretty quickly I would decide to do something else. Immediately, IMMEDIATELY! I know too many people who go on too long. I will not do that. It would not be fair on my employers, my friends and my family.

After ten years in the world championship is it not hard to maintain motivation?

Yes, it can be difficult. I think at the moment I am the driver who has spent the longest time in the world championship without a break. Juha Kankkunen went almost two years without driving, Didier almost the same. Colin and Tommi have not been around for as long as I have. In fact, I have always felt it is harder to stay at the top than to get there. It takes one or two years to get to the top. But then to stay there all the time is hard.

Why?

When you are young and you have just arrived, all you have to do is try and win. But when you have reached the peak, everyone tries to beat you. You have to maintain your motivation if you want to stay out in front. Each rally becomes an exam and you have to be 100% prepared for every exam. When you have won so many rallies and several titles, you have to be really strong and very strict with yourself to maintain this situation. It is important for it not to become a routine. So you have to fight and fight.

26.2

26.4

26.1-4 Australia 1991: Driving beyond his limits a bit too often, he suffers the most serious accident of his career to date.

26.2 Greece 1993: This was his worst season, at the wheel of a Jolly Club Lancia Delta Integrale.

26.5-27.1 Monte-Carlo 1995: A second win on the Monte and a first for Subaru, but Carlos chose to leave the team at the end of the year after several differences of opinion with David Richards.

26.3 Safari 1992: First win on the African event and his second world championship.

26.6 Greece 1997: The last world championship win and a one-two finish for the Ford Escort WRC.

26.7 New Zealand 1998: Winning this rally at the other end of the world, the man from Madrid became the holder of the greatest number of victories (22.)

26.3

26.7

27.1

Do you think you are as fast as in the past?

If I have confidence in the car, yes. This year for example, I was very confident on the loose, but not yet 100% on tarmac. I can be quick anywhere on all surfaces. That has always been my ambition; to be quick on the snow in Sweden and on the loose in Finland and the Acropolis, and on tarmac; even in the fog on the RAC. In all conditions!

This year you set a new record of 22 wins. What is your big ambition for the future?

To win another title! And to help Toyota to win more constructors' titles. And to still enjoy my driving. At 36, I know that if I am still having fun, then everything is alright.

Do you want to beat Kankkunen's number of championship wins?

Not necessarily. I have been very lucky to win several titles already. And I continue to fight. I do not think I have always been lucky in my career. Winning rallies is great. But the record is not the main thing, but all the same....(smiles.) For me the important thing is to be the only driver capable of winning all sorts of rallies as different as the Monte Carlo, Corsica, the Safari, Finland or the RAC for example. The Grand Slam of rallies for a driver. My next ambition would be to win in Sweden and to be the first non-Scandinavian driver to win on snow. Makinen has said he would like to win all the rallies at least once. That would really prove the ability of a driver.

You work hard; as much as when you started?

Of course. In fact all the drivers work a lot. The difference might be that if I have six tyres to test, I will test all of them. If I have three different set-ups, I will try all three. That's normal. It is my job and I am a pro. I have to do it. Nobody likes testing, but it is part of the job. However, I do not agree with those people who say, "Carlos has

Winning rallies is great. But the record is not the main thing.

done it because he works hard." Not only do you have to work hard, you also need to have the talent, a good team, a good car, a good co-driver and good tyres. To win you need it all!

You are very famous in Spain. Is that difficult to live with?

On the contrary, it is very easy. When you come back from abroad you realise that people know what you have done and they appreciate it. That gives you more motivation. I am very proud to carry the Spanish colours. I am Spanish.

Do you get enough time in between the rallies and your other commitments to devote time to your family?

No, we do not get enough time together. Especially with the children. I do not see them grow up and that is the worst thing about my job. I forgot to say earlier that the other factor which could make me give up driving is my children. Not because of the risks, that would be stupid. But because I miss them and they miss me. When you are away from home for 300 days a year it really is a lot. It is too much and the hardest thing to do is leave the family behind.

Indeed, are these 14 rally seasons not too long?

It is too much, and that opinion is nothing new. This is the only sport without a break. But we are getting political now. Twelve or thirteen would be ideal, to at least have a proper break. F1, motorbikes, football, everyone has one. Look, after the RAC we start winter testing straight away for Sweden and Monte Carlo. But we are not supposed to raise the issue. We try to talk to the FIA

about it, but I do not want to discuss that. All I can say is fourteen is too many, not just for the drivers, but also for the teams and even the press. We have to find the right balance and that means less.

But interest in rallying is growing.

The interest increases thanks to more TV, more people promoting the sport. But we need even more professional people to promote rallying in the same way as Formula 1. Other than that, the format of the events is good. FIA has done an excellent job. Technically I am not happy with the current power levels we have, nor with the weight limits for the cars. We should have a bit more for these WRC in order to find a better balance. At the moment, especially on tarmac it is not great. So... but I do not want to talk about the FIA.

What are your plans for your final seasons in the sport?

Since I was 10 or 11 years old, I think I always wanted to be a driver. Maybe not always in terms of doing it as a sport at the highest level, but just to be a driver. I have always liked cars and the relationship with them. I am a big fan of racing, rallying, F1, Le Mans. I am sure I will stay with TTE. We will have to see what we can do together.

So, how do you sum up your career?

That is for you to judge, not me. I am very happy. I have worked hard, sometimes in winning cars and sometimes not. Actually, I think the day I decided to give up studying law, I made quite a good decision.

1998
BIB

It was a good anniversary year for Michelin. Its 25 years in the world rally championship were celebrated with two more championship titles and the marque's 150th win, which was clocked up on the New Zealand rally. All those wins can be seen as the fruits of constant innovation.

Michelin...
...by appointment to racers

The good men of Michelin are undaunted when it comes to travelling the world in support of their crews. Twelve trailers, 30 technicians, 4000 tyres... before each rally, a long yellow road train stretches out from Clermont Ferrand and heads off for Jyvaskyla in Finland, Delphi in Greece or Porto in Portugal. Only the oceans can stop the trucks: for Australia, Argentina, Kenya, New Zealand and Indonesia, the piles of tyres travel by boat in containers. By land or sea, the objective is always the same: to arrive on time and get setup, more often than not in an isolated car park or scrap of wasteland, because plenty of space is needed for the Michelin compound to set itself up with enough place to work in comfort.

It has been going on officially for twenty five years, since the world championship began in 1973 and

with the Corsican win for Andruet- "Biche" in their little Renault Alpine.

"All our partners want the same thing," explains Pierre Dupasquier, director of motorsport. "They want performance, confidentiality and a manufacturer who is capable of helping them meet their long term objectives, while also reacting very quickly in the short term." Most of the company's involved in the world championship use Michelin: Mitsubishi, Toyota, Ford, Peugeot, Hyundai and Skoda. Only Subaru and Seat opted instead for Pirelli.

The relationship between Michelin and the manufacturers is a strong one. It is more of a partnership but Michelin charges for its services. The efficiency of the relationship and therefore its performance is no doubt due in part to this arrangement. As Francois Michelin said in his book (he was not one for talking much,) "the customer is the be all and end all of everything." The satisfaction works both ways.

Before the truck caravan heads out from Clermont-Ferrand, a great deal of preparation work has been carried out. A few days or a few weeks before each rally, each team, working away quietly on its own, will have come up with its tyre choice after some tough test sessions. The pebbles that pepper the Australian tracks have little in common with the tyre slicing rocks found on the Safari. The snow, which is nearly always melting in Monte-Carlo bears no comparison to the thick ice of the Swedish stages. However, the less than smooth tarmac in Corsica has much in common with the roads behind San Remo. The fourteen events on the calendar, including Indonesia, which was eventually cancelled, can be divided into seven different terrains. It is therefore necessary to judge, estimate, compare and try and try again all the different tread patterns, more or less aggressive, more or less asymmetric, the different sidewall heights, various widths, type of compound and even the length of

studs, plus various other parameters which are strictly secret. "A driver can tell immediately if one tyre is a tenth of a second per kilometre quicker or slower than another," claims Ayme Chatard, the boss of the rally department. "It is a very fine line, but it is par for the course when you think that these days a rally can be won by as little as five seconds." However, it would be far too simple, just to go for the tyre which is quickest on the clock. The engineer is there to temper the ardour of the driver, who will always tend to favour the quickest tyre without thinking about the wear issue. Also to be taken into consideration is the fact that the temperature at the top of the Col de Turini, recce'd in mid-December can be as much as ten degrees out compared with the temperature on the day of the rally itself. It all comes down to the mystery of tyre compounds.

Once the tyres have been tested, chosen, manufactured, transported, the tyres finally arrive at the

"A driver can tell immediately if one tyre is a tenth of a second per kilometre quicker or slower than another"

start of the event. Each team sends a van to collect its tyres. The Michelin men stick to their own kit of white shirt with blue and yellow stitching, but one engineer and one fitter is assigned to each major team. The race is on. Makinen, Sainz, Auriol and Kankkunen usually have a choice of eight different types of tyre, not to mention the fine detail of the hand-cut options. On the Monte, probably the most complex rally from a tyre point of view, there are also four different sizes of tyre: the 20-65-18 for the dry, the 18-65-18 for partial snow, the 15-65-16 for slush and the 10-65-16 for full snow. Translate the markings and win a pile of tyres! The first figure in millimetres corresponds to the width of the footprint, the second in centimetres to the overall diameter and the third in inches, to the size of the rim. Is that clear now?

The tyre is of fundamental importance. "It is the final element to be decided on before the stage," notes Ayme Chatard. Remember for example, the 1985 Monte-Carlo and Vatanen against Rohrl. Vatanen was back in second place after his co- driver got confused, clocked in early and picked up an 8 minute penalty. At the start of the Puget-Theniers stage, Vatanen watches Rohrl take off in front of him on snow tyres. He instantly decides to make the opposite choice, overtaking his struggling opponent in the middle of the stage to take an unexpected win. All thanks to the tyres. When all goes well, the winning tyre is simply considered to have done its job and no more. However, if things go badly, out of the driver-car-tyre trio, the rubber will always shoulder the blame and who cares if the driver pushed a bit too hard or if the electronic diff got itself in a knot, forcing the tyre to wear quicker than it should have done, or if rock hard suspension had forced the tyre to take on the role of a shock absorber.

The best response is of course, hard work, innovation and intelligence. Not everyone drives like Mr. Michelin in his CX, covering 330,000 km in fourth gear, admiring the beautiful views of the French countryside. Makinen and his little friends are in a hurry, a big hurry. And that does not bother the Michelin Man, Bibendum, whose lardy looks are only there to fool the opposition. Michelin, the world number one, hides behind its legendary discretion (the doors to the factory are rarely opened to visitors) in order to move forward.

It all started with Mr. Dunlop of course. The veterinary surgeon was fed up with riding his bone crushing bicycle on unmade country roads. He had the bright idea of replacing the metal rims covered in rubber with an air chamber to reduce the bumps. However, following on with the lightning strike of the first car tyre, Michelin soon racked up the firsts: first aeroplane tyre (1914,) first train tyre (1932,) first metro tyre (1952,) first tubeless tyre (1967,) first green tyre (1992.) Less important but destined to make the headlines, Michelin also equipped the "Never Happy," a rocket car which was the first to hit 100 km/h and several years later, Michelin also equipped the American Space Shuttle.

Naturally, the history of rallying was on-going through all these landmark achievements. The radial tyre of course was an extrapolation of what was being done for road cars. Then we had the slick tyre: "we created the slick because there is no need to make a tyre with grooves and holes when there is nothing that needs to be pushed aside," underlines Pierre Dupasquier. Almost every time, new regulations would be introduced to wipe out the advantage of these revolutionary discoveries. But others would fight their way through. There is for example the fascinating tale of ATS, which made its debut in the 1987 Acropolis Rally.

The ATS is an anti-puncture product. "The principle goes back to the 50s," says Ayme Chatard. "We started to use it on motor bikes in the Paris-Dakar in the 80s and when we saw it was working well, we introduced it for rallies." Inside the tyre lies a patented foam. Under normal conditions the pressure of the tyre squashes the foam against the rim. In the event of a puncture, the foam, reacting with micro-bubbles produced by a complex composition of gases, expands to plug the hole. The driver can keep going without an appreciable drop in performance. Sometimes, the driver might not have even realised he had a puncture. It's magic! Makinen used ATS

Miki Biasion (Lancia) Safari 1988.

almost 30 times in 1998. A puncture which involves changing a wheel can cost two minutes minimum. The competition would take several years to come up with a similar system.

More recently, the F8 system, the code name for

uriol (Toyota) Argentina 1994,

Jean Claude Andruet (Alpine) Monte-Carlo 1973, Timo Salonen (Peugeot) Grèce 1985.

"It's magic... Makinen used ATS almost 30 times in 1998"

"the Leak" has given Michelin at least a six month advantage over the opposition. Here again, the idea pretty much just needed to be thought of . The problem was simple. Tyres operate best at a certain pressure, but the more miles they do, the hotter they get and the pressure rises so how could the pressure be regulated? Simple; arrange a small controlled leak. "It worked rather well," said the Michelin men. So well in fact that it was banned.

The FIA keeps a very close eye on the progress made by all the manufacturers, in the so called name of safety or for a more balanced sport. Slicks? Banned. Tyre width? Controlled. "We would like to have the widest tyres possible, for greater efficiency," says Aime Chatard. But they have to fit through a template, which is too small to handle the 300 horsepower plus which many of the engines push out. That's the game and a fascinating one at that and it is the same for everyone. Champagne often awaits the Michelin men at the end of the day. "Nunc est bibendum," as it said in the Michelin ads. "It is time to drink."

Over 150 wins

By going through a permutation of tyres in the range on offer (the classic Z tyres, or the ZA, the very special WB which are narrower than the others in order to cut through the mud) Carlos Sainz won a very special rally in New Zealand. It was Michelin's 150th win in 25 years of the world championship. Of course, Sainz is not the only one to have won, hand in hand with Bibendum. Listed below are all the drivers who have won a world championship rally on Michelin tyres in date order. Andruet (Alpine), Thérier (Alpine, Porsche 911), Darniche (Alpine, Lancia Stratos), Nicolas (Alpine, Peugeot 504, Porsche 911, Peugeot 504 V6), Andersson (Peugeot 504), Mikkola (Peugeot 504, Audi Quattro), Blomqvist (Saab 99, Audi Quattro), Fassina (Lancia Stratos), Toivonen (Talbot Lotus),

Ragnotti (Renault 5), Fréquelin (Talbot Lotus), Röhrl (Opel Ascona 400, Audi Quattro), Vatanen (Opel Ascona 400, Peugeot 205 T16), Salonen (Peugeot 205 T16, Mazda 323), Kankkunen (Peugeot 205 T16, Lancia Delta intégrale), Moutinho (Renault 5), Saby (Peugeot 205 T16, Lancia Delta), Béguin (BMW M3), Wittmann (Lancia Delta), Alen (Lancia Delta, Lancia Delta intégrale), Biasion (Lancia Delta intégrale, Ford Escort), Auriol (Ford Sierra, Lancia Delta intégrale, Toyota Celica, Toyota Corolla WRC), Haider (Opel Kadett GSI), Recalde (Lancia Delta intégrale), Carlsson (Mazda 323), Ericsson (Lancia Delta intégrale, Mitsubishi Galant), Oreille (Renault 5 GT), Airikkala (Mitsubishi Galant), Tauziac (Mitsubishi Galant), Eriksson (Mitsubishi Galant, Mitsubishi Lancer), Jonsson (Toyota Celica), Aghini (Lancia intégrale), Delecour (Ford Escort), McRae (Subaru Legacy), Duncan (Toyota Celica), Makinen (Ford Escort, Mitsubishi Lancer), Sainz (Ford Escort, Ford Escort WRC, Toyota Corolla WRC), Burns (Mitsubishi Carisma).

All these victories resulted in 13 drivers' and 13 constructors' championships.

Tyreography of a season

Both championships, drivers' and constructors' was Michelin's reward at the end of this season. Here is a look at the season through the tyre man's eyes - a sort of tyreography where constant improvement is the main feature.

Monte-Carlo: Not much snow. Sainz wins with a new weapon, the Michelin N for cold and damp conditions.

Sweden: A totally Michelin podium with Makinen on top, using the new asymmetric studded Michelin GE.

Kenya: The ATS anti-

puncture system was used on some sections, despite the fact it is not normally considered suitable for long distances in hot conditions. Burns makes the most of them to take his first win.

Spain: A new version of the type N tyre, with considerably reduced deformation at high speed. Ten out of the top ten are on Michelin with Auriol in the lead.

Argentina: New evolutions of the type ZA and success as usual for Makinen

New Zealand: Brand new evolution of the ZA tyre for damp conditions and a Toyota one-two finish.

Finland: Reinforcement for the Michelin Z, grooved for high speed precision. Makinen wins again.

Sanremo: Two weapons contribute to Makinen's win over local boy Liatti. The ATS system worked well with Makinen setting a fastest time on puncture. The FP ("fort potentiel" or strong potential) version of the N tyre, specially developed for this rally, increases cornering speed.

Australia: Two tyres held the key to the fight between the three candidates for the championship: the latest evolution of the re-cut ZA and the WD, specially designed to clear the small gravel which is so typical of these stages.

Tommi Makinen (Mitsubishi) Finland 1997.

MITSUBISHI

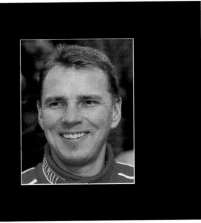

He wants to be the first driver ever to have won every rally at least once. Nothing more. He is serious about it. Tommi Makinen might be a Finn, but he has demonstrated that his talent extends further than the usual Scandinavian repertoire of gravel and snow. From the day he won in Catalunya, he understood he was an all-terrain talent. Of course, he keeps racking up wins in the 1000 Lakes, he is chasing Kankkunen's record of four world championships. He is insatiable and currently dreams of winning the Monte Carlo and there is no reason why it should not happen, as everything seems to be inevitable for Tommi.

1. Tommi MAKINEN

IDENTITY CARD

- Nationality: *Finnish*
- Date of Birth: *26th June 1964*
- Place of Birth: *Puuppola (Finland)*
- Resident: *Puuppola and Monaco*
- Marital Status: *Single*
- Children: *one son (Henry)*
- Hobbies: *golf, skiing, hiking*
- Co-Driver: **Risto MANNISENMAKI**
                      (Finnish)

STATISTICS

- First Rally: 1987
- Number of Rallies: 69
- Number of victories: 15

CAREER

1990 - 20th in championship
1991 - 29th in championship
1993 - 10th in championship
1994 - 10th in championship
1995 - 5th in championship
1996 - WORLD CHAMPION
1997 - WORLD CHAMPION
1998 - WORLD CHAMPION

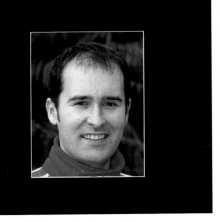

His career nearly died before it took off. For a long time, it looked as though the Mitsubishi yen counters would only come up with enough money for one driver. So for a long time, Richard Burns had to live on hope, while Uwe Nittel, a less talented but better backed German, filled the gap and more often than not the ditches too. Finally the money arrived and the amiable Englishman quickly made up for lost time, most notably by winning the Safari. He is so young and so promising that Subaru, who had given him his start, dug deep into their wallets to buy him back as Number One for next season. History sometimes repeats itself.

2. Richard BURNS

IDENTITY CARD

- Nationality: *British*
- Date of Birth: *17th January 1971*
- Place of Birth: *Reading (England)*
- Resident: *Reading (England)*
- Marital Status: *Single*
- Children: -
- Hobbies: *motorbikes, mountain-bikes*
- Co-Driver: **Robert REID**
                      (British)

STATISTICS

- First Rally: 1990
- Number of Rallies: 34
- Number of victories: 2

CAREER

1994 - 19th in championship
1995 - 9th in championship
1996 - 9th in championship
1997 - 7th in championship
1998 - 6th in championship

TEAM MITSUBISHI RALLIART

- Director:
  Andrew COWAN
- Sporting Director:
  Phil SHORT

MITSUBISHI LANCER EVOLUTION V

TECHNICAL SPECIFICATION

- Engine
  Type | 4 cylinder
       | 16 valves DOHC
       | DOHC
  Bore x Stroke | 85.0 x 88.0 mm
  Capacity | 1997 cc
  Induction | ECI multi
  Turbo | Mitsubishi
  Max. Power | 300 ps
             | at 6000 rpm
  Max. Torque | 52 kg/m
              | at 3500 rpm
- Transmission
  Type | permanent four
       | wheel drive
  Gearbox | 6 speed
          | sequential
          | (INVECS)

- Suspension
  Front - McPherson struts
  with helicoidal springs
  Rear - Independent with
  pull rods and helicoidal springs
- Dampers | Ohlins
- Steering | Assisted
           | rack and pinion
- Brakes
  Front - Ventilated discs with
                    6 piston calipers
  Rear - Ventilated discs with
                    4 piston calipers
- Tyres | Michelin
- Dimensions
  Length | 4350 mm
  Width | 1770 mm
  Wheelbase | 2510 mm
  Front track | 1510 mm
  Rear track | 1505 mm

POSITION
WORLD CHAMPIONSHIP FOR MANUFACTURERS

Year	Pos	Year	Pos	Year	Pos	Year	Pos
1973	16	1980	15	1987	-	1994	-
1974	11	1981	14	1988	14	1995	2
1975	11	1982	8	1989	4	1996	2
1976	10	1983	16	1990	3	1997	3
1977	10	1984	14	1991	3	**1998**	**1st**
1978	13	1985	-	1992	5		
1979	13	1986	-	1993	5		

In his earlier incarnation as McCrash, he could make Calder, the sculptor who crushed cars, jealous. He was the roll-a-drive who seemed to be at his happiest when upside down; Colin the son of his father, a former British champion; Colin, a driver cocooned and protected in a team built around him: there are indeed a lot of negative images attached to him. It was too unfair. There were some amazing drives in Greece and Corsica and wins on all surfaces proved that Colin McRae could be an exceptional and safe driver. It is a pity that his 1998 Subaru was not up to the job.

3. Colin McRAE

IDENTITY CARD

- Nationality: *British*
- Date of Birth: *5th August 1968*
- Place of Birth: *Lanark (Scotland)*
- Resident: *Scotland, Monaco*
- Marital Status: *married*
- Children: -
- Hobbies: *water-skiing, motocross*
- Co-Driver: **Nicky GRIST** *(British)*

STATISTICS

- First Rally: 1986
- Number of Rallies: 73
- Number of victories: 16

CAREER

1992 - 8th in championship
1993 - 5th in championship
1994 - 4th in championship
1995 - WORLD CHAMPION
1996 - 2nd in championship
1997 - 2nd in championship
1998 - 3rd in championship

 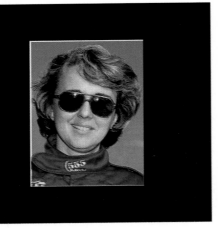

Piero Liatti is a timid Italian and thrown into the deep end among the English, he seems as ill at ease as a fish out of water. It is not easy to get on top of things when one can only manage a few words of what is pretty much a universal language. Not to mention being thrown into a team built around Colin McRae. Piero Liatti had been taken on at the insistence of Pirelli. He managed to show at times, in Corsica, Catalunya and Italy, that on tarmac at least, he fully deserved his drive. Unfortunately the Subaru situation was not the best and added to that, he had more than his fair share of bad luck.

4. Piero LIATTI

IDENTITY CARD

- Nationality: *Italian*
- Date of Birth: *7th May 1962*
- Place of Birth: *Biella (Italy)*
- Resident: *Monaco, Biella (Italy)*
- Marital Status: *married*
- Children: *one daughter (Lucrezia)*
- Hobbies: *skiing, motorbikes, mountain biking*
- Co-Driver: **Fabrizia PONS** *(Italian)*

STATISTICS

- First Rally: 1985
- Number of Rallies: 34
- Number of victories: 1

CAREER

1992 - 11th in championship
1993 - 26th in championship
1995 - 8th in championship
1996 - 5th in championship
1997 - 6th in championship
1998 - 7th in championship

555 SUBARU WORLD RALLY TEAM

- Director:
  David RICHARDS

- Technical Director:
  David LAPWORTH

OTHER NOMINATED DRIVERS

Jarmo KYTOLEHTO

Alister McRAE

SUBARU IMPREZA 555 WRC

TECHNICAL SPECIFICATION

- Engine
  Type — Flat four
  Bore x Stroke — 92.0 x 75.0 mm
  Capacity — 1994 cc
  Turbo — IHI
  Max. Power — 300 ps
  at 5500 rpm
  Max. Torque — 48 kg/m
  at 4000 rpm

- Transmission
  Type — Permanent four
  wheel drive
  Gearbox — Manual/semi
  automatic
  six speed
  (PRODRIVE)

- Suspension
  Front - McPherson strut
  Rear - McPherson strut,
  with longitudinal and transverse arms

- Dampers — Bilstein
- Steering — Assisted rack
  and pinion
- Brakes
  Front - Ventilated discs with four
  piston calipers
  Rear - Ventilated discs with four
  piston calipers
- Tyres — Pirelli
- Dimensions
  Length — 4340 mm
  Width — 1770 mm
  Height — 1390 mm
  Weight — 1230 kg
  Wheelbase — 2520 mm
  Front track — 1590 mm
  Rear track — 1590 mm

POSITION
WORLD CHAMPIONSHIP FOR MANUFACTURERS

1983	7	1987	10	1991	6	**1995**	**1st**
1984	9	1988	9	1992	4	**1996**	**1st**
1985	12	1989	12	1993	3	**1997**	**1st**
1986	8	1990	4	1994	2	1998	3

TOYOTA

Is he still as quick? Not necessarily. Age, money, family, these are all factors that dampen a young man's ardour. Is he still as good? Probably. With age and experience, Carlos Sainz has learnt to think things through, which has allowed him once more to fight for the title. Always as assured, hard working to the point of being pernickety, which is probably an essential quality for a world champion, he has overtaken Juha Kankkunen's record for the most number of wins. And he has not finished yet.

5. Carlos SAINZ

IDENTITY CARD

- Nationality: *Spanish*
- Date of Birth: *12th April 1962*
- Place of Birth: *Spain*
- Resident: *Madrid (Spain)*
- Marital Status: *married*
- Children: *2 (Bianca and Carlos)*
- Hobbies: *football, squash, tennis*
- Co-Driver: **Luis MOYA** *(Spanish)*

CAREER

1988 - 11th in championship
1989 - 8th in championship
1990 - **WORLD CHAMPION**
1991 - 2nd in championship
1992 - **WORLD CHAMPION**
1993 - 8th in championship
1994 - 2nd in championship
1995 - 2nd in championship
1996 - 3rd in championship
1997 - 3rd in championship
1998 - 2nd in championship

STATISTICS

- First Rally: 1987
- Number of Rallies: 109
- Number of victories: 22

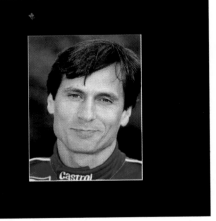

Strange to think his premature retirement almost became a permanent state. Kicked out of the world championship after Toyota was banned for a year after some slightly naughty and too powerful turbochargers were used, Didier Auriol left for Millau to wait for a brighter future. His detractors would say that his world title had in any case robbed him of some motivation. He was taken back by Toyota to develop and then drive the Redemption car. It was a successful comeback and Didier is almost out of reach when he is in perfect harmony with his equipment.

6. Didier AURIOL

IDENTITY CARD

- Nationality: *French*
- Date of Birth: *18th August 1958*
- Place of Birth: *Montpellier (France)*
- Resident: *Millau (France)*
- Marital Status: *married*
- Children: *2 (Robin and Diane)*
- Hobbies: *Golf, mountain bikes*
- Co-Driver: **Denis GIRAUDET**
                      (French)

CAREER

1988 - 6th in championship
1989 - 4th in championship
1990 - 2nd in championship
1991 - 3rd in championship
1992 - 3rd in championship
1993 - 3rd in championship
1994 - WORLD CHAMPION
1995 - Excluded from championship
1996 - 25th in championship
1997 - 11th in championship
1998 - 5th in championship

STATISTICS

- First Rally: 1984
- Number of Rallies: 94
- Number of victories: 18

TOYOTA CASTROL TEAM

- Director:
  Ove ANDERSSON
- Technical Director:
  Dagobert ROHRER

OTHER NOMINATED DRIVERS

Freddy LOIX

Thomas RADSTROM

TOYOTA COROLLA WRC

TECHNICAL SPECIFICATION

- **Engine**
  Type — in line four cylinder, 16 valves DOHC
  Bore x Stroke — 85.44 x 86 mm
  Capacity — 1972.3 cc
  Turbo — Toyota, CT20
  Max. Power — 300 ps at 5700 rpm
  Max. Torque — 51 kg/m at 4000 rpm
- **Transmission**
  Type — permanent four wheel drive
  Gearbox — six speed sequential

- **Suspension**
  Front - McPherson strut
  Rear - McPherson strut
- **Dampers** — Ohlins
- **Steering** — Assisted
- **Brakes**
  Front - Ventilated discs
  Rear - Ventilated discs
- **Tyres** — Michelin
- **Dimensions**
  Length — 4100 mm
  Width — 1770 mm
  Height — 1365 mm
  Weight — 1230 kg
  Wheelbase — 2465 mm
  Front track — 1564 mm
  Rear track — 1556 mm

POSITION
WORLD CHAMPIONSHIP FOR MANUFACTURERS

1973	9	1980	7	1987	7	**1994**	**1st**
1974	4	1981	8	1988	5	1995	-
1975	7	1982	5	1989	2	1996	-
1976	6	1983	6	1990	2	1997	-
1977	5	1984	4	1991	2	1998	2
1978	6	1985	5	1992	2		
1979	5	1986	6	**1993**	**1st**		

He could play the role of the venerable old champion, sitting on his four world thrones, playing with son Tino, or having fun in tractor pulling contests or working hard, managing his possible successors, smoking cigars and playing golf. Juha Kankkunen does a bit of all that but he continues to rally as well, as he approaches 40 years of age. His desire is such that, at one stage, he agreed to drive the equally venerable old Ford for almost nothing. That was his problem: in an outdated car with a down on power engine, Juha Kankkunen rarely had the opportunity to show he was still quick.

7. Juha KANKKUNEN

IDENTITY CARD

- Nationality: *Finlandaise*
- Date of Birth: *2 avril 1959*
- Place of Birth: *Laukaa (Finlande)*
- Resident: *Laukaa (Finlande)*
- Marital Status: *Marié*
- Children: *un fils (Tino)*
- Hobbies: *Golf, pêche, randonnée*
- Co-Driver: **Juha REPO** *(Finlandais)*

STATISTICS

- First Rally: 1979
- Number of Rallies: 127
- Number of victories: 21

CAREER

1983 - 16th in championship
1984 - 24th in championship
1985 - 5th in championship
1986 - WORLD CHAMPION
1987 - WORLD CHAMPION
1989 - 3rd in championship
1990 - 3rd in championship
1991 - WORLD CHAMPION
1992 - 2nd in championship
1993 - WORLD CHAMPION
1994 - 3rd in championship
1995 - Excluded from championship
1996 - 7th in championship
1997 - 4th in championship
1998 - 4th in championship

 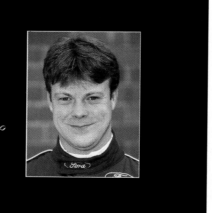

They say it is a handicap if you want to win. They say Bruno Thiry is too nice. It is true that he has put up with a lot. Remember in the days when Sainz was at Ford, he allowed his car to be cannibalised without complaining, he drove for a handful of Belgian francs, he was pushed aside without a murmur and he shrugged his shoulders when the limits of his old Escort were mentioned. Bruno Thiry is good. And it would be right and fitting if just once he could put the winner's wreath around his little boy lost shoulders, to wipe away the tears he shed one day when he so cruelly missed out on winning the Tour of Corsica.

8. Bruno THIRY

IDENTITY CARD

- Nationality: *Belgian*
- Date of Birth: *8th October 1962*
- Place of Birth: *Saint-Vith (Belgium)*
- Resident: *Les Awirs (Belgium)*
- Marital Status: *married*
- Children: *two sons (Adrien and Mathieu)*
- Hobbies: *cycling, mountain bikes*
- Co-Driver: **Stéphane PREVOT** *(Belgian)*

STATISTICS

- First Rally: 1989
- Number of Rallies: 47
- Number of victories: 0

CAREER

1992 - 16th in championship
1993 - 17th in championship
1994 - 5th in championship
1995 - 6th in championship
1996 - 6th in championship
1998 - 9th in championship

FORD WORLD RALLY TEAM

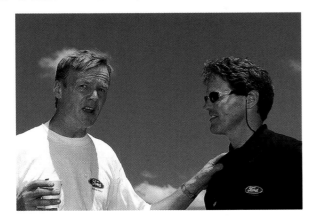

- Director:
  Martin WHITAKER
- Team Manager:
  Malcolm WILSON
- Technical Director:
  Marc AMBLARD

OTHER NOMINATED DRIVERS

Ari VATANEN

FORD ESCORT WRC

TECHNICAL SPECIFICATION

- **Engine**
  Type   4 cylinder
          16 valves
  Capacity   1993 cc
  Turbo   Ford
  Max. Power   300 ps
  Max. Torque   50 kg/m
          at 4000 rpm
- **Transmission**
  Type   Permanent four
          wheel drive
  Gearbox   6 speed
          sequential
          (FORD/MTRACK)
- **Suspension**
  Front - McPherson strut
  Rear - McPherson strut

- **Dampers**   Bilstein
- **Steering**   Assisted rack
          and pinion
- **Brakes**
  Front - Ventilated discs with
          four pistons
  Rear - Ventilated discs with
          four pistons
- **Tyres**   Michelin
- **Dimensions**
  Length   4211mm
  Width   1770 mm
  Height   1425 mm
  Weight   1230 kg
  Wheelbase   2550 mm
  Front track   1530 mm
  Rear track   1530 mm

POSITION
WORLD CHAMPIONSHIP FOR MANUFACTURERS

1973	3	1980	3	1987	5	1994	3
1974	3	1981	3	1988	2	1995	3
1975	6	1982	4	1989	13	1996	3
1976	3	1983	-	1990	8	1997	2
1977	2	1984	12	1991	4	1998	4
1978	2	1985	11	1992	3		
1979	**1st**	1986	5	1993	2		

How do you become a rally driver when speed limits are strictly enforced at 90 km/h and that radar traps lurk behind every fifth tree? Easy. Harri Rovanpera, the latest in a long line of Finnish talent, trots out the usual recipe. The frozen lakes provide a skid course while the country tracks, which are free from police, provide as many blind yumps as you care to tackle. Then there is the college system, where the older established drivers help the most talented youngsters. Thus we have with us Harri Rovanpera, who hopes that Seat will get their act together soon.

9. Harri ROVANPERA

IDENTITY CARD

- Nationality: *Finnish*
- Date of Birth: *8th April 1966*
- Place of Birth: *Jyvaskyla (Finland)*
- Resident: *Jyvaskyla (Finland)*
- Marital Status: *married*
- Children: -
- Hobbies:
- Co-Driver: **Risto PIETILAINEN** *(Finnish)*

STATISTICS

- First Rally: 1993
- Number of Rallies: 25
- Number of victories: 0

CAREER

1998 - 15th in championship

Marc Duez was only there to develop the Cordoba, the Seat WRC brought in as a successor to the Ibiza two litre car. He was supposed to be the man in the shadows, studious and hidden and he settled for that, without showing any regret for his own career, which was somewhat in the doldrums. But then, Oriol Gomez could not hold a candle to Harri Rovanpera. The fact he was Spanish saved him for a while, until the idea of running Marc Duez became the only sensible option, but only provisionally as has so often been the fate of this sacrificial driver.

10. Marc DUEZ

IDENTITY CARD

- Nationality: *Belgian*
- Date of Birth: *18th April 1957*
- Place of Birth: *Verviers (Belgium)*
- Resident: *Monaco*
- Marital Status: *married*
- Children:
- Hobbies:
- Co-Driver: **Luc Manset** *(Belgian)*

STATISTICS

- First Rally: 1987
- Number of Rallies: 24
- Number of victories: 0

CAREER

1989 - 13th in championship
1991 - 16th in championship
1998 - no classified

SEAT SPORT

- President:
  Vicente AGUILERA
- Director:
  Jaime PUIG
- Team Manager:
  Antonio RODRIGUEZ
- Chief Engineer:
  Benoît BAGUR

OTHER NOMINATED DRIVERS

Oriol GOMEZ

Gwyndaf EVANS

SEAT WRC

TECHNICAL SPECIFICATION

- **Engine**
  Type   4 cylinder, 16 valves
  Capacity   1995 cc
  Injection   Magnetti Marelli type MR 3
  Turbo   Garett
  Max. Power   300 ps at 5300 rpm
- **Transmission**
  Type   Permanent four wheel drive
  Gearbox   6 speed sequential
- **Suspension**
  Front - McPherson strut
  Rear - McPherson strut
- **Dampers**   Ohlins

- **Steering**   Assisted
- **Brakes**
  Front - Ventilated discs
      Tarmac: diameter
      76 mm, 6 piston calipers
      Loose: diameter
      304 mm, 4 piston calipers
  Rear ventilated discs,
      Diameter
      304 mm, 4 piston calipers
- **Tyres**   Pirelli
      Asphalte : 225/650-18
      Terre : 195/65-15
- **Dimensions**
  Length   4150mm
  Width   1770 mm
  Height   1500 mm
  Weight   1230 kg

POSITION
WORLD CHAMPIONSHIP FOR MANUFACTURERS
*2 litres

1977	14	1994*	10	**1996***	**1st**	**1998***	**1st**
1993*	12	1995*	4	**1997***	**1st**		

"Leaving snowdrifts in his wake..."

MONTE-CARLO

All the pencils were sharpened, the overalls were brand new, the cars immaculate and everything was ready. It was back to school time and life was full of uncertainties. Would the Toyotas be ready? With two titles already, would Makinen still be hungry? Would the Fords have progressed? Would the Subarus be as tough as ever? Had McRae calmed down? How would Burns get on as full-time Number Two at Mitsu? There were all sorts of

factors to take into consideration, not least the arrival of Peugeot, complicated by the fact they would only be tackling four events. In fact, putting aside the Subarus, victory on this first event would be a case of calm and steady winning the day: Makinen majestic in the early stages, then throwing it all away to hand victory to a cool and calculating Sainz.

The Sainz comes marching in

It was a good old style Monte-Carlo that was in full flow on the first leg where snow, ice and the odd dry patch all vied for attention. Right away and despite a good show from Panizzi in the second stage, the weather accounted for the Peugeots. Auriol who had set the first fastest time, crashed in the second, after the team sent him off on rain tyres, when snowones would have been a better choice, damaging the steering rack. It waschanged, but the Corolla felt all wrong. Never mind tenths of a second, the gaps after the six timed sections on the first day were often of the order of whole handfuls of seconds, which is not that common these days. After the display of French brio it was Makinen's turn to strut his stuffin the pouring rain here, the snow there and even a little bit of ice. No one could keep up. When they reached Gap, the gap from Makinen was a not inconsiderable 1.08.5 to Sainz and another ten seconds to Liatti. But it all turned pear shaped for the leader, right from the first special stage on day two. Sainz took command on the drying roads and despite the return to form of the Subarus and Peugeots and the way Kankkunen was going for it, he took his Toyota Corolla to a first win.

Gentleman Tommi

He was ill when he arrived, but thought he

44.1

was not. He was wrong, still suffering with a bad dose of bronchitis which he had been trying to shakeoff since the end of the previous season. The '97 RAC, where he shook off his illness to take his second world title, seemed a long way back in the past. Tommi Makinen's winter break had been one long misery of medicalexaminations, days of enforced inactivity when he had to sit helpless while team-mate Richard Burns did

the bulk of winter testing. The Finn thought he could see the light at the end of the tunnel just before the Monte. Sadly, his early morning jogging sessions in the watery sunshine might have caused the relapse. Who could tell with such a pernicious ailment. But the world champion is a stubborn sort of bloke and if the first day of the rally is difficult then all the better. After taking a few stages to get his eye in, he gradually picks up the pace to take charge at the half-distance, leaving a few crumbling snow drifts in his wake. "Burns did a great job," he explained by way of thankinghis young team mate. The Lancer is perfect. "With this bug, I am the onewho cannot keep up with him!" What would he have done if he had been on form? Outside, the Lombarde, an evil icy wind is blowing in sheets of drizzle which covers the mechanics as they slip around in the mud, before sliding underneath the Mitsubishi to dig around in its entrails. Any contact with a metal surface is punished with the cold. Makinen pops out of the support truck, and quickly takes off his red parka and gets behind the wheel in one fluid movement. The door slams, the engine grinds into life and one more stage awaits the sick driver. The Mitsubishi Lancer wheels dig into the slush, with their rain tyres, because higher up, between Les Savoyons and Sigoyer, the ice shines in the spotlights. "To go quickly on this section, it helps if you don't like yourself too much....the risk!" is what the old rallymen say. All the other top drivers decided to go with the reassurance of lightly studded tyres. The irony is that it is Makinen who puts the hammer down, nailing a first time

44.2

Mission accomplished for Peugeot

They came out of it with honour. The task imposed on Francois Delecour and Gilles Panizzi in their 306 Maxis was pretty straightforward as they lined up to start the Monte Carlo Rally. "We made our objectives clear before the start," announced Jean-Pierre Nicolas, Peugeot's rally boss. "A podium if it was completely dry, a top five finish if it was a bit damp, and a struggle to make the top ten if it snowed, even for only ten kilometres." "Delec" finished ninth, one place ahead of Zebulon-Panizzi. They had done the business in style, with both 306 Maxis finishing wheel to wheel on the last stage, after the brothers lost precious minutes changing a puncture tyre. Then, as so often in sport, there are a few "ifs" to throw into the equation. If Delecour-Grataloup had not gone off on the firsttimed section of the second completely snowbound stage; if that puncture had not come along to slow the Panizzi boys; and especially if the snow had not come down with its mate, black ice. But the Monte is held in winter on mountain roads. So you can lock up the ifs and throw away the key.

Luckily the Monte ended on that perfectly dry tarmac which allows the two lions to claw their way to a brilliant finish. And there was also that one single fabulous exploit. On the first day, on the snowy descent from Turini, the two brothers from Menton did a 14.38.4 (av. speed 68.44 km/h over 16.70 km) setting the best two wheel drive time in the 1998 Monte and setting a course record. So, the imposing figure of Jean-Pierre Nicolas, notebook in hand, could trumpet their achievements: "Adding together the times of the first three stages on the final leg, which were dry, we can see that Auriol was quickest with 27.17, two seconds better than Liatti, 3 ahead of Delecour and 4 better than Panizzi. On the Turini descent, Panizzi had been 10s quicker than Auriol, which had made the difference on the climb. We were well within our target!" In the dry. Above all, the men from Velizy knew that, of the four appearances planned on this year's world championship trail, the Monte-Carlo was the least favourable to them. Catalunya, Corsica and SanRemo should suit them much better.

45.1
Finland's Tommi Makinen was a brief but impressive leader on the first leg until an accident forced his retirement.

45.2
Richard Burns is a real revelation. His Carisma was the most effective form of transport in these conditions.

45.1

on the stage of a staggering 21.01.4, fully 44.8 seconds ahead of second placed man Liatti over the 27 kilometre run. Of course Sainz was quick. But once again he went off. Shame, never mind, shouldn't have done it. "I lost 30 seconds." Not Makinen though. "I knew that between the ice there were some wet patches. I thought that might be enough to make the difference as the new Michelin rain tyres are also excellent on ice." Everything seems so simple when one is world champion. Then, flashing his cheeky smile, he had one more thought before going off to find a warm duvet. "There is still a long way to go. And if it is as complicated as today, it is far from being won. We will have to wait for the Sisteron stage."

Not won indeed, because the Makinen saga would turn out to be as short as it was sweet. At the start, against a snow covered landscape, on stage seven, the first of the day, Makinen went off in a big way and retired. It was quick and permanent. But we are dealing with a world champion here and he made all the right mea culpa noises; "late braking, too optimistic, my fault!" and so on. However, a few days later, some Finns got hold of a recording of the in-car conversation from the Mitsubishi. It was clear for all to hear that terrible moment of hesitation from Risto Mannisenmaki. The young man lacks the experience and charisma of Seppo Harjanne, that old trooper with the Father Christmas beard, who brought Makinen through the ranks to the world championship. There was no doubt about the error. Makinen knew it, but he said nothing. Doff your hat to a true gentleman.

46.1

46.2

46.3

46.4

46.5

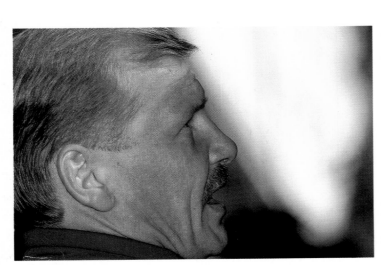

46.6

47.1

MONTE-CARLO
"Leaving snowdrifts in his wake..."

46. 1-2

Colin McRae indulged in a bit too much ditch hooking in his efforts to win, while Richard Burns proved to be quick and reliable.

46. 3-6

The old fox Juha Kankkunen gave Ford second place, but he still has not managed to put the Monte-Carlo winner's trophy on his mantlepiece.

46. 4-5

Frenchmen Didier Auriol and Francois Delecour threw away any chance of victory by crashing.

46. 7

His mastery of the course meant that Spain's Carlos Sainz was unbeatable on the two snow-covered stages.

47. 1

Carlos Sainz and Luis Moya did the business on returning to Toyota.

47. 2

Winner in 1997, Piero Liatti can consider himself lucky to have got to the finish, after rolling on Sisteron.

47.2

RALLYE MONTE-CARLO
1998 1 *1998*

TOP ENTRIES

1 Tommi Makinen
Risto Mannisenmaki
MITSUBISHI LANCER EV.4

2 Richard Burns
Robert Reid
MITSUBISHI CARISMA GT

3 Colin McRae
Nicky Grist
SUBARU IMPREZA WRC

4 Piero Liatti
Fabrizia Pons
SUBARU IMPREZA WRC

5 Carlos Sainz
Luis Moya
TOYOTA COROLLA WRC

6 Didier Auriol
Denis Giraudet
TOYOTA COROLLA WRC

7 Juha Kankkunen
Juha Repo
FORD ESCORT WRC

8 Bruno Thiry
Stéphane Prévot
FORD ESCORT WRC

10 Uwe Nittel
Tina Thorner
MITSUBISHI CARISMA GT

11 Henrik Lundgaard
Freddy Pedersen
TOYOTA CELICA GT-FOUR

12 Gustavo Trelles
Jorge Del Buono
MITSUBISHI LANCER EV.4

14 François Delecour
Daniel Grataloup
PEUGEOT 306 MAXI

15 Harri Rovanperä
Voitto Silander
SEAT IBIZA 16V KIT CAR

16 Gilles Panizzi
Hervé Panizzi
PEUGEOT 306 MAXI

17 Oriol Gomez
Marc Marti
SEAT IBIZA 16V KIT CAR

18 Adruzilo Lopes
Luis Lisboa
PEUGEOT 306 MAXI

19 Luis Climent
Alex Romani
MITSUBISHI LANCER EV.3

20 Marc Duez
Gilles Thimonier
MITSUBISHI LANCER EV.4

21 Armin Kremer
Klaus Wicha
SUBARU IMPREZA

22 Christophe Spiliotis
Colette Neri
SUBARU IMPREZA

25 Cyril Henny
Aurore Brand
PEUGEOT 306 MAXI

26 César Baroni
Dominique Savignoni
MITSUBISHI LANCER EV.4

28 Manfred Stohl
Peter Muller
MITSUBISHI LANCER EV.3

41 Jurgen Barth
Jean-Claude Perramond
SUBARU IMPREZA

66TH MONTE-CARLO RALLY

1st leg of the 1998 world rally championships for constructors and drivers
1st leg of the constructors' "2 litre", production car drivers' and teams' world cups

Date: *19 - 21 January 1998*

Route: *1454.53 km divided into 3 legs, with 18 stages all on tarmac (359.19 km)*
1st leg: Monday 19th January, Monaco - Gap, 6 stages (119.59 km)
2nd leg: Tuesday 20th January, Gap - Monaco, 7 stages (148.01 km)
3rd leg: Wednesday 21st January, Monaco - Monaco, 5 stages (91.59 km)

Starters: *106 (55 Group A + 51 Group N)*
Finishers: *60 (33 Group A + 27 Group N)*

Carlos Sainz' third win in the Principality was not his toughest.

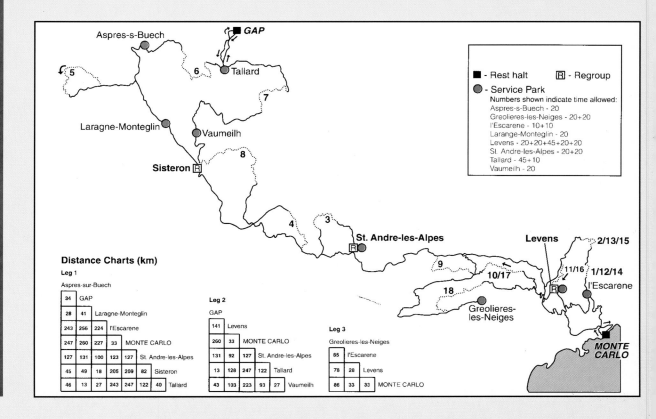

- Rest halt   **R - Regroup**
- Service Park
Numbers shown indicate time allowed:
Aspres-s-Buech - 20
Greolieres-les-Neiges - 20+20
l'Escarene - 10+10
Larange-Monteglin - 20
Levens - 20+20+45+20+20
St. Andre-les-Alpes - 20+20
Tallard - 45+10
Vaumeilh - 20

Distance Charts (km)

Leg 1

Aspres-sur-Buech							
34	GAP						
28	41	Laragne-Monteglin					
243	256	224	l'Escarene				
247	260	227	33	MONTE CARLO			
127	131	100	123	127	St. Andre-les-Alpes		
45	49	18	205	209	82	Sisteron	
46	13	27	243	247	122	40	Tallard

Leg 2

GAP					
141	Levens				
260	33	MONTE CARLO			
131	92	57	St. Andre-les-Alpes		
13	128	247	122	Tallard	
43	103	223	93	27	Vaumeilh

Leg 3

Greolieres-les-Neiges			
85	l'Escarene		
78	28	Levens	
86	33	33	MONTE CARLO

SPECIAL STAGE TIMES

ES.1 Luceram-Peira Cava 1 (9,65 km)
1. Auriol 7'35"1; 2. Kremer 7'45"1; 3. McRae 7'45"8; 4. Liatti 7'48"4; 5. Makinen 7'48"8; Gr.N Bedini 8'19"9; F2 Rovanpera et Gomez 8'16"3

ES.2 Peira Cava-La Bollène Vésubie 1 (16,7 km)
1. Panizzi 14'38"4; 2. Sainz 14'43"2; 3. Liatti 14'45"5; 4. Thiry 14'51"8; 5. Delecour 14'56"8; Gr.N Stohl 15'07"4

ES.3 Lambruisse-Clumanc (15 km)
1. Makinen 11'01"; 2. Auriol 11'03"7; 3. Burns 11'03"8; 4. Liatti 11'06"3; 5. Kankkunen 11'08"8; Gr.N Stohl 11'48"7; F2 Delecour 11'20"1

ES.4 Chaudon Norante-Et.Thermal Digne (19,53 km)
1. Makinen 13'00"7; 2. Burns 13'10"1; 3. Sainz 13'14"2; 4. Liatti 13'14"5; 5. Auriol 13'19"6; Gr.N Stohl 14'27"; F2 Rovanpera 13'53"3

ES.5 L'Epine-Rosans (31,15 km)
1. Makinen 19'05"8; 2. McRae 19'05"9; 3. Sainz 19'15"8; 4. Burns 19'28"4; 5. Kankkunen 19'33"; F2 Delecour 20'18"5

ES.6 Les Savoyons-Sigoyer (27,56 km)
1. Makinen 21'01"4; 2. Liatti 21'46"2; 3. Sainz 21'47"4; 4. Kankkunen 21'54"2; 5. McRae 22'01"4; Gr.N Climent 24'42"7; F2 Delecour 23'15"9

ES.7 Bayons (22,55 km)
1. Sainz 19'05"9; 2. Kankkunen 19'18"1; 3. Thiry 19'39"1; 4. Auriol 19'42"6; 5. Burns 20'25"9; Gr.N Duez 31'38"9; F2 Panizzi, 20'40"4

ES.8 Sisteron - Thoard (36,72 km)
1. Kankkunen 30'07"4; 2. Sainz 30'20"0; 3. Burns 30'24"7; 4. Nittel 30'37"7; 5. Thiry 30'39"7; Gr.N Duez 31'41"4; F2 Delecour 31'55"7

ES.9 Entrevaux - Saint-Pierre (29,71 km)
1. Liatti 19'58"8; 2. McRae 19'59"8; 3. Burns 20'21"5; 4. Thiry 20'27"6; 5. Auriol 20'29"2; Gr.N Stohl 22'30"8; F2 Delecour 20'30"4

ES.10 Toudon - Saint-Antonin 1 (20,71 km)
1. Liatti 15'25"2; 2. McRae 15'29"9; 3. Panizzi 15'30"4; 4. Auriol 15'31"2; 5. Thiry 15'42"0; Gr.N Baroni 17'07"9; F2 Delecour 15'51"9

ES.11 Saint-Jean-La-Rivière - Levens 1 (11,97 km)
1. McRae 8'23"1; 2. Liatti 8'25"6; 3. Auriol 8'27"1; 4. Sainz 8'28"1; 5. Thiry 8'29"6; Gr.N Baroni 9'20"4; F2 Delecour 8'32"3

ES.12 Lucéram - Peira-Cava 2 (9,65 km)
1. Auriol 7'20"9; 2. Thiry 7'24"3; 3. Sainz 7'25"4; 4. Panizzi 7'26"4; 5. Kankkunen 7'28"1; Gr.N Baroni 8'10"5; F2 Delecour 7'30"2

ES.13 Peira-Cava - La Bollène Vésubie 2 (16,70 km)
1. Thiry 12'01"8; 2. Delecour 12'04"0; 3. Auriol 12'05"6; 4. Panizzi 12'09"8; 5. Kankkunen 12'09"9; Gr.N Marcon 13'32"1

ES.14 Lucéram - Peira-Cava 3 (9,65 km)
1. Thiry 7'12"; 2. Auriol 7'12"4; 3. Sainz 7'13"1; 4. Panizzi 7'15"2; 5. Liatti 7'15"9; Gr.N Marcon 7'56"8

ES.15 Peira-Cava - La Bollène Vésubie 3 (16,70 km)
1. Auriol 11'42"5; 2. Delecour 11'46"; 3. Panizzi 11'47"2; 4. Thiry 11'48"4; 5. Liatti 11'49"2; Gr.N Marcon 12'45"

ES.16 Saint-Jean-La-Rivière - Levens 2 (11,97 km)
1. Liatti 8'13"4; 2. McRae 8'13"9; 3. Delecour 8'15"4; 4. Auriol 8'18"; 5. Panizzi 8'18"9; Gr.N Baroni 8'57"1

ES.17 Toudon - Saint-Antonin 2 (20,71 km)
1. Auriol 15'06"9; 2. Burns 15'08"9; 3. McRae 15'08"9; 4. Liatti 15'12"5; 5. Delecour 15'15"3; Gr.N Baroni 16'34"5

ES.18 Les 4 Chemins (32,56 km)
1. McRae 22'13"9; 2. Auriol 22'17"8; 3. Liatti 22'25"; 4 Burns, 22'28"3; 5 Kankkunen, 22'30"9; Gr.N Baroni 24'51"4; F2 Delecour 22'42"6

RESULTS AND RETIREMENTS

	Driver/Co-Driver	Car	N°	Gr	Total Time
1	Carlos Sainz - Luis Moya	Toyota Corolla WRC	5	A	4h28m00,5s
2	Juha Kankkunen - Juha Repo	Ford Escort WRC	7	A	4h28m41,3s
3	Colin McRae - Nicky Grist	Subaru Impreza WRC	3	A	4h29m01,5s
4	Piero Liatti - Fabrizia Pons	Subaru Impreza WRC	4	A	4h29m13,5s
5	Richard Burns - Robert Reid	Mitsubishi Carisma GT	2	A	4h29m23,2s
6	Bruno Thiry - Stéphane Prévot	Ford Escort WRC	8	A	4h30m20,9s
7	Uwe Nittel - Tina Thorner	Mitsubishi Carisma GT	10	A	4h34m21,3s
8	Armin Kremer - Klaus Wicha	Subaru Impreza WRC	21	A	4h37m40,1s
9	Gilles Panizzi - Hervé Panizzi	Peugeot 306 Maxi	16	A	4h39m24,0s
10	François Delecour - Daniel Grataloup	Peugeot 306 Maxi	14	A	4h40m02,2s
ES.3	Oriol Gomez - Marc Marti	Seat Ibiza 16v Kit Car	17	A	Accident
ES.6	Gustavo Trelles - Jorge Del Buono	Mitsubishi Lancer Ev.3	12	N	Accident
ES.7	Tommi Makinen - Risto Mannisenmaki	Mitsubishi Lancer Ev.4	1	A	Accident
ES.7	Henrik Lundgaard - Freddy Pedersen	Toyota Celica GT-Four	11	A	Accident

PREVIOUS WINNERS

1973 Andruet - "Biche"
ALPINE RENAULT A 110

1975 Munari - Mannucci
LANCIA STRATOS

1976 Munari - Maiga
LANCIA STRATOS

1977 Munari - Maiga
LANCIA STRATOS

1978 Nicolas - Laverne
PORSCHE 911 SC

1979 Darniche - Mahé
LANCIA STRATOS

1980 Rohrl - Geistdorfer
FIAT 131 ABARTH

1981 Ragnotti - Andrié
RENAULT 5 TURBO

1982 Rohrl - Geistdorfer
OPEL ASCONA 400

1983 Rohrl - Geistdorfer
LANCIA RALLY 037

1984 Rohrl - Geistdorfer
AUDI QUATTRO

1985 Vatanen - Harryman
PEUGEOT 205 T16

1986 Toivonen - Cresto
LANCIA DELTA S4

1987 Biasion - Siviero
LANCIA DELTA HF 4WD

1988 Saby - Fauchille
LANCIA DELTA HF 4WD

1989 Biasion - Siviero
LANCIA DELTA INTEGRALE

1990 Auriol - Occelli
LANCIA DELTA INTEGRALE

1991 Sainz - Moya
TOYOTA CELICA GT-Four

1992 Auriol - Occelli
LANCIA DELTA HF INTEGRALE

1993 Auriol - Occelli
TOYOTA CELICA TURBO 4WD

1994 Delecour - Grataloup
FORD ESCORT RS COSWORTH

1995 Sainz - Moya
SUBARU IMPREZA 555

1996 Bernardini - Andrié
FORD ESCORT COSWORTH

1997 Liatti - Pons
SUBARU IMPREZA WRC

MICHELIN

EVENT LEADERS

ES.1: Auriol
ES.2 - ES.3: Liatti
ES.4 - ES.6: Makinen
ES.7 - ES.18: Sainz

BEST PERFORMANCES

	1	2	3	4	5	6
Auriol	4	3	2	3	2	1
Makinen	4	-	-	-	1	-
Liatti	3	2	2	4	2	1
McRae	2	4	2	-	1	2
Thiry	2	1	1	3	3	-
Sainz	1	2	5	1	-	3
Kankkunen	1	1	-	1	5	2
Panizzi	-	2	3	1	2	9
Delecour	-	2	1	-	2	1
Kremer	-	1	-	-	-	-

CHAMPIONSHIP CLASSIFICATIONS

Drivers :
1. Carlos Sainz 10
2. Juha Kankkunen 6
3. Colin McRae 4
4. Piero Liatti 3
5. Richard Burns 2
6. Bruno Thiry 1

Constructors:
1. Toyota 10
2. Ford 7
2. Subaru 7
4. Mitsubishi 2

Group N:
1. Manfred Stohl 13
2. Luis Climent 8
3. César Baroni 5

Two Litres:
1. Peugeot 16
2. Seat 4
3. Citroën 1

Teams' Cup :
No team classified

GOSSIP

• TOYOTA

"You should not expect miracles from us this season. We will try and get up with the top teams. Winning the title will be difficult." In his quiet tones, in complete contrast to his gentle giant appearance, Ove Andersson was being falsely modest once the win was in the bag. After a one year ban and a timid return in the middle of 1997, one of the best rally teams (39 wins from 1973 to early 1998, two constructors' world titles and four drivers' championships) had made a big impression. In January 1997 the World Rally Car turned a wheel for the first time. A year later it won a tarmac rally for only the second time.

• SKODA

Skoda chose the Monte-Carlo to make a discrete but oh so important announcement: in 1998 the Czech marque would enter an Octavia World Rally Car. The decision to move up to the blue riband rally class was taken in early January by the board. With SEAT due to arrive towards the end of the season, the VAG group was really taking its rallying seriously.

• MICHELIN

The tyre manufacturer certainly went in for the grand plan. To kit out nine of the thirteen factory cars, it brought over 3,500 tyres to meet every possible level of grip which the Monte might throw at it. That meant its entire range, from maxi-snow all the way through to rubber wear for hot dry tarmac. What is more, Michelin packed in a total of 14 test sessions over the winter. This major effort paid off as most of the drivers expressed delight with the new tyre developments.

• BURNS

He was the revelation of Monte-Carlo. Richard Burns had never tackled this event before and he finished fifth, having been as high as third for a while. "I like this event," he explained, wreathed in smiles at the finish. "I like it more than I thought I would at the start and I am delighted to finish in the points." His Mitsu Number One, Makinen did not hold back from eulogising the technical choices Burns had made in preparation for the event.

"*A bad fairy related to Swedish*

rolls... "

SWEDISH

Sweden cut it fine, only bringing out its traditional snowy white blanket at the last minute, laying down white sheets on already ice-covered roads. It was looking good for any enterprising Swede. Thomas Radstrom and his excellent Toyota Corolla World Rally Car put on a fabulous festival of ice dancing, before crashing out of the event and handing victory to an unsuspecting Makinen. As far as the Championship was concerned, Sainz' second place in the rally kept him in the lead ahead of the equal-pointing Makinen and Kankkunen.

52.1

Makinen a cut above

Even before the start, there are some who must make amends. Tommi Makinen might have been the big hero of Monte-Carlo with a majestic lead, but he also had a majestic "off." If he does not want to get left behind in the championship, the reigning champion and winner here in '96 must at least get his Mitsubishi high up in the points. He is backed as favourite to do so. Auriol also wishes to put the recent past behind him. His Monte-Carlo rally had been hard to swallow, he admitted it. This time, he is not under pressure so watch out. Then there is Kenneth Eriksson out for the big triple in his Subaru finale, having won here in 95 and 97. "I want to go out on a high note." Then there is the Toyota wild card entry for taciturn local, Radstrom. Finally we have the podium trio from the Monte-Carlo Rally; Sainz, Kankkunen, McRae. They all want to make their mark in round two. Starting at the head of the field for the first leg, they will be playing the role of snow plough for the others. A hell of a disadvantage for them and a great advantage for Thomas Radstrom, who makes the most of the opportunity. In the first leg, he almost has a clean sweep in his Toyota Corolla, which is kitted out with the latest Michelin snow tyre, the GE. Of the eight stages that day, Radstrom took six of them. "He's got this rally in his blood," affirmed Auriol. He also had the advantage of running eighth on the road. The party would soon be over. Next day, on the longest stage, the Swede gets it wrong. "It was very difficult," he admitted later. "The snow was turning to soup, but we went off because I misunderstood a pace note." He thus hands the lead to Makinen, who wanted nothing more as he was just about to attack. When the Finn switches to this mode it is some-

52.2   52.3   52.4

52.2-4
Eriksson was never capable of matching the pace set by the two Finns, Makinen and Kankkunen.

thing between a suicide run and a surprise attack; which is over almost before anyone has realised what is going on. In the preceding stage, he fits Michelin's ultimate weapon; an asymmetric studded tyre, developed over the winter, as used by Radstrom on his previous day's dazzling display. Radstrom and McRae (electrics) were out, Sainz and Thiry could not stop spinning, Eriksson was off the pace and Auriol was more interested in his bad luck than his stage times. Makinen had it all his own way and the Swedish Rally cruised to its conclusion with second placed Sainz keeping the championship lead.

Auriol: bad luck or no luck at all

As expected, the Swedish Rally is cold, but not as we know it. A dry cold which soaks into the bones and at the end of the day, as night drew in, temperatures would flit around the -15 degree mark. So, after constantly inhaling snow in its radiator grille, taking in all the negative vibes from the cold and sliding over black ice all day, the Toyota Corolla of Didier Auriol and Denis Giraudet obviously had enough. It was just at the start of the second timed section of the first leg that a thick, acrid and grey smoke cloud billowed majestically from the central vent in the dashboard.

They quizzed the team by radio as to the proper procedure for a blazing car; getting out sounds good, before former ambulance driver Auriol transformed himself into fireman and traced the fault to the heated windscreen and sorted it. "Short circuit" he cursed later in grumpy mood. He had every reason to be grumpy as the delay cost him 20 seconds.

This little episode was only the start of a series of misadventures which befell Didier Auriol and Denis Giraudet. Here is a run-down, and it's not exhaustive! Friday: fire in the dashboard, which damages water injection pump, which puts excessive heat through the turbo; gear selector playing up. Saturday: fuel pump cuts out intermittently, forcing Auriol and Giraudet to change it themselves between two stages. Sunday: engine cuts out only to restart after two minutes of immobility; loss of power under acceleration; gear indicator fails; windscreen wipers and washers come on when the brakes are applied.

It seemed that the little Frenchman had picked up a bad fairy in Monte-Carlo and it was now wreaking revenge for being taken to the frozen north. It was no doubt

related to these Swedish trolls that make an appearance in the forests every time those rally cars make their crablike sideways progress through the trees. At the end of the event Auriol looked more resigned than downhearted. After all, what could he do when, of the three Toyota Corolla WRC entered, his was the only one which seemed to have its own ghost, along with a pack of black cats or may be just a colony of computer bugs. To finish sixth in these circumstances was something of an achievement. Auriol never gave up and when his Corolla ran cleanly, he put up some good times. If you took out all the stages where the gremlins struck, he would have been toughing it out with Sainz and Kankkunen for a place on the podium.

The Radstrom party

He is Swedish and yet another of those with small oval spectacles, perched on a nice straight nose which stood out from a face as podgy as the love handles which tussle with the belt of his overalls. One

said he was starting eighth every time, with Sainz, Kankkunen and McRae acting as his road sweepers, taking the top layer of snow off the tracks and making the stages immaculate. There was no doubt this was the quickest snow plough trio in the world. "Road conditions are deciding the order," said McRae, seeking solace with an easy way to explain away a great drive. Once again, what really impressed was the performance of the Toyota, with Radstrom in the lead and Sainz third at the end of the first leg and Auriol who should have been upthere with them. Brilliant in Monte-Carlo, the Corolla was simply staggering in Scandinavia. As for Ove Andersson, he could but congratulate himself on nominating the Swede to score the constructors' championship points instead of Auriol. At the start of the second leg, it was Radstrom's turn to play pathfinder. "I'm not worried. It just means I am leading!" However, the Swede was no longer dominant and then went off for good in the middle of the day. Nevertheless, his performance did not go unnoticed.

53.1

gets the impression the lad was a bit too keen on his mum's meat and two veg. Whatever, she produced a superb rally driver, who won here in 1994, when this was not a championship event. Since then, he has been under Toyota's wing and his mission here was simple; to bring home some points. After the first stage, where Sainz was allowed to top the time sheet, no doubt to lull him into a false sense of security, the rally became a Radstrom riot as he took six of the eight stages. It has to be

52.1
All the troubles which befell the Toyota WRC team appeared to land on Didier Auriol's car.

53.1
Thanks to the elimination of Thomas Radstrom, Makinen got his revenge for Monte-Carlo.

54.1

54.2

54.3

55.1

SWEDISH
"A bad fairy related to Swedish trolls..."

54.1

But for the engine problems which caused his retirement, McRae could have featured on the podium.

54.2

Carlos Sainz was untouchable in the final stage. Second place was enough to keep his championship lead.

54.3

A good performance from Finland's Marcus Gronholm, who would be give n a Toyota Corolla WRC from the Portuguese Rally.

54.4

Tommi Makinen owed victory in part to Michelin, whose tyres were particularly well suited to the Mitsubishi.

55.1

In the final stage, Kankkunen could not resist Carlos Sainz' charge.

55.2

Three times winner of this event, Kenneth Eriksson was never really on the pace in this his last drive with Subaru.

55.2

2 SWEDISH RALLY
THE INTERNATIONAL

47TH SWEDISH RALLY

TOP ENTRIES

1 Tommi Makinen
Risto Mannisenmaki
MITSUBISHI LANCER EV.4

2 Richard Burns
Robert Reid
MITSUBISHI CARISMA GT

3 Colin McRae
Nicky Grist
SUBARU IMPREZA WRC

4 Kenneth Eriksson
Staffan Parmander
SUBARU IMPREZA WRC

5 Carlos Sainz
Luis Moya
TOYOTA COROLLA WRC

6 Thomas Rädström
Lars Bäckman
TOYOTA COROLLA WRC

7 Juha Kankkunen
Juha Repo
FORD ESCORT WRC

8 Bruno Thiry
Stéphane Prévot
FORD ESCORT WRC

9 Didier Auriol
Denis Giraudet
TOYOTA COROLLA WRC

10 Piero Liatti
Fabrizia Pons
SUBARU IMPREZA WRC

11 Marcus Grönholm
Timo Rautiainen
TOYOTA CELICA GT FOUR

12 Sebastian Lindholm
Timo Hantunen
FORD ESCORT WRC

14 Uwe Nittel
Tina Thorner
MITSUBISHI CARISMA GT

15 Mats Jonsson
Johnny Johansson
FORD ESCORT COSWORTH

16 Pasi Hagstrom
Tero Gardemeister
TOYOTA CELICA GT-FOUR

17 Harri Rovanperä
Voitto Silander
SEAT IBIZA 16v KIT CAR

18 Per Svan
Johan Olsson
OPEL ASTRA GSI

19 Oriol Gomez
Marc Marti
SEAT IBIZA 16v KIT CAR

20 Alister McRae
David Senior
VW GOLF GTI KIT CAR

21 Toni Gardemeister
Paavo Lukander
NISSAN SUNNY GTI

22 Kenneth Backlund
Tord Andersson
MITSUBISHI LANCER EV.4

23 Gustavo Trelles
Jorge Del Buono
MITSUBISHI LANCER EV.4

24 Juha Kangas
Jani Laaksonen
MITSUBISHI CARISMA GT

25 Stig-Olov Walfridson
Benny Melander
MITSUBISHI LANCER EV.4

26 Juuso Pykalisto
Esko Mertsalmi
MITSUBISHI CARISMA GT

27 Jorgen Jonasson
Pecka Svensson
SEAT IBIZA 16v KIT CAR

28 Jonas Kruse
Per Schlegel
RENAULT MEGANE MAXI

31 Luis Climent
Alex Romani
MITSUBISHI LANCER EV.3

32 Alexandre Nikonenko
Victor Timkovsky
FORD ESCORT WRC

2nd leg of the 1998 world rally championships for constructors and drivers
2nd leg of the constructors' "2 litre", production car drivers' and teams' world cups

Date: *6 - 8 February 1998*

Route: *1430.31 km divided into 3 legs with 19 stages on snow covered loose surface roads (381.34 km)*
1st leg: Friday 6th February, Karlstad - Torsby - Karlstad, 8 stages (147.28 km)
2nd leg: Saturday 7th February, Karlstad - Borlange, 6 stages (139.82 km)
3rd leg: Sunday 8th February, Borlange - Karlstad, 5 stages (94.24 km)

Starters: *78 (44 Group A + 34 Group N)*

Finishers: *42 (24 Group A + 18 Group N)*

Bruno Thiry's lack of experience on these roads did not help his cause .

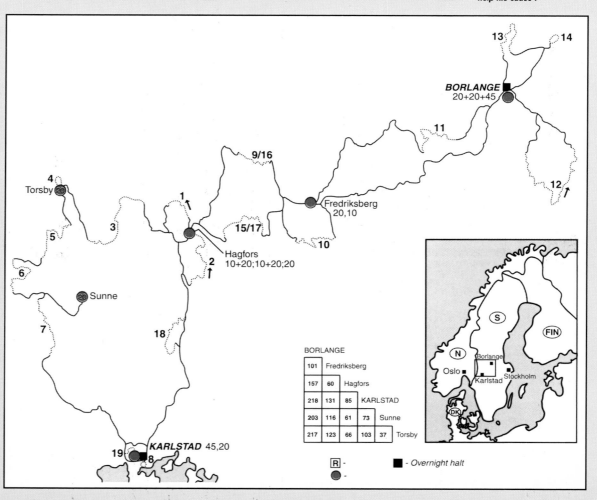

SPECIAL STAGE TIMES

ES.1 Malta (11,88 km)
1. Sainz 5'55''4; 2. Rädström, 5'55''9; 3. Makinen 5'57''8; 4. Gronhölm 5'59''3; 5. Auriol 5'59''6; Gr.N Backlund 6'16''9; F2 Rovanpera 6'23''9

ES.2 Sunnemo (30,87 km)
1. Rädström 15'33''3; 2. Makinen 15'41'3; 3. Sainz 15'48''7; 4. Auriol 15'50''9; 5. McRae 15'53''; Gr.N Walfridson 16'27''4; F2 Jonasson 16'53''2

ES.3 Hamra (35,42 km)
1. Rädström 19'30''7; 2. Makinen 19'36''6; 3. Auriol 19'45''8; 4. Grönhölm 19'46''1; 5. McRae 19'46''3; Gr.N Walfridson 20'25''4; F2 A.McRae 21'05''1

ES.4 Vassjön (4 km)
1. Makinen 3'11''1; 2. Auriol 3'12''; 3. Eriksson 3'12''2; 4. Rädström 3'12''3; 5. Kankkunen 3'12''5; Gr.N Backlund 3'18''1; F2 Svan 3'26''

ES.5 Bjälverud (21,58 km)
1. Rädström 11'17''8; 2. Makinen, à 11'20''8; 3. Grönhölm, à 11'25''5; 4. Sainz 11'26''3; 5. Auriol 11'27''9; Gr.N Backlund 11'53''7; F2 Gardemeister 12'22''2

ES.6 Mangen (22,09 km)
1. Rädström 12'40''; 2. Makinen 12'43''9; 3. Grönhölm 12'45''6; 4. Auriol 12'49''5; 5. Kankkunen 12'54''3; Gr.N Walfridson 13'15''5; F2 Gardemeister 13'48''9

ES.7 Langjohanstorp (19,44 km)
1. Rädström, 10'09''8; 2. Makinen 10'11''6; 3. Sainz 10'13''5; 4. Kankkunen 11'13''8; 5. Eriksson 10'16''6; Gr.N Backlund 10'40''9; F2 Jonasson 10'51''2

ES.8 Inre Hamn (2 km)
1. Rädström 1'22''2; 2. Grönhölm 1'23''3; 3. Makinen 1'23''5; 4. Burns 1'23''6; 5. Sainz 1'24''; Gr.N Backlund 1'28''3; F2 Svan 1'30''4

ES.9 Sagen (14,76 km)
1. Burns 8'08''2; 2. Kankkunen 8'17''7; 3. McRae 8'17''7; 4. Rädström 8'18''2; 5. Thiry 8'19''6; Gr.N Walfridson; F2 Svan 8'43''6

ES.10 Fredriksberg (24,80 km)
1. Burns, 14'20''3 2. Kankkunen 14'20''9; 3. Sainz 14'22''2; 4. Makinen 14'24''; 5. McRae 14'25''1; Gr.N Backlund 14'53''8; F2 Svan 15'26''5

ES.11 Nyhammar (27,79 km)
1. Kankkunen 15'19''4; 2. Makinen 15'24''3; 3. Burns 15'27''9; 4. Eriksson 15'28''3; 5. McRae 15'29''3; Gr.N Walfridson 16'06''2; F2 Joki 16'23''8

ES.12 Jutbo (47,65 km)
1. Makinen, 27'55''3; 2. Kankkunen 28'18''7; 3. Eriksson 28'25''2; 4. Auriol 28'41''7; 5. Grönhölm 28'42''1; Gr.N Walfridson 29'24''7; F2 Nilsson 30'36''7

ES.13 Skog (22,82 km)
1. Makinen 13'04''1; 2. Kankkunen 13'04''6; 3. Sainz 13'07''8; 4. Eriksson et Auriol 13'12''; Gr.N Walfridson 14'00''2; F2 Jonasson 14'20''3

ES.14 Lugnet (2 km)
1. Makinen 1'58''4; 2. Kankkunen 2'00''3; 3. Sainz 2'00''4; 4. Eriksson 2'01''4; 5. Auriol 2'01''5; Gr.N Backlund 2'06''4; F2 Gardemeister 2'12''8

ES.15 Rämmen 1 (23,81 km)
1. Sainz 12'26''1; 2. Kankkunen 12'28''4; 3. Auriol 12'31''2; 4. Burns 12'34''5; 5. Eriksson 12'37''9; Gr.N Backlund 13'11''5; F2 Gardemeister 13'27''8

ES.16 Sagen 2 (14,76 km)
1. Burns 7'56''6; 2. Sainz 7'57''6; 3. Kankkunen 7'58''5; 4. Makinen 8'00''9; 5. Hagström 8'05''8; Gr.N Walfridson 8'25''3; F2 Joki 8'32''

ES.17 Rämmen 2 (23,81 km)
1. Sainz 12'23''1; 2. Makinen 12'24''9; 3. Grönhölm 12'28''9; 4. Auriol 12'31''6; 5. Burns 12'32''2; Gr.N Walfridson 13'08''; F2 Gardemeister 13'16''8

ES.18 Mangstorp (22,49 km)
1. Sainz 12'08''7; 2. Kankkunen 12'14''5; 3. Auriol 12'15''; 4. Burns 12'20''1; 5. Eriksson 12'28''5; Gr.N Backlund 12'59''5; F2 Jonasson 13'25''8

ES.19 I2 (9,37 km)
1. Sainz 5'46''2; 2. Kankkunen 5'49''1 ; 3. Makinen 5'51''5; 4. Auriol 5'52''5; 5. Gronhölm 5'53''3; Gr.N Walfridson 6'10''; F2 Jonasson 6'27''2

RESULTS AND RETIREMENTS

	Driver/Co-Driver	Car	N°	Gr	Total Time
1	Tommi Makinen - Risto Manisenmaki	Mitsubishi Lancer Ev.4	1	A	3h32m51,6s
2	Carlos Sainz - Luis Moya	Toyota Corolla WRC	5	A	3h33m43,2s
3	Juha Kankkunen - Juha Repo	Ford Escort WRC	7	A	3h33m50,4s
4	Kenneth Eriksson - Staffan Parmander	Subaru Impreza WRC	4	A	3h35m23,3s
5	Marcus Grönholm - Timo Rautiainen	Toyota Celica GT-Four	11	A	3h36m21,5s
6	Didier Auriol - Denis Giraudet	Toyota Corolla WRC	9	A	3h37m09,8s
7	Uwe Nittel - Tina Thörner	Mitsubishi Carisma GT	14	A	3h37m35,2s
8	Bruno Thiry - Stéphane Prévot	Ford Escort WRC	8	A	3h38m35,1s
9	Piero Liatti - Fabrizia Pons	Subaru Impreza WRC	10	A	3h40m38,5s
10	Mats Jonsson - Johnny Johansson	Ford Escort Cosworth	15	A	3h41m05,5s
ES.2	Gustavo Trelles - Jorge Del Buono	Mitsubishi Lancer Ev.3	23	N	Engine
ES.2	Luis Climent - Alex Romani	Mitsubishi Lancer Ev.3	31	N	Suspension
ES.6	Harri Rovanperä - Voitto Silander	Seat Ibiza 16v Kit Car	17	A	Engine
ES.11	Per Svan - Johan Olsson	Opel Astra GSI	18	A	Accident
ES.12	Thomas Rädström - Lars Bäckman	Toyota Corolla WRC	6	A	Accident
ES.12	Colin McRae - Nicky Grist	Subaru Impreza WRC	3	A	Electrical
ES.12	Alister McRae - David Senior	VW Golf GTI Kit Car	20	A	Engine

PREVIOUS WINNERS

1973	Blomqvist - Hertz SAAB 96 V 4
1975	Waldegaard - Thorszelius LANCIA STRATOS
1976	Eklund - Cederberg SAAB 96 V 4
1977	Blomqvist - Sylvan SAAB 99 EMS
1978	Waldegaard - Thorszelius FORD ESCORT RS
1979	Blomqvist - Cederberg SAAB 99 TURBO
1980	Kullang - Berglund OPEL ASCONA 400
1981	Mikkola - Hertz AUDI QUATTRO
1982	Blomqvist - Cederberg AUDI QUATTRO
1983	Mikkola - Hertz AUDI QUATTRO
1984	Blomqvist - Cederberg AUDI QUATTRO
1985	Vatanen - Harryman PEUGEOT 205 T16
1986	Kankkunen - Piironen PEUGEOT 205 T16
1987	Salonen - Harjanne MAZDA 323 TURBO
1988	Alen - Kivimaki LANCIA DELTA HF 4WD
1989	Carlsson - Carlsson MAZDA 323 4WD
1991	Eriksson - Parmander MITSUBISHII GALANT VR-4
1992	Jonsson - Backman TOYOTA CELICA GT-FOUR
1993	Jonsson - Backman TOYOTA CELICA TURBO 4WD
1994	Radstrom - Backman TOYOTA CELICA TURBO 4WD
1995	Eriksson - Parmander MITSUBISHI LANCER Ev.2
1996	Makinen - Harjanne MITSUBISHI LANCER Ev.3
1997	Eriksson - Parmander SUBARU IMPREZA WRC

EVENT LEADERS

ES.1: Sainz
ES.2 - ES.11: Rädström
ES.12 - ES.19: Makinen

BEST PERFORMANCES

	1	2	3	4	5	6
Rädström	6	2	-	2	-	-
Sainz	5	1	5	1	1	2
Makinen	4	7	3	2	-	2
Burns	3	-	1	3	1	3
Kankkunen	1	7	1	1	2	4
Auriol	-	1	3	6	3	1
Grönholm	-	1	3	2	-	-
Eriksson	-	-	2	3	3	2
McRae	-	-	1	-	4	3
Thiry	-	-	-	-	1	1
Hagstrom	-	-	-	-	1	1

CHAMPIONSHIP CLASSIFICATIONS

Drivers:
1. Carlos Sainz 16
2. Tommi Makinen 10
2. Juha Kankkunen 10
4. Colin McRae 4
5. Piero Liatti 3
5. Kenneth Eriksson 3

Constructors:
1. Toyota 16
2. Mitsubishi 12
3. Ford 11
4. Subaru 10

Group N:
1. Manfred Stohl 13
1. Stig-Olov Walfridson 13
3. Luis Climent 8
3. Kenneth Bäcklund 8

Two Litres:
1. Peugeot 16
2. Seat 14
3. Volkswagen 3

Team's Cup:
1. Scuderia Grifone 10

GOSSIP

• MICHELIN
Michelin got it all: victory, the whole podium and 19 fastest times out of 19 stages! It would be difficult to do better, especially as this came hot on the heels of Monte success. The company was praised by all those who used its product, Makinen claiming he owed the win to the tyres. The top snow tyre is the GE. It has an asymmetric pattern and only a different length of stud separated those used by Radstrom on Friday and then Makinen on Saturday. Finland's Gronhölm was a magnificent fifth overall in his "old" Toyota Celica which was fitted with GA62 tyres that any snow rally fans can buy over the counter. Pirelli was really feeling the heat. The previous year, the Italian company had won the first two events.

• SUBARU
It was a big let down for Subaru. Liatti, ninth at the finish, was completely off the pace in terms of his driving for the whole event. McRae might have made the podium but for recalcitrant electricals on the second leg. Eriksson admitted he had got it wrong and had a bad set-up. It should be noted that all the Imprezas struggled with a chronic lack of power and Eriksson also had to fight a flawed gearbox towards the end of the rally.

• ERIKSSON
Kenneth Eriksson, winner here in 1997 was tackling his final rally for Subaru. "For the rest of the season, Subaru only offered me a small programme of events and a testing job." So, as from the Portuguese Rally at the end of March, he would be slipping into Hyundai overalls. Despite the economic crisis in Asia, the Korean constructor had decided to tackle ten of the eleven remaining rounds with its Kit Car Coupe, before stepping up its involvement in the world rally championship. "In 1999," continued Eriksson, "The Hyundai World Rally Car should be up and running before tackling a full season in 2000 with a works team. That is why I preferred to leave Subaru."

SAFARI

After Sainz in Monte-Carlo and Makinen in Sweden, it was Burns' turn to take top honours. It was a welcome first world status win for the English beanpole, whose talent became

more and more apparent with every passing rally. All the same, he did profit from the misfortune of others on the Safari, where usually a finish provides a good result. But finishing is the big challenge. So, we had three events and three winners. An exciting championship was in prospect.

anorexic giraffe..."

Burns night

Right from the first leg, Makinen and Burns in their Mitsubishis were leaving the others to eat their dust. A local fable tells of a war between baboons and bees and these two drivers put on a mechanical version, monkeying around ahead of the chasing swarm of insects. Nothing stopped their ineffable progress. Even the plague of punctures of years past did not bother them. "Not one spare wheel came out of its holder," said a Michelin technician charged with looking after the Mitsubishis, bristling with pride. "There are plenty of cuts on the sidewalls, but not enough to puncture them." Once again the Michelin Man has got it right. In the past,

the stranded car with its airless tyre was a common sight as the crew grunted with effort on the jack, burnt their forearms on the red hot discs, while scraping their knuckles on the wheelnuts. Each time it happened, another two minutes went down the drain. The only one to cling on to the leaders was McRae and he was the worst affected by the consequences of one of these irritating punctures. He cleaned the stages in vain, the Mitsus continued to keep their distance. Behind them it was all a bit untidy, like a herd of disorientated gnus running blindly through the brush.

As for Auriol, bad luck his most faithful companion so far this season, was lurking in the boot of his Corolla in the form of a loose can rattling around until it broke a battery terminal. Five minutes lost and he does not look happy. "Why, why is it always me?" he swore, his head simmering in the heat.

On the morning of the second day, Makinen, sticking to his

60.1
Harri Rovanpera's surprising fifth place meant he scored drivers' world championship points for the first time.

60.2
Once again, Colin McRae was let down by an engine failure.

61.1-2
Richard Burns and Ari Vatanen: an explosion of happiness on the podium.

usual tactic, put the hammer down once again. On the first stage of the day, he set a breathtaking time which left the pack to choke on his dirt as he pulled out an advantage of almost five minutes on his young compadre. In the dense fog of dust, despite the cars starting at three minute intervals, Sainz rolled, Auriol punctured, while McRae, Liatti and Kankkunen simply had to give best. "I drove well," declared the world champion with that cheeky grin. "There was quite a bit of traffic on the open roads, but nothing too serious." His dominance was robbing the rally of any interest, but not for long. He might have done better to see the signs rather than rejoice at the simultaneous retirement of second placed McRae and of Liatti. "The engine overheated," moaned the Scotsman. His team could only pick up what was left of it as it spat oil and filled their lungs with smoke. Liatti was stranded in the tenth stage. "The engine seized," as did the voice of Fabrizia Pons when explaining their fate.

The Mitsu boys did not heed the warning signs. In the next stage, the final one of the leg, the cam belt on Makinen's Lancer broke, taking the engine with it. "No noise, no sign, no warning. Just bang!" Over the course of two stages, the balance of the Safari had been overturned. Burns, thus made it into Nairobi in the lead, ahead of the indestructible Vatanen, driving his "nothing special" Ford with caution. The final leg was a mere formality. Cushioned by a nice 6.01 advantage over Vatanen, the Englishman did not even have to fight off the advances of the Ford dri-

61.1

61.2

vers in second and third places. Vatanen, hel-ped by Kankkunen, seemed to be too busy to shake off the leechlike Auriol. Third, the Frenchman had attempted one last vain attempt to go for second place, but technical problems put him off his stride. In the final section, Vatanen, the high class stand-in, handed second place to team leader Kankkunen, which put him into the lead of this uncertain and fascinating champion-ship.

Vatanen gets Thiry's seat

Some Belgian jokes are not really funny. Thiry can curse his luck for having come into the line of fire of a tool box or a roll over cage or a spare wheel, all in the back of his own Escort. What led to this strange series of events which robbed him of his attempt on the Safari? At the start of the year, Kenya had been hit by a deluge of rain. Torrents had raged, rivers had run but now, all that was left were a few muddy sections. It was in one of these, on 16th February, that Juha Kankkunen got bogged down in his spare car, while recceing the stage. It proved impossible to get it out of the mire, even with the help of the service cars. With both Ford crews still having a lot of stages to look at, "Mister K" took the wheel of Thiry's car, while the Belgian and his co-driver got in the back. It was a question of size, not rank. The two bulky Finns could only fit in the front. As night fell, the rain came down hard again and Kankkunen, despite his immense expe-rience, was unable to avoid a deep pothole.

In the back, Thiry was thrown against the tool box-wheel-roll hoop trio and bounced off with five broken ribs. Ford immediately organised a replacement. "I am absolutely heartbroken for Bruno," explained team manager Malcolm Wilson. "He was so loo-king forward to his first Safari. While waiting for him to be with us again in Portugal, we are happy to welcome Ari Vatanen. His expe-rience could play a vital role." Indeed, less than two days after the accident, Ford confir-med the arrival of the great Ari. For his part, he was delighted and his knowledge of Africa in particular and rallying in general could only be a benefit. The Finn knows the Safari having won it once with Opel in 1983 and taken part on four occasions, so the Kenyan tracks held no fears for him. However, dea-ling with the world championship, his oppo-nents and his pace was a different matter. In November '97 he had made an uninspired comeback in the RAC at the wheel of a Escort WRC. But logic does not apply in Africa and the rain gods had offered him the eternal comeback drive.

Burns baptized

Richard Burns' face is ravaged with worry. He jumps out of the car, opens the bonnet and peers in with engineers and mechanics by his side. The collective ears hear nothing wrong. The driver manages a weak smile: "I thought I heard a noise. It must have been in my head." It is midday in the Kenyan sun at the entrance to the Plains Park service area. In the distance, a train blows a never ending

warning whistle to move the animals straying across its tracks. It is the only sound in this vast expanse of green nothing, but Burns has succumbed to the worry of hearing things. Real or not, the clickety click gnaws away at the mind. It is a well known torment for those on the path to victory. The tall car-rot-top who resembles nothing more than an anorexic giraffe with the face of a cooked rather than tanned camel, is tenser than a Masai warrior hunting a lion. It is never easy to run first on the road to success. "I have never been as nervous as I was today. I really wanted to win." Therein lay his strength. It is not his only quality. At the age of 28 he already has an impressive range of talents. "He is a tireless worker," explains a watery-eyed Andrew Cowan, the top man at Mitsubishi. "He has made astonishing pro-gress." For the wily horse dealing Scotsman, this was also his success. He spotted the pre-cocious talent of this gangly youth who won the British championship in 1993, realising he was a charger. He snaffled him away from the Subaru stockade and set him up in his team in '96. Training and working the tho-roughbred, he got him to win the non-cham-pionship 1996 New Zealand rally. He took a while to stand out from the crowd, but made his mark on the 1997 RAC, pulling off a full contract for the following year. During the winter, while Makinen convalesced, Burns took on the development of the current Mitsubishi, while also putting the new Evo V through its first paces. He only needed to claim his first rally scalp and since Kenya, the rally establishment has one more member.

SAFARI
"The silhouette of an anorexic giraffe..."

62.1
*Didier Auriol proved to be more
competitive than his team-mate.*

62.2
*On a puncture-free run, Richard Burns
maintained a relentlessly rapid pace.*

62.3
*Winner of the Safari back in 1983,
it did not take Ari Vatanen long to get
back into the swing of things.*

62.4
*Several damper failures delayed
the WRC Corollas on their Safari debut.*

62.1

62.2

62.3

62.4

63.1

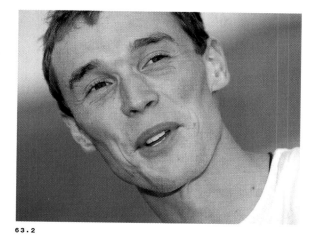

63.2

63.1
The Ford team might not have the quickest car,
but they certainly have the most reliable one.

63.2
In Kenya, Richard Burns picked up one of the most
prestigious wins of the season.

63.3-4
At the start of the second stage, an evidently slightly
nervous Carlos Sainz had a time consuming roll.

63.5
Had Makinen pushed his car too hard ?
He was now fourth in the championship.

63.3

63.5

SAFARI
"The silhouette of an anorexic giraffe..."

64.1
Called in as a last minute replacement for Bruno Thiry, Ari Vatanen was delighted to find himself at the wheel of a works car.

64.2
Tommi Makinen was untouchable until his engine cried no more.

64.3
The Seat Ibiza was surprisingly well adapted to the African tracks.

65.1
Just when he felt he could finish second, Didier Auriol suffered as

65.2

64.1

64.2

65.1

64.3

3

TOP ENTRIES

1 Tommi Makinen
 Risto Mannisenmaki
 MITSUBISHI LANCER EV.4

2 Richard Burns
 Robert Reid
 MITSUBISHI CARISMA GT

3 Colin McRae
 Nicky Grist
 SUBARU IMPREZA WRC

4 Piero Liatti
 Fabrizia Pons
 SUBARU IMPREZA WRC

5 Carlos Sainz
 Luis Moya
 TOYOTA COROLLA WRC

6 Didier Auriol
 Denis Giraudet
 TOYOTA COROLLA WRC

7 Juha Kankkunen
 Juha Repo
 FORD ESCORT WRC

8 Ari Vatanen
 Fred Gallagher
 FORD ESCORT WRC

9 Emmanuel Katto
 Frank Gitau
 TOYOTA CELICA GT-FOUR

10 Frédéric Dor
 Kevin Gormley
 SUBARU IMPREZA

11 Harri Rovanperä
 Voitto Silander
 SEAT IBIZA 16V KIT CAR

12 Kris Rosenberger
 Per Carlsson
 VW GOLF GTI KIT CAR

14 Manfred Stohl
 Kay Gerlach
 MITSUBISHI LANCER EV.3

15 Oriol Gomez
 Marc Marti
 SEAT IBIZA 16V KIT CAR

16 Raimund Baumschlager
 Klaus Wicha
 VW GOLF GTI KIT CAR

17 Patrick Njiru
 Gillian Webb
 SUBARU IMPREZA

18 Luis Climent
 Alex Romani
 MITSUBISHI LANCER EV.3

20 Rudi Stohl
 Jurgen Berti
 AUDI QUATTRO COUPÉ S2

46TH SAFARI RALLY

3rd leg of the 1998 world rally championships for constructors and drivers
3rd leg of the constructors' "2 litre", production car drivers' and teams' world cups

Date: *28 February - 2 March 1998*

Route: *2226.01 km divided into 3 legs with 16 sections run on loose surface roads (1068.98 km)*
1st leg: Saturday 28th February, Nairobi - Plains Park - Nairobi, 6 sections (347.54 km)
2nd leg: Sunday 1st March, Nairobi - Equator Park - Nairobi, 5 sectors (378.29 km)
3rd leg: Monday 2nd March, Nairobi - Plains Park - Nairobi, 5 sectors (343.15 km)

Starters: *48 (27 Group A + 21 Group N)*

Finishers: *19 (12 Group A + 7 Group N)*

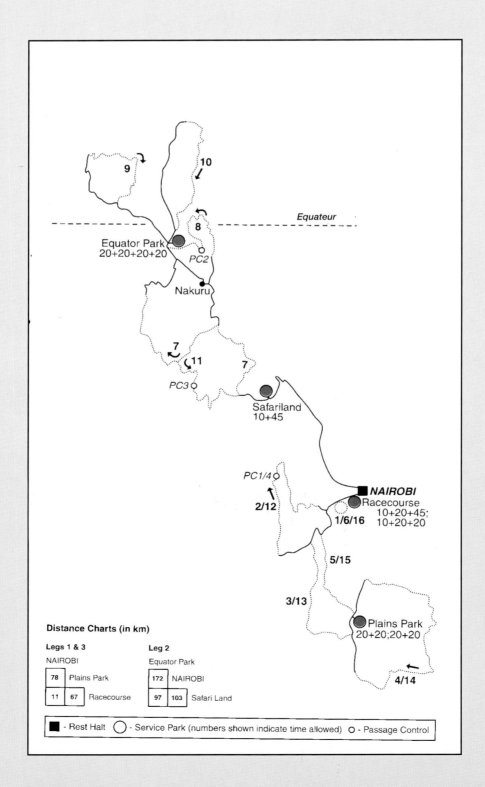

Distance Charts (in km)

Legs 1 & 3

NAIROBI

| 78 | Plains Park |
| 11 | 67 | Racecourse |

Leg 2

Equator Park

| 172 | NAIROBI |
| 97 | 103 | Safari Land |

■ - Rest Halt   ◯ - Service Park (numbers shown indicate time allowed)   ○ - Passage Control

After a cautious start, Luis Climent took the Group N
win at his first attempt.

SPECIAL STAGE TIMES

SC.1 Super Spéciale 1(4,30 km)
1. Burns 3'06''; 2. Makinen 3'07''; 3. Auriol 3'09''; 4. Liatti et Sainz 3'10''; Gr.N Climent 3'36''; F2 Rovanpera 3'34''

SC.2 Oltepsei 1 (108,12 km)
1. Makinen 47'45''; 2. Burns 48'; 3. Liatti 48'59''; 4. Sainz 50' 5. Auriol 50'06''; Gr.N Climent 1h02'35''; F2 Rosenberger 1h01'15''

SC.3 Hunter's Lookout 1 (71,90 km)
1. McRae 35'18''; 2. Makinen 35'32''; 3. Burns 35'46''; 4. Auriol 35'50''; 5. Liatti 36'32''; Gr.N Njiru 48'35''; F2 Rovanpera 45'52''

SC.4 Olkejiado 1 (109,87 km)
1. McRae 55'48''; 2. Makinen 56'21''; 3. Burns 57'02''; 4. Makinen 57'19''; 5. Kankkunen 57'40''; Gr.N Climent 1h10'43''; F2 Baumschlager 1h06'34''

SC.5 Kajiado 1 (48,96 km)
1. McRae 20'45''; 2. Makinen 21'14''; 3. Vatanen 21'32''; 4.Burns 21'39''; 5. Auriol 21'46''; Gr.N Njiru 27'47''; F2 Gomez 26'22''

SC.6 Super Spéciale 2 (4,30 km)
1. McRae 3'06''; 2. Makinen et Burns 3'07''; 4. Kankkunen 3'08''; 5. Sainz 3'11''; Gr.N Climent et Rosenberger 3'39''; F2 Gomez 3'36''

SC.7 Crater Lake Road (79,42 km)
1. Makinen 36'03''; 2. Vatanen 37'56''; 3. McRae 39'16''; 4. Burns 40'08''; 5. Liatti 41'08''; Gr.N Climent 49'12''; F2 Rovanpera 48'02''

SC.8 Solai 1 (66,49 km)
1. Makinen 32'04''; 2. Sainz et Vatanen 42'44''; 4. McRae 32'52''; 5. Burns 33'16''; Gr.N Stohl 44'03''; F2 Rovanpera 40'07''

SC.9 Nyaru (87,19 km)
1. Liatti 55'39''; 2. Sainz 55'52''; 3. Kankkunen 56'23''; 4. Makinen 56'26''; 5. McRae 56'29''; Gr.N Climent 1h06'58''; F2 Baumschlager 1h04'58''

SC.10 Marigat (78,70 km)
1. Auriol 34'51''; 2. Makinen 34'53''; 3. Burns 35'08''; 4. Sainz 37'35''; 5. Kankkunen 37'43''; Gr.N Stohl 42'41''; F2 Baumschlager 42'18''

SC.11 Solai 2 (66,49 km)
1. Sainz 32'11''; 2. Auriol 32'36''; 3. Burns 33'13''; 4. Vatanen 33'16''; 5. Kankkunen 35'09''; Gr.N Climent 42'47''; F2 Rovanpera 40'35''

SC.12 Oltepesi 2 (108,12 km)
1. Burns 49'46''; 2. Kankkunen 49'51''; 3. Vatanen 50'08''; 4. Auriol 51'11''; 5. Sainz 51'53''; Gr.N Climent 1h02'56''; F2 Rovanpera 1h01'46''

SC.13 Hunter's Lookout 3 (71,90 km)
1. Vatanen 35'31''; 2. Burns 36'31''; 3. Kankkunen 36'36''; 4. Auriol 39'08''; 5. Hirji 47'15''; Gr.N Stohl 47'34''; F2 Baumschlager 48'48''

SC.14 Olkejiado 2 (109,87 km)
1. Kankkunen 56'42''; 2. Vatanen 57'03''; 3. Burns 57'54''; 4. Auriol 58'33''; 5. Rovanpera 1h08'26''; Gr.N Stohl 1h10'35''

SC.15 Kajiado 2 (48,96 km)
1. Kankkunen 21'47''; 2. Vatanen 22'04''; 3. Burns 22'29''; 4. Auriol 23'43''; 5. Stohl 28'15''; F2 Rosenberger 28'19''

SC.16 Super Spéciale 3 (4,30 km)
1. Burns 3'09''; 2. Kankkunen 3'13''; 3. Vatanen 3'14''; 4. Auriol 3'17''; 5. Rosenberger 3'37''; Gr.N Climent 3'49''

RESULTS AND RETIREMENTS

	Driver/Co-Driver	Car	N°	Gr	Total Time
1	Richard Burns - Robert Reid	Mitsubishi Carisma GT	2	A	8h57m34s
2	Juha Kankkunen - Juha Repo	Ford Escort WRC	7	A	9h07m01s
3	Ari Vatanen - Fred Gallagher	Ford Escort WRC	8	A	9h07m26s
4	Didier Auriol - Denis Giraudet	Toyota Corolla WRC	6	A	9h12m00s
5	Harri Rovanperä - Voitto Silander	Seat Ibiza GTI 16v Kit Car	11	A	11h03m12s
6	Raimund Baumschlager - Klaus Wicha	VW Golf GTI Kit Car	16	A	11h17m35s
7	Luis Climent - Alex Romani	Mitsubishi Lancer Ev.3	18	N	11h25m37s
8	Kris Rosenberger - Per Carlsson	VW Golf GTI Kit Car	12	A	11h43m21s
9	Marco Brighetti - Abdul Sidi	Subaru Impreza	19	A	11h53m35s
10	Karim Hirji - Frank Nekusa	Toyota Celica GT-Four	21	A	12h01m03s
SC.5	Frédéric Dor - Kevin Gormley	Subaru Impreza	10	A	Turbo
SC.6	Patrick Njiru - Gillian Webb	Subaru Impreza	17	A	Transmission
SC.9	Emmanuel Katto - Frank Gitau	Toyota Celica GT-Four	9	A	Accident
SC.10	Piero Liatti - Fabrizia Pons	Subaru Impreza WRC	4	A	Engine
SC.10	Colin McRae - Nicky Grist	Subaru Impreza WRC	3	A	Engine
SC.11	Tommi Makinen - Risto Manisennmaki	Mitsubishi Lancer Ev.4	1	A	Engine
SC.11	Oriol Gomez - Marc Marti	Seat Ibiza 16v Kit Car	15	A	Out of Time
SC.13	Carlos Sainz - Luis Moya	Toyota Corolla WRC	5	A	Suspension

GOSSIP

• AURIOL

Fourth place was good for the soul of Didier Auriol. Once again he was the victim of bad luck, but when it left him alone, the Frenchman was easily the better of the two Toyota drivers and made his way to the front. Third at the start of the final leg, he set off in pursuit of second place. "The roads were very bad and we had too many punctures. Then the dampers were too soft and I had to back off. Finally, I decided to take it easy to make sure there was at least one Toyota at the finish."

• SEAT

For their first Safari, the Seat Ibizas did a great job. Rovenpera was fifth and won the two litre category. It was the first time an Ibiza had figured in the top six of a world championship rally and it was also a first for the young Finn. Reigning champions in the two litre world cup, the Spanish constructor also took the lead away from Peugeot. "For us,it was a case of coming to learn the ropes," explained Benoit Bagur, the chief engineer, "as part of our preparations for running a WRC next year." Mission accomplished.

• TYRES

The Safari is a tyre nightmare and victory often goes to the driver who knew how best to look after his rubber. Michelin brought a new tyre this year, with more resistance to side-wall cuts, which is the main worry here. The manufacturer also offered its drivers the possibility to run with tyres fitted with ATS, an anti-puncture mousse, although they do not work on long stages or when it is very hot. A major handicap here. It did have one advantage however and that was the one minute forty it takes a crew to change a wheel.

• VW

Seat's toughest opposition in the two litre class came from the two semi-works Golf Kit Cars, driven by the Austrians Baumschlager and Rosenberger. Entered by Sawfish Racing, the Golfs did a more than respectable job as Baumschlager finished sixth.

PREVIOUS WINNERS

1973	Mehta - Drews DATSUN 240 Z
1974	Singh - Doig MITSUBISHI COLT LANCER
1975	Andersson - Hertz PEUGEOT 504
1976	Singh - Doig MITSUBISHI COLT LANCER
1977	Waldegaard - Thorszelius FORD ESCORT RS
1978	Nicolas - Lefebvre PEUGEOT 504 V6 COUPÉ
1979	Metha - Doughty DATSUN 160 J
1980	Metha - Doughty DATSUN 160 J
1981	Metha - Doughty DATSUN VIOLET GT
1982	Metha - Doughty DATSUN VIOLET GT
1983	Vatanen - Harryman OPEL ASCONA 400
1984	Waldegaard - Thorzelius TOYOTA CELICA TURBO
1985	Kankkunen - Gallagher TOYOTA CELICA TURBO
1986	Waldegaard - Gallagher TOYOTA CELICA TURBO
1987	Mikkola - Hertz AUDI 200 QUATTRO
1988	Biasion - Siviero LANCIA DELTA INTÉGRALE
1989	Biasion - Siviero LANCIA DELTA INTEGRALE
1990	Waldegaard - Gallagher TOYOTA CELICA GT-FOUR
1991	Kankkunen - Piironen LANCIA DELTA INTEGRALE
1992	Sainz - Moya TOYOTA CELICA TURBO 4WD
1993	Kankkunen - Piironen TOYOTA CELICA TURBO 4WD
1994	Duncan - Williamson TOYOTA CELICA TURBO 4WD
1995	Fujimoto - Hertz TOYOTA CELICA TURBO 4WD
1996	Makinen - Harjanne MITSUBISHI LANCER EV.3
1997	McRae - Grist SUBARU IMPREZA WRC

MICHELIN

EVENT LEADERS

SC.1: Burns
SC.2 - SC.10: Makinen
SC.11 - SC.16: Burns

BEST PERFORMANCES

	1	2	3	4	5	6
McRae	4	-	1	1	1	1
Makinen	3	5	-	2	-	-
Burns	3	3	5	2	1	-
Kankkunen	2	2	2	1	3	4
Vatanen	1	4	3	1	-	3
Sainz	1	2	-	3	2	1
Auriol	1	1	1	5	2	2
Liatti	1	-	1	1	2	2
Rovanperä	-	-	-	-	1	3
Rosenberger	-	-	-	-	1	1
Hirji	-	-	-	-	1	-
Stohl	-	-	-	-	-	1

CHAMPIONSHIP CLASSIFICATIONS

Drivers:
1. Carlos Sainz 16
1. Juha Kankkunen 16
3. Richard Burns 12
4. Tommi Makinen 10
5. Didier Auriol 4
5. Ari Vatanen 4
5. Colin McRae 4

Constructors:
1. Mitsubishi 22
2. Ford 21
3. Toyota 19
4. Subaru 10

Group N:
1. Luis Climent 21
2. Manfred Stohl 21
3. Stig-Olov Walfridson 13

Two Litres:
1. Seat 24
2. Peugeot 16
3. VW 13

Teams'Cup:
1. Scuderia Grifone 10
1. Sawfish Racing 10

"*In his mirror, a grille with the look o*

a startled duckling..."

Right from the third stage, Colin McRae took control of an event he would dominate without ever coming under serious attack. Only Freddy Loix, making his comeback this season, at the wheel of a works WRC Toyota Corolla, attempting for a while to challenge the Scotsman, until his gearbox plays up and takes away any semblance of

a chance on the final leg. Second at the end of the day, Sainz consolidates his lead in a championship which is proving to be enthralling, with no less than three different winners, on both driver and constructor front, from the three rallies held so far. With this win, McRae sent out a timely reminder that he too would be in the running for the title.

off. "I ran wide in a corner. I hit a tree and the damage was too bad to continue." From then on, only Loix could threaten McRae. The leader, glancing in his rear view mirror, would see the ever larger radiator grille with that look of a startled duckling. It was the third works Toyota Corolla WRC. Despite five punctures, when the anti-puncture mousse did its stuff, an off into the eucalyptus trees which chewed up the right hand side bodywork, the little devil really went for it, knocking out four fastest times in a row, gradually moving up from fifth to second. But it was not to be for the Belgian. In the last leg, while Sainz was on a right royal charge, taking time off McRae in handfuls, Loix lost fifth and sixth gears. Meanwhile, on stage 26, Sainz was taking one second per kilometre off the leader. Before the last eleven kilometre test, 6 minutes and eight seconds separated the two men after 369.13 timed kilometres. Sainz was quickest again, his fifth out of the eight stages run that day and took 4'7 off the gap, leaving the Scotsman to win by 2'1 only! However, the matador still had the championship under control; his 22 points givinghim a 6 point lead over Kankkunen, who coming seventh did not score any, 7 points ahead of Burns and 8 ahead of McRae. The big loser on this event was Tommi Makinen who came sixth. Luckily for the reigning champion, the competition was closer than ever and there were still ten rallies to go.

The timely return of the McRae-Subaru combo

Colin McRae's win was a timely reminder that it would be impossible to fight out a world championship without him. Especially as the whole scene had changed from 1997 to 1998. A year earlier, the Subarus had arrived in Portugal having dominated the beginning of the season, winning the Monte-Carlo (Liatti,) Sweden (Eriksson) and the Safari (McRae.) This year, not one event had gone their way. In January, for the Monte, the Subaru Impreza was not up to McRae's ambitions and he came away from the Principality with a hard won third place. The snowy Swedish month of February was not kind to him either, with wiring loom problems on his capricious mount, which was not to his liking, letting him down on the way to the podium. Then came the Safari where, as the Equator is crossed and double crossed, one is never sure what season it is. It was too cartesian for the blue beauty which expired in a cloud of smoke of a similar hue. So at the end of the first three rallies in those winter months, McRae only had four miserable points stuffed in his sporran. Not much to go title chasing with.
Arriving in Portugal, the Scotsman is more than fired up, especially as he can count on plenty of local support. The on-stage clapo-

McRae out on his own

Didier Auriol's ever-present new girlfriend is here again: Lady Badluck is her name and right from day one, she never stopped hitting on her man. The water injection and rev counter on his Corolla failed on the super-stage but it did not stop the Frenchman from being quickest. Run as a Sunday aperitif at Lousada, in front of 20,000 crazy fans, this great time counted for little, but it was very good for the morale. The serious business did not start until the next day and it was kicked off with a great time from Marcus Gronholm, a talented but often too fiery temperament. A bit of a knock not long after that, a broken wheel, the ATS mousse catches fire and just like that, eight minutes are lost. This incident caused Gronholm to lose momentum and that was all McRae needed to seize the initiative. Throughout the first leg, the Scotsman played his usual game; part inspired lunacy, part sensible. Apart from his skill at the wheel, he owed his dominance of the fourth round of the championship to an astute tyre choice. "I expected the going to be a bit warmer in the morning," said Makinen at the mid-point of a lacklustre

70.1
Once again, Didier Auriol retired with mechanical problems.

70.2
Best privateer, Gregoire de Mevius was the class of the "Teams' Cup."

70.3
Without getting involved in the fight for victory, Richard Burns and Robert Reid were now in third place in the drivers' championship.

first leg. "Mitsubishi, like many of the other teams, opted for tyres which were a bit too hard. Colin made a good choice." Helped by Pirellis perfectly suited to the conditions, McRae stamped his authority on the third stage to take the lead and from then on the tyres helped him along nicely. Things were made even easier, as those in his wake ran into difficulties. Gearbox and transmission problems for Toyota; having to learn or re-learn the event for Liatti and Vatanen; poor form at Ford; poor tyre choice at Mitsubishi. Makinen retired after an

meter shows heis by far the most popular competitor. The crowd was dense everywhere aswell as being passionate, bright and even respectful, but above all, knowledgeable. And, apart from the Portuguese drivers, they worship but one idol: Colin McRae. They love his passion, his will and his virulent attacking style, which made him a virtual conquistador. "My tactic is to win, "he repeated endlessly. He only had one way of winning: to drive quickly, never giving his Subaru a breather now it was back on form. "This is my hundredth world championship rally," admitted a somewhat destabilised Sainz. "Despite that experience, fighting off McRae in this mood is sometimes impossible." McRae has changed. In the past, his state of grace transformed into fury often ended upside down in a ditch. But that was then and this is now. Now, even under pressure from Loix and then Sainz, he knows how to keep thinking clearly and realistically. "Winning in Portugal was very important for us," he said once he had won. "Without the ten points we picked up here, the championship would have been a disaster for us." McRae is back.

Freddy has fun

Three little sentences, but they said it all. "Not a bad day, I'm back up to speed, eh guys? Me, I've got no real objective. I'll carry on trying to upset the others!" It is pure Freddy Loix, blowing his own trumpet and getting away with it. He made these remarks at the end of the second leg, the one where his great talent got him right up on terms with McRae, ready for a challenge. That day he had set off in attack mode, certain that happiness belongs to the innocent and victory to the conquerors. It was a great performance, but the tight lipped McRae had little to say about it, save for: "It proves that the nickname, "Fast Freddy" deserves to be known outside Belgium. Along with Burns, Loix was the revelation of this start to the season. Courted by Toyota, the young man with the eternal smile had already proved his worth in the past with two fourth places in 1976 in Catalunya and SanRemo and a brilliant second place in Portugal in 1997. But above all, his performance in Portugal, after months of inactivity, surprised and impressed, just missing out on second place which looked to have his name on it, until the gearbox let him down. These factors would later combine to make him top Toyota driver for the event in Catalunya to the detriment of Didier Auriol. "Portugal has renewed my confidence. I was able to prove that, after three months out of the car, I am still quick and what is more I did it on the loose, when I am often considered a tarmac specialist." There was only one ambition for Catalunya and that was victory and as he declared it, his usually reedy voice put the point across in a determined fashion.

Having led from stage three, McRae could have won easily, but for a puncture, which forced him to pull out all the stops to beat Toyota mounted Sainz and Loix.

72.1

72.2

73.1

73.2

73.4

PORTUGAL
"In his mirror, a grille with the look of a startled duckling..."

72.1

Ding...Dong.. 21 years after his first attempt, Ari Vatanen finally finishes the Portuguese Rally.

72.2

A sensible drive from Richard Burns meant that Mistubishi maintained its championship lead.

73.1

The gap between Sainz and McRae at the finish is the closest ever recorded in the history of the championship.

73.2

Kankkunen under the local television spotlight at Fafe, led the chase to McRae for a long time, until his differential failed.

73.3

Competing in the Teams' Cup, Poland's Holowczyc put up an impressive performance.

73.4

But for gearbox problems, Freddy Loix could have won his first world championship rally.

31ST PORTUGUESE RALLY

TOP ENTRIES

1 **Tommi Makinen - Risto Mannisenmaki**
MITSUBISHI LANCER EV.4

2 **Richard Burns - Robert Reid**
MITSUBISHI CARISMA GT

3 **Colin McRae - Nicky Grist**
SUBARU IMPREZA WRC

4 **Piero Liatti - Fabrizia Pons**
SUBARU IMPREZA WRC

5 **Carlos Sainz - Luis Moya**
TOYOTA COROLLA WRC

6 **Didier Auriol - Denis Giraudet**
TOYOTA COROLLA WRC

7 **Juha Kankkunen - Juha Repo**
FORD ESCORT WRC

8 **Ari Vatanen - Fred Gallagher**
FORD ESCORT WRC

9 **Freddy Loix - Sven Smeets**
TOYOTA COROLLA WRC

10 **Marcus Grönholm - Timo Rautiainen**
TOYOTA COROLLA WRC

11 **Krzysztof Holowczyc - Maciej Wislawski**
SUBARU IMPREZA WRC

12 **Thomas Radström - Lars Backman**
TOYOTA COROLLA WRC

14 **Uwe Nittel - Tina Thörner**
MITSUBISHI CARISMA GT

15 **Rui Madeira - Nuno Da Silva**
TOYOTA CELICA GT-FOUR

16 **Harri Rovanperä - Risto Pietilainen**
SEAT IBIZA 16V KIT CAR

17 **Andrea Dallavilla - Danilo Fappani**
SUBARU IMPREZA

18 **Kenneth Eriksson - Staffan Parmander**
HYUNDAI COUPÉ KIT CAR

19 **Adruzilo Lopes - Luis Lisboa**
PEUGEOT 306 MAXI

20 **Luis Climent - Alex Romani**
MITSUBISHI LANCER EV.3

21 **Gustavo Trelles - Martin Christie**
MITSUBISHI LANCER EV.4

22 **Abdullah Bakhashab - Bobby Willis**
TOYOTA CELICA GT-FOUR

23 **Jean-Pierre Richelmi - Thierry Barjou**
SUBARU IMPREZA

24 **Mark Higgins - Philip Mills**
NISSAN ALMERA GTI KIT CAR

25 **Raimund Baumschlager - Klaus Wicha**
VW GOLF GTI KIT CAR

26 **Manfred Stohl - Peter Muller**
MITSUBISHI LANCER EV.3

27 **Gregoire De Mevius - Jean-Marc Fortin**
SUBARU IMPREZA WRC

29 **Fernando Peres - Ricardo Caldeira**
FORD ESCORT WRC

30 **Oriol Gomez - Marc Marti**
SEAT IBIZA 16V KIT CAR

31 **Kris Rosenberger - Per Carlsson**
VW GOLF GTI KIT CAR

32 **José Carlos Macedo - Miguel Borges**
RENAULT MEGANE MAXI

33 **Frédéric Dor - Didier Breton**
SUBARU IMPREZA WRC

34 **Hamed Al-Wahaibi - Terry Harryman**
MITSUBISHI LANCER EV.4

35 **Pedro Azeredo - Fernando Prata**
RENAULT MEGANE MAXI

36 **Wayne Bell - Iain Stewart**
HYUNDAI COUPÉ Kit Car

37 **Pedro Matos Chaves - Sergio Paiva**
TOYOTA COROLLA WRC

38 **Alexander Nikonenko - Victor Timkovsky**
FORD ESCORT WRC

39 **Marc Duez - Luc Manset**
SEAT IBIZA GTI 16V KIT CAR

4th of the 1998 world rally championships for constructors and drivers
4th of the constructors' "2 litre", production car drivers' and teams' world cups

Date: *22 - 25 March 1998*

Route: *1701.81 km divided into three legs with 28 stages on loose surface roads (330.18 km)*
1st leg: Sunday 22nd and Monday 23rd March, Porto - Viseu, 10 stages (134.66 km)
2nd leg: Tuesday 24th March, Viseu - Porto, 10 stages (144.94 km)
3rd leg: Wednesday 25th March, Porto - Porto, 8 stages (100.58 km)

Starters: *116 (76 Group A + 40 Group N)*

Finishers: *47 (32 Group A + 15 Group N)*

A great drive from the Russian Alexander Nikonenko, who finished third in the Teams' Cup.

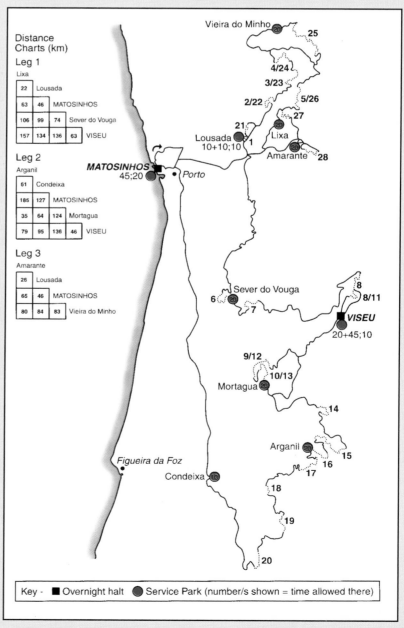

Distance Charts (km)

Leg 1
Lixa

22	Lousada		
63	46	MATOSINHOS	
106	99	74	Sever do Vouga
157	134	136	63	VISEU

Leg 2
Arganil

61	Condeixa		
185	127	MATOSINHOS	
35	64	124	Mortagua
79	95	136	46	VISEU

Leg 3
Amarante

26	Lousada	
65	46	MATOSINHOS
80	84	83	Vieira do Minho

Vieira do Minho — 25
4/24
3/23
2/22
5/26
27
21;
Lousada 10+10;10 — 1
Lixa
Amarante — 28
MATOSINHOS 45;20
Porto
Sever do Vouga
6 — 7
8
8/11
VISEU 20+45;10
9/12
10/13
Mortagua
14
Arganil — 15
16
17
18
Figueira da Foz
Condeixa
19
20

Key - ■ Overnight halt ● Service Park (number/s shown = time allowed there)

SPECIAL STAGE TIMES

ES.1 Lousada Super spéciale (3,88 km)
1. Auriol 3'06''9; 2. Radström 3'07''1; 3. McRae 3'07''7; 4. Sainz 3'07''8; 5. Grönholm 3'07''9; Gr.N Trelles 3'18''9; F2 Lopes 3'18''9

ES.2 Santa Quitéria 1 (9,02 km)
1. Grönholm 6'16''7; 2. McRae 6'21''0; 3. Auriol 6'21''8; 4. Loix 6'22''1; 5. Sainz 6'22''5; Gr.N Campos 6'48''3; F2 Lopes 6'33''5

ES.3 Fafe-Lameirinha 1 (15,18 km)
1. McRae 10'08''8; 2. Kankkunen 10'17''8; 3. De Mévius 10'19''6; 4. Makinen 10'20''0; 5. Sainz 10'20''06; Gr.N Campos 11'05''6; F2 Lopes 10'43''4

ES.4 Luilhas (10,53 km)
1. McRae 7'51''0; 2. Makinen 7'55''7; 3. Liatti 7'56''2; 4. Kankkunen 7'56''8; 5. Loix 7'58''2; Gr.N Stohl 8'39''2; F2 Lopes 8'15''7

ES.5 Vizo-Celorico de Basto (11,79 km)
1. McRae 7'34''3; 2. Grönholm 7'35''1; 3. Kankkunen 7'35''5; 4. Makinen 7'36''2; 5. Radström 7'37''8; Gr.N Campos 8'10''5; F2 Lopes 7'58''

ES.6 Sever do Vouga (14,73 km)
1. McRae 11'28''6; 2. Sainz 11'33''8; 3. Liatti et Nittel 11'35''2; 5. Radström 11'35''5; Gr.N Manfrinato 12'26''08; F2 Lopes 12'10''9

ES.7 Ladario-Oliveira de Frades (11,22 km)
1. McRae 8'17''6; 2. Sainz 8'18''0; 3. Kankkunen 8'19''2; 4. Makinen 8'22''2; 5. Burns, 8'24''1; Gr.N Trelles 9'18''; F2 Rovanpera 9'11''3

ES.8 Viseu (22,42 km)
1. Kankkunen 14'02''2; 2. McRae 14'04''6; 3. Makinen 14'08''5; 4. Loix 14'08''9; 5. Radström 14'10''0; Gr.N et F2 14'43''3 (temps forfaitaire)

ES.9 Mortazel 1 (18,74 km)
1. Loix 12'38''4; 2. McRae 12'40''2; 3. Makinen 12'46''9; 4. Sainz 12'47''00; 5. Burns 12'50''1; Gr.N Climent 13'55''4; F2 Rovanpera 13'47''6

ES.10 Mortagua 1 (17,15 km)
1. McRae 11'51''5; 2. Sainz 11'54''1; 3. Makinen 11'54''2; 4. Loix 11'55''0; 5. Kankkunen 11'55''8; Gr.N Climent 13'19''4; F2 Rovanpera 11'39''5

ES.11 Bertelhe (11,98 km)
1. Makinen 7'14''0; 2. Kankkunen 7'15''9; 3. Auriol 7'17''0; 4. Sainz 7'17''9; 5. McRae 7'18''8; Gr.N Stohl 8'06''9; F2 Lopes 7'47''6

ES.12 Mortazel 2 (18,74 km)
1. McRae 12'37''6; 2. Loix 12'40''3; 3. Burns 12'41''0; 4. Sainz 12'45''3; 5. Liatti 12'45''7; Gr.N Trelles 14'06''; F2 Gomez 14'03''7

ES.13 Mortagua 2 (17,15 km)
1. Burns 11'48''7; 2. Vatanen 11'51''8; 3. McRae 11'53''4; 4. Kankkunen 11'54''0; 5. Liatti 11'54''7; Gr.N Climent 12'58''; F2 Gomez 13'08''

ES.14 Tabua (13,46 km)
1. Burns 8'32''8; 2. Loix 8'34''5; 3. Sainz 8'35''1; 4. Liatti 8'40''7; 5. Vatanen, 8'40''7; Gr.N Manfrinato 9'15''; F2 Rovanpera 9'10''8

ES.15 Arganil-Secarias (28,80 km)
1. McRae 19'42''8; 2. Sainz 19'44''5; 3. Loix 19'45''0; 4. Kankkunen 19'54''8; 5. Burns 19'56''4; Gr.N Trelles 21'45''6; F2 Lopes 21'33''9

ES.16 Salegueiro-Lomba (10,41 km)
1. Sainz 6'53''3; 2. Loix 6'55''2; 3. Kankkunen 6'56''6; 4. McRae 6'58''3; 5. Burns 6'58''4; Gr.N Trelles 7'49''2; F2 Lopes 7'43''4

ES.17 Gois (12,78 km)
1. Loix 7'51''3; 2. Burns 7'52''6; 3. Sainz et Burns 7'55''1; 5. Liatti 7'56''1; Gr.N Manfrinato 8'41''9; F2 Lopes 8'25''9

ES.18 Lousa (10,47 km)
1. Loix 7'07''4; 2. Sainz 7'10''9; 3. Burns 7'12''5; 4. McRae 7'16''5; 5. Liatti 7'17''3; Gr.N Manfrinato 7'41''9; F2 Lopes 7'42''

ES.19 Pedrogao Grande (10,65 km)
1. Loix 6'59''0; 2. Sainz et Burns 7'02''1; 4. McRae 7'05''0; 5. De Mévius 7'15''6; Gr.N 7'47''9; F2 Lopes 7'42''

ES.20 Figueiro dos Vinhos (10,50 km)
1. Loix 7'49''5; 2. Liatti 7'53''7; 3. Burns 7'55''9; 4. Vatanen 7'56''7; 5. Sainz 7'56''8; Gr.N Stohl 7'28''7; F2 Lopes 8'27''2

ES.21 Lousada-Campelos (8,05 km)
1. Sainz 5'59''7; 2. McRae 6'01''6; 3. Burns 6'02''1; 4. Kankkunen 6'02''7; 5. Loix 6'04''1; Gr.N Trelles 6'25''3; F2 Lopes 6'27''9

ES.22 Santa-Quiteria 2 (9,02 km)
1. McRae 6'23''7; 2. Kankkunen 6'26''0; 3. Loix 6'26''4; 4. Sainz et Burns 6'27''0; Gr.N Climent 6'55''1; F2 Lopes 6'43''7

ES.23 Fafe-Lameirinha 2 (15,18 km)
1. Sainz 10'16''0; 2. McRae 10'16''9; 3. Loix 10'18''0; 4. Kankkunen 10'18''1; 5. Burns 10'21''5; Gr.N Climent 11'12''7; F2 Lopes 11'02''7

ES.24 Luilhas 2 (10,53 km)
1. Loix 8'03''1; 2. Kankkunen 8'05''8; 3. Burns 8'05''4; 4. Sainz 8'06''4; 5. Vatanen 8'10''5; Gr.N Climent 8'50''9; F2 Lopes 8'46''3

ES.25 Vieira-Cabeceiras (27,35 km)
1. Sainz 16'54''5; 2. Kankkunen 17'00''8; 3. McRae 17'00''8; 4. Vatanen 17'09''1; 5. Liatti, 17'11''8; Gr.N Sanchez 18'48''4; F2 Lopes 18'34''9

ES.26 Vizo-Celorico de Basto 2 (11,79 km)
1. Kankkunen 7'30''7; 2. Sainz 7'31''8; 3. Burns 7'37''0; 4. Liatti 7'40''1; 5. Vatanen 7'41''7; Gr.N Climent 8'18''5; F2 Lopes 8'07''8

ES.27 Seixoso (7,61 km)
1. Sainz 5'23''5; 2. Kankkunen 5'25''8; 3. Burns 5'28''7; 4. McRae 5'29''6; 5. Loix 5'31''1; Gr.N Climent 5'49''9; F2 Lopes 5'50''3

ES.28 Amarante (11,05 km)
1. Sainz 8'27''3; 2. McRae 8'32''0; 3. Kankkunen 8'33''2; 4. Liatti 8'33''6; 5. Vatanen 8'35''7; Gr.N Climent 9'24''6; F2 Lopes 9'20''5

RESULTS AND RETIREMENTS

Driver/Co-Driver	Car	N°	Gr	Total Time
1 Colin McRae - Nicky Grist	Subaru Impreza WRC	3	A	4h20m58,1s
2 Carlos Sainz - Luis Moya	Toyota Corolla WRC	5	A	4h21m00,2s
3 Freddy Loix - Sven Smeets	Toyota Corolla WRC	9	A	4h21m43,9s
4 Richard Burns - Robert Reid	Mitsubishi Carisma GT	2	A	4h21m51,2s
5 Ari Vatanen - Fred Gallagher	Ford Escort WRC	8	A	4h24m18,3s
6 Piero Liatti - Fabrizia Pons	Subaru Impreza WRC	4	A	4h24m22,3s
7 Juha Kankkunen - Juha Repo	Ford Escort WRC	7	A	4h24m35,0s
8 Gregoire De Mévius - Jean-Marc Fortin	Subaru Impreza WRC	27	A	4h27m57,1s
9 Rui Madeira - Nuno da Silva	Toyota Celica GT-Four	15	A	4h31m22,2s
10 Krzysztof Holowczyc - Maciej Wislawski	Subaru Impreza WRC	11	A	4h32m56,2s
ES.1 Raimund Baumschlager - Klaus Wicha	VW Golf GTI Kit Car	16	A	Gearbox
ES.4 Marc Duez - Luc Manset	Seat Ibiza 16v Kit Car	39	A	Engine
ES.6 Kenneth Eriksson - Staffan Parmander	Hyundai Coupé Kit Car	18	A	Engine
ES.9 Mark Higgins - Philip Mills	Nissan Almera GTI Kit Car	24	A	Accident
ES.10 Marcus Gronhölm - Timo Rautiainen	Toyota Corolla WRC	10	A	Suspension
ES.12 Tommi Makinen - Risto Mannisenmaki	Mitsubishi Lancer Ev.4	1	A	Accident
ES.12 Thomas Radström - Lars Backman	Toyota Corolla WRC	12	A	Accident
ES.15 Uwe Nittel - Tina Thörner	Mitsubishi Carisma GT	14	A	Engine
ES.16 Harri Rovanperä - Risto Pietiläinen	Seat Ibiza GTI 16v Kit Car	16	A	Engine
ES.16 Didier Auriol - Denis Giraudet	Toyota Corolla WRC	6	A	Gearbox

GOSSIP

• VATANEN

He did what he was supposed to, still sitting in for Thiry, injured in a recce accident for the Safari. He brought his Ford home in fifth place giving the team two points in the constructors' championship. Remarkably consistent, Vatanen had played the stand-in role to perfection in Kenya, finishing third after handing his second place to Kankkunen, before scoring more points in Portugal, before declaring: "I am delighted."

• TEAM ORDERS

Following the Australian Formula 1 Grand Prix, where team orders came into play between the two McLaren drivers, FIA announced before the rally that arrangements such as these which were to the detriment of the sport were no longer allowed. Nevertheless, the way Loix let Sainz by towards the end of the event highlighted the issue once again. His gearbox seemed to cause trouble at a very opportune moment. Asked before the start, how he might react to a potential request from his team manager, Loix had his own very special way of looking at it. "I would be very happy to be given instructions, as it would mean I was ahead of Sainz or Auriol!"

• LOPES

Having made an appearance in Monte-Carlo, Portugal's Adruzilo Lopes had flown in the two litre category, helped on his way by the retirement on Tuesday of his main rival, Harri Rovenpera. Even so, the Finn's Seat was no match for Lopes' Peugeot 306 Maxi. The French constructor was now yet again pushing Seat for the two litre world cup.

• HYUNDAI

Portugal '98 was the first official rally appearance of the Hyundai factory, in the safe hands of English preparation company MSD. Two Kit Car Coupes were entered for Sweden's Kenneth Eriksson and the veteran Australian (although making his European debut!) Wayne Bell. Nine other events were programmed for the Korean constructor this year: Acropolis, New Zealand, Finland, San Remo, Australia, RAC (with the same drivers;) Catalunya and Corsica (with Eriksson and Alister McRae) and Argentina (only with Eriksson.) This was the first step before competing with a World Rally Car for some events in '99 and for a full season in 2000.

PREVIOUS WINNERS

1973	Thérier - Jaubert	ALPINE RENAULT A 110
1974	Pinto - Bernacchini	FIAT 124 ABARTH
1975	Alen - Kivimäki	FIAT 124 ABARTH
1976	Munari - Maiga	LANCIA STRATOS
1977	Alen - Kivimäki	FIAT 131 ABARTH
1978	Alen - Kivimäki	FIAT 131 ABARTH
1979	Mikkola - Hertz	FORD ESCORT RS
1980	Röhrl - Geistdörfer	FIAT 131 ABARTH
1981	Alen - Kivimäki	FIAT 131 ABARTH
1982	Mouton - Pons	AUDI QUATTRO
1983	Mikkola - Hertz	AUDI QUATTRO
1984	Mikkola - Hertz	AUDI QUATTRO
1985	Salonen - Harjanne	PEUGEOT 205 T16
1986	Moutinho - Fortes	RENAULT 5 TURBO
1987	Alen - Kivimäki	LANCIA DELTA HF 4WD
1988	Biasion - Cassina	LANCIA DELTA INTEGRALE
1989	Biasion - Siviero	LANCIA DELTA INTEGRALE
1990	Biasion - Siviero	LANCIA DELTA INTEGRALE
1991	Sainz - Moya	TOYOTA CELICA GT-FOUR
1992	Kankkunen - Piironen	LANCIA HF INTEGRALE
1993	Delecour - Grataloup	FORD ESCORT RS COSWORTH
1994	Kankkunen - Grist	TOYOTA CELICA TURBO 4WD
1995	Sainz - Moya	SUBARU IMPREZA
1996	Madeira - Da Silva	TOYOTA CELICA GT-FOUR
1997	Makinen - Harjanne	MITSUBISHI LANCER Ev.4

EVENT LEADERS

ES.1: Auriol
ES.2: Gronhölm
ES.3 - ES.28: McRae

BEST PERFORMANCES

	1	2	3	4	5	6
McRae	9	8	3	4	1	2
Sainz	6	7	2	5	4	1
Loix	6	3	3	3	3	1
Kankkunen	2	4	5	6	1	2
Burns	2	1	7	2	4	6
Gronhölm	1	2	-	-	-	1
Makinen	1	1	2	3	1	0
Auriol	1	-	2	-	-	1
Liatti	-	1	3	3	4	7
Vatanen	-	1	-	1	4	3
Radström	-	1	-	-	4	-
De Mevius	-	-	1	1	1	-
Nittel	-	-	1	-	-	1

CHAMPIONSHIP CLASSIFICATIONS

Drivers:
1. Carlos Sainz 22
2. Juha Kankkunen 16
3. Richard Burns 15
4. Colin McRae 14
5. Tommi Makinen 10

Constructors:
1. Mitsubishi 25
1. Toyota 25
3. Ford 23
4. Subaru 21

Group N:
1. Manfred Stohl 29
2. Luis Climent 24
3. Gustavo Trelles 13
3. Stig-Olov Walfridson 13

Two Litres:
1. Seat 30
2. Peugeot 26
3. VW 17

Teams' Cup:
1. Scuderia Grifone 20
2. Sawfish Racing 10
3. Stomil Mobil 1 Rally Team 6

"*Scores to be settled, corrida*

ashion..."

CATALUNYA

Didier Auriol returned to his old self on the Catalan tarmac. Imperial and untouchable, the Toyota driver proved that he had lost none of his talent or determination, silencing in the most convincing way possible those who had bad-mouthed him after his unlucky start to the season. In Spain he was in a different league to the rest and while the 1994 champion refutes the tarmac specialist tag, he certainly made it all look so easy on this terrain. Among the others were the two wheel drive, two litre French cars with the Peugeot 306

77.1

making its comeback to the world stage and the Citroen Xsara its debut. As is often the case on tarmac, they were to play a leading role in the proceedings.

78.1

Auriol and then the rest

It all started in the by now familiar and sinister fashion. At the finish of the first stage, Didier Auriol parked his Toyota, his face racked with disappointment and acceptance of his fate. He wound down the window to say: "problem with the water injection, front right puncture," and drove off again. He tried to understand and to react but it was in vain. Bad luck dogged him still. But Didier Auriol is not the sort to ever give up. The first stage had gone badly. Never mind, there were still eighteen to go. From then on he set four fastest times in a row taking the lead from the beginning. So what happened to the evil eyed curse? Gone, flown away, but the talent was still there. On that first day, nobody could match his pace. Smiling a lot and just a little bit proud of himself and rightly so, he became chatty. "I am pushing very hard, as usual. I have not changed my driving style at all. It is the car which is working better. I am trying to concentrate. Sometimes I have been pushing a bit too hard. I am sure it looks impressive from the outside."

78.2

77.1

As soon as he passed the chequered flag, Tommi Makinen went to the Circuito de Catalunya where he met Jacques Villeneuve to test the Canadian's Williams Renault

He played the piece in just the right tempo from start to finish, passing smoothly from a grandiose fortissimo to a delicate moderato on a stage made very dangerous because of the stones and earth covering the surface. It was an intelligent performance. Once the danger had passed, he pushed hard once again, behind the surprising Citroen Xsaras which, along with the 306 and Thiry, who had to wear a corset for his broken ribs, provided the excitement at the beginning of the event.

Because apart from the flying Toyota driver, all the other main players in the world championship were a bit off form on the slopes of the Pyrenees. Even Sainz, two spins, even Makinen, fiddling with the set up of his new Lancer Evo V, even McRae struggling with his tyres. It was also clear from the look on the faces of this lot, that once again, the two wheel drive boys were as usual upsetting the hierarchy which is so dear to them. And now there are not only two 306, there are also the two Xsaras. "On tarmac, they're as quick as hell!" said an admiring Kankkunen. All change the next day and the heavy artillery lead the assault. Playtime is over and the intrepid French two wheel drivers have to give best to the muscle, the tattoos and the 4 x 4s. You have had your little joke with your shiny little nippy cars but now you must leave the points to us. This meant that the six stages fought out in the foothills of the grandiose Sierra del Montsant and its wonderful smell of wild mint, that zigzagged between the vineyards and olive groves made for a marvellous rally, albeit in the wake of Auriol the Amazing. As it is undoubtedly true that happy people have no history, he had a dull time of it, simply sailing along with a mastery that meant he constantly increased his lead. "I can't slow down, the pace is too high." Behind him, Peugeot and Citroen - Puras had been admirable up until then at least - were stripped bare and then, by the end of the leg, Loix, Sainz and Makinen finally got their cars sorted having found the right set up. As the stages go by, they move up from 7th, 8th and 9th to 2nd, 3rd and 4th. They are back where it suits them, but the gaps are tiny. From one Belgian to another, Loix in second place to Thiry in eighth the gap is only a minute.

The final leg came down to a tangle between the pretenders to the throne. Sainz goes out through his own efforts, with a puncture which followed a knock. He finished stage 16 on a rim when his tyre came off completely. Makinen was charging in search of the 6 points on offer for second place. Loix is stubborn and will refuse to give up. Strange noises in the Mitsubishi transmission force the Finn to back off. It does not matter at the end of the day, because he like everyone else for that matter, had lived through a strange rally spent so far, so very far away from the leader. It was a transformed Auriol. He was the boss and made his point taking the best time on the final stage.

Auriol all smiles

"Naturally, it is frustrating when you develop a car and get it just right and then it works for others but not for you. That is not easy to live with, but you have to accept it and hope that better days are just around the corner." Lost in a huge leather armchair, on the eve of the rally, Didier Auriol tries to look on the bright side. But he is not finding it easy. The early part of his season has been tarnished with misfortune which has corroded his soul. The final insult; Ove Andersson decided shortly before this event that Loix and not Auriol would be the designated Toyota points scorer, alongside the permanent fixture that is Carlos Sainz. The decision shows a singular lack of faith. Three days later, Didier Auriol returns to the winner's enclosure, three years after his last victory in the 1995 Tour of Corsica. He did not do things by halves this time either! For months now, each rally has thrown up a bitter struggle, more bitter than the unripened Catalan chestnuts. There were scores to be settled, corrida style with no mercy for the losers. However, on this event, Auriol-Giraudet won pretty much as they pleased. In the lead after

the second stage, he ceaselessly increased his lead. Better still, with a final advantage of 53'4 over Loix, Auriol pulled out the biggest winning margin of the season, apart from the Safari. "If a job's worth doing, it is worth doing well," he laughed. Then, to put the cherry on the cake, there was only one of the 19 stages where he was not in the top six. "I was very consistent, consistently in front! There was hardly a stage where I did not take 15 seconds, four or five at the worst." So, Auriol is happy with his work which proved he had been written off way too early. His car turned out to be perfect, ideally moulded to fit around his small, athletic, jockey style stature. "I have said it for years; when I am on form, then I am very quick. I had a very good feeling." Then he pulled himself up short: "But it is always very difficult to win as many of us are capable of doing it." All the same, this was a very timely win. "I am very happy for myself. It is not a case of revenge, but I wanted to prove that when everything goes well, I am up for the win." No doubt he dreamt of more.

Kit Cars lose the bet

François Delecour can always remind his audience of his earlier pearls of wisdom: "I had told you, the World Rally Cars have made too much progress. Even on tarmac, they are now out of our reach." He was not wrong and one of the main lessons to be learned from this rally was to be had by comparing the performance of the little French cars from Peugeot and Citroen with that of the latest world championship 4 x 4. Once the event was over, the two teams returned to their neighbouring bases in Velizy with mixed feelings, somewhere between disappointment and the desire to prove that it was not all over. However, before the off, Jean-Pierre Nicolas had said: "We hope to do as well as in 1997, when we came third." It was not to be and the best of the two 306 Maxis, was sixth in the hands of the two Panizzi brothers, just behind Bugalski-Chiaroni.

At Citroen, not only did the Xsaras go the distance, they also achieved their aim, as Bugalski won the two litre category, beating Peugeot on the way in their own little war. On the performance front, the pretty 306 and Xsara only managed three best times, one for Panizzi, a second for Puras and another for Bugalski. Finally, having only just missed out on victory in 1997, it would seem that the kit cars have now missed their chance.

79.1

78.1
This time, when Freddy Loix moved into attack mode, Didier Auriol was already out of reach.

78.2
This victory allowed Didier Auriol and Denis Giraudet to find their feet within the team.

79.1
Philippe Bugalski proved very competitive for his first attempt at this event.

79.2
The Pirelli tyres were a lot to blame for Subaru's poor performance.

79.2

CATALUNYA
"Scores to be settled, corrida fashion..."

80.1

Delayed right from the start, Francois Delecour never managed to get himself back in the game.

80.2

A quick peek inside the cockpit of the ever incisive Panizzi brothers.

80.3

In its first appearance on the world stage, the Citroen Xsara dominated the 2 litre category, just as the Peugeot 306 had done twelve months earlier.

81.1-4

Catalunya marked the debut of a new Evolution 5 version of the Lancer, in the hands of Tommi Makinen.

81.2

Thomas Radstrom still has a lot to learn to be competitive on tarmac.

81.3

On tarmac, the Seat Ibiza is still no match for the French Kit-Cars.

80.1

80.2

80.3

81.1

81.2

81.3

81.4

34TH SPANISH RALLY

TOP ENTRIES

1 Tommi Makinen - Risto Mannisenmaki
MITSUBISHI LANCER EV.5

2 Richard Burns - Robert Reid
MITSUBISHI CARISMA GT

3 Colin McRae - Nicky Grist
SUBARU IMPREZA WRC

4 Piero Liatti - Fabrizia Pons
SUBARU IMPREZA WRC

5 Carlos Sainz - Luis Moya
TOYOTA COROLLA WRC

6 Freddy Loix - Sven Smeets
TOYOTA COROLLA WRC

7 Juha Kankkunen - Juha Repo
FORD ESCORT WRC

8 Bruno Thiry - Stéphane Prévot
FORD ESCORT WRC

9 Didier Auriol - Denis Giraudet
TOYOTA COROLLA WRC

10 Thomas Radstrom - Lars Backman
TOYOTA COROLLA WRC

11 Marcus Gronholm - Timo Rautiainen
TOYOTA COROLLA WRC

12 François Delecour - Daniel Grataloup
PEUGEOT 306 MAXI

14 Rui Madeira - Nuno da Silva
TOYOTA COROLLA WRC

15 Gilles Panizzi - Hervé Panizzi
PEUGEOT 306 MAXI

16 Andrea Dallavilla - Danilo Fappani
SUBARU IMPREZA WRC

17 Philippe Bugalski - Jean-Paul Chiaroni
CITROËN XSARA KIT CAR

18 Harri Rovanpera - Risto Pietilainen
SEAT IBIZA 16V KIT CAR

19 Jesus Puras - Carlos Del Barrio
SEAT IBIZA 16V KIT CAR

20 Oriol Gomez - Marc Marti
SEAT IBIZA 16V KIT CAR

21 Luis Climent - Alex Romani
RENAULT MAXI MEGANE

22 Krzysztof Holowczyc - Maciej Wislawski
SUBARU IMPREZA WRC

23 Andrea Navarra - Renzo Casazza
SUBARU IMPREZA

24 Patrick Snijers - Daniel De Canck
FORD ESCORT WRC

25 Manuel Muniente - Joan Ibanez
PEUGEOT 306 MAXI

26 Uwe Nittel - Tina Thorner
MITSUBISHI CARISMA GT

27 Kenneth Eriksson - Staffan Parmander
HYUNDAI COUPÉ KIT CAR

28 Adruzilo Lopes - Luis Lisboa
PEUGEOT 306 MAXI

29 Alister McRae - David Senior
HYUNDAI COUPÉ KIT CAR

30 Gustavo Trelles - Martin Christie
MITSUBISHI LANCER EV.5

31 Pavel Sibera - Petr Gross
SKODA OCTAVIA KIT CAR

32 Manfred Stohl - Peter Muller
MITSUBISHI LANCER EV.3

33 Alexander Nikonenko - Victor Timkovsky
FORD ESCORT WRC

34 Volkan Isik - Ilham Dokumcu
TOYOTA CELICA GT-FOUR

35 Abdullah Bakhashab - Bobby Willis
TOYOTA CELICA GT-FOUR

38 Renaud Verreydt - Jean-François Elst
SUBARU IMPREZA WRC

**5th leg of the 1998 world rally championships for constructors and drivers
5th leg of the constructors' "2 litre", production car drivers' and teams' world cups**

Date: *19 - 22 April 1998*

Route: *1471.74 km divided into three legs with 19 stages run on tarmac roads (400.71 km)*
1st leg: Monday 20th April, Lhoret de Mar - Lhoret de Mar, 7 stages (121.53 km)
2nd leg: Tuesday 21st April, Lhoret de Mar - Lhoret de Mar, 6 stages (172.92 km)
3rd leg: Wednesday 22nd April, Lhoret de Mar - Lhoret de Mar, 6 stages (106.26 km)

Starters: *116 (62 Group A + 54 Group N)*

Finishers: *46 (28 Group A + 18 Group N)*

Renaud Verreydt had an astonishing rally, dominating all the WRC Corolla privateers until a puncture robbed him of 10th place.

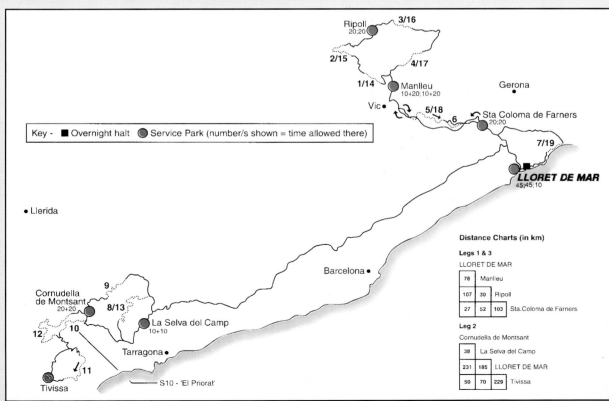

Key - ■ Overnight halt ● Service Park (number/s shown = time allowed there)

Distance Charts (in km)

Legs 1 & 3

LLORET DE MAR			
78	Manlleu		
107	30	Ripoll	
27	52	103	Sta.Coloma de Farners

Leg 2

Cornudella de Montsant			
38	La Selva del Camp		
231	185	LLORET DE MAR	
50	70	229	Tivissa

SPECIAL STAGE TIMES

ES.1 La Trona 1 (12,86 km)
1. Thiry 8'31"9; 2. Burns 8'32"3; 3. Sainz 8"34"4; 4.Panizzi 8'34"6; 5. Loix 8'35"8; Gr.N Trelles 9'11"8

ES.2 Alpens-Les Llosses 1 (21,95 km)
1. Auriol 13'44"4; 2. Puras 13'47"9; 3. Panizzi 13'48'9; 4. Bugalski 13'49"7; 5. Burns 13'49"8; Gr.N Climent 13'57"4

ES.3 Coll De Santigosa 1 ((10,62 km)
1. Auriol 6'49"1; 2. Thiry 6'51"; 3. Liatti 6'51"8; 4.Burns 6'52"8; 5. Sainz, Makinen et Panizzi 6'52"5; Gr.N Trelles 7'20"7

ES.4 Coll de Bracons 1 (19,89 km)
1. Auriol 13'02; 2. Bugalski 13'04"8; 3. Puras 13'04"9; 4. Delecour et Panizzi 13'06"; Gr.N Stohl 14'22"

ES.5 La Fullaca-Sant Hilari 1 (21,98 km)
1. Auriol 14'11"; 2. Bugalski 14'11"9; 3. Puras 14'12"1; 4. Sainz 14'14"4; 5. Burns 14'15"1; Gr.N Trelles 15'16"2

ES.6 Cladells (15,27 km)
1. McRae 10'13"; 2. Liatti 10'14"2; 3. Burns 10'16"9; 4. Makinen 10'17"7; 5. Auriol 10'18"5; Gr.N Trelles 11'05"4; F2 Panizzi 10'24"4

ES.7 Sant Feliu-Tossa 1 (18,96 km)
1. Puras 12'16"5; 2. Bugalski 12'17"6; 3. Auriol 12'21"3; 4. Thiry 12'22"; 5. Delecour 12'23"1; Gr.N Trelles 13'26"

ES.8 La Riba 1 (32,72 km)
1. Loix et Makinen 20'40"6; 3. Sainz 20'42"2; 4. Delecour 20'43"; 5. Auriol 20'44"5; Gr.N Trelles 22'18"1

ES.9 Prades (13,77 km)
1. Panizzi 8'25"2; 2. Delecour 8'25"4; 3. Loix 8'28"1; 4. Auriol et Sainz 8'28"2; Gr.N Trelles 9'05"4

ES.10 El Priorat (20,67 km)
1. Auriol 14'42"9; 2. Loix 14'45"5; 3. Sainz 14'51"; 4. Makinen 14'51"4; 5. Bugalski 14'52"1; Gr.N Trelles 15'51"5

ES.11 Santa Marina (27,47 km)
1.Bugalski 17'09"7; 2. Delecour 17'11"9; 3. Liatti 17'14"; 4. Auriol 17'15"2; 5. Loix 17'17"3; Gr.N Trelles 19'08"8

ES.12 La Figuera-Escaledei (45,57 km)
1. Auriol 29'05"3; 2. Bugalski 29'10"1; 3. Sainz 29'10"8; 4. Makinen 29'12"2; 5. Loix 29'14"2; Gr.N Trelles 31'49"8

ES.13 La Riba 2 (32,72 km)
1. Loix 20'36"9; 2. Makinen 20'38"1; 3. Auriol 20'42"; 4. Sainz 20'42"9; 5. McRae 20'46"6; Gr.N Trelles 22'33"2; F2 Bugalski 20'48"6

ES.14 La Trona 2 (12,86 km)
1. Loix 8'31"3; 2. Auriol 8'32"1; 3. Makinen 8'33"3; 4. Sainz 8'34"8; 5. Thiry 8'35"7; Gr.N Stohl 9'20"7; F2 Panizzi 8'39"8

ES.15 Alpens-Les Llosses 2 (21,95 km)
1. Auriol 13'41"5; 2. Makinen 13'43"6; 3. Thiry 13'45"6; 4.Burns 13'49"3; 5.Loix 13'50"3; Gr.N Stohl 15'07"; F2 Panizzi 13'52"3

ES.16 Coll de Santigosa 2 (10,62 km)
1. Makinen 6'45"5; 2. Burns 6'46"2; 3. Auriol 6'47"4; 4. Panizzi 6'48"; 5. Bugalski 6'48"1; Gr.N Trelles 7'23"7

ES.17 Coll de Bracons 2 (19,89 km)
1. Auriol 13'02"; 2. Makinen 13'02"7; 3. Lopes 13'05"6; 4. Loix 13'06"6; 5. Panizzi 13'07"1; Gr.N Trelles 14'04"5

ES.18 La Fullaca-Sant Hilari 2 (21,98 km)
1. Loix 14'08"3; 2. Auriol 14'13"3; 3. Makinen 14'14"9; 4. Burns 14'16"1; 5. Sainz 14'16"8; Gr.N Trelles 15'23"2; F2 Panizzi 14'18"4

ES.19 Sant Feliu-Tossa 2 (18,96 km)
1. Auriol 12'18"5; 2. Delecour 12'18"5; 3. Bugalski 12'19"5; 4. Loix 12'20"4; 5. Panizzi 12'22"4; Gr.N Stohl 13'32"7

RESULTS AND RETIREMENTS

	Driver/Co-Driver	Car	N°	Gr	Total Time
1	Didier Auriol - Denis Giraudet	Toyota Corolla WRC	9	A	4h18m36,9s
2	Freddy Loix - Sven Smeets	Toyota Corolla WRC	6	A	4h19m30,3s
3	Tommi Makinen - Risto Mannisenmaki	Mitsubishi Lancer Ev.5	1	A	4h19m46,3s
4	Richard Burns - Robert Reid	Mitsubishi Carisma GT	2	A	4h20m10,4s
5	Philippe Bugalski - Jean-Paul Chiaroni	Citroën Xsara Kit Car	17	A	4h20m28,3s
6	Gilles Panizzi - Hervé Panizzi	Peugeot 306 Maxi	15	A	4h20m44,0s
7	Carlos Sainz - Luis Moya	Toyota Corolla WRC	5	A	4h21m05,7s
8	François Delecour - Daniel Grataloup	Peugeot 306 Maxi	12	A	4h21m24,6s
9	Uwe Nittel - Tina Thörner	Mitsubishi Carisma GT	26	A	4h22m45,6s
10	Rui Madeira - Nuno da Silva	Toyota Corolla WRC	14	A	4h25m24,5s
ES.3	Harri Rovänperä - Risto Pietiläinen	Seat Ibiza GTI 16v Kit Car	18	A	Engine
ES.6	Pavel Sibera - Petr Gross	Skoda Octavia Kit Car	31	A	Accident
ES.8	Jesus Puras - Carlos del Barrio	Citroën Xsara Kit Car	19	A	Engine
ES.9	Marcus Grönholm - Timo Rautiainen	Toyota Corolla WRC	11	A	Accident
ES.12	Piero Liatti - Fabrizia Pons	Subaru Impreza WRC	4	A	Accident
ES.12	Luis Climent - Alex Romani	Renault Maxi Mégane	21	N	Accident
ES.15	Colin McRae - Nicky Grist	Subaru Impreza WRC	3	A	Transmission
ES.16	Juha Kankkunen - Juha Repo	Ford Escort WRC	7	A	Accident
ES.17	Bruno Thiry - Stéphane Prévot	Ford Escort WRC	8	A	Engine

PREVIOUS WINNERS

1991	Schwarz - Hertz
	TOYOTA CELICA GT-FOUR
1992	Sainz - Moya
	TOYOTA CELICA TURBO 4WD
1993	Delecour - Grataloup
	FORD ESCORT RS COSWORTH
1994	Bertone - Chiapponi
	TOYOTA CELICA TURBO 4WD
1995	Sainz - Moya
	SUBARU IMPREZA
1996	McRae - Ringer
	SUBARU IMPREZA
1997	Makinen - Harjanne
	MITSUBISHI LANCER EV.4

GOSSIP

• MITSUBISHI

In Catalunya, Burns and Makinen got their hands on the all-new Mitsubishi, the Lancer Evo. V. With an improved engine putting out more power, different suspension, a new electronic management system which provided the crew with more information (putting more duplicate dials in front of the co-driver,) some parts were enlarged, when compared to its predecessor, notably air intakes and car width. This was aimed at overcoming the car's small performance deficit on tarmac. It is worth noting that this Evo. V is still built to Group A rules, rather than as a WRC, as the Japanese constructor can still market its entire production.

• PURAS

Jesus Puras, Citroen's regular driver in Spain, was at the wheel of the second works double chevron car. As usual, he did more than shine, finishing the first leg in second place, setting a best time on the way. Nevertheless, right from the first stage of the second leg, the rapid Spaniard had to retire. "He hit a ditch very hard," explained Citroen Sportboss Guy

Frequelin. "The sump exploded, oil went everywhere and the engine broke."

• CITROEN

It was 25 years since a Citroen had done a fastest time in a World Championship event. To find the predecessor to the Xsaras of Puras and Bugalksi, one has to go back to the days of the DS and the 1973 Morocco Rally.

• LIATTI

"The agony is over," said a frustrated Piero Liatti after he went off the road. All rally long he fought against a failing turbo and slow-tyres. The final chapter came on stage 12. Trying to cut a corner, the Italian only noticed a large rock at the last moment. He steered wide to miss it but he instantly lost control of his Subaru and he hit a concrete post on the other side. The front suspension was pulled apart and the left rear wheel was ripped off. The Impreza would go no further.

CHAMPIONSHIP CLASSIFICATIONS

Drivers:
1. Carlos Sainz 22
2. Richard Burns 18
3. Juha Kankkunen 16
4. Didier Auriol 14
4. Tommi Makinen 14
4. Colin McRae 14

Constructors:
1. Mitsubishi 32
2. Toyota 31
3. Ford 23
4. Subaru 21

Group N:
1. Manfred Stohl 37
2. Gustavo Trelles 26
3. Luis Climent 24

Two Litres:
1. Peugeot 36
2. Seat 33
3. VW 17

Teams' Cup:
1. Scuderia Grifone 30
2. Sawfish Racing 10
2. Stomil Mobil 1 Rally Team 10

EVENT LEADERS

ES.1: Thiry
ES.2 - ES.19: Auriol

BEST PERFORMANCES

	1	2	3	4	5	6
Auriol	9	2	3	2	2	-
Loix	4	1	1	2	4	-
Bugalski	1	4	1	1	2	3
Makinen	1	4	2	3	-	2
Thiry	1	1	1	1	1	4
Puras	1	1	2	-	-	-
Panizzi	1	-	1	3	3	4
McRae	1	-	-	-	1	-
Delecour	-	3	-	2	1	1
Burns	-	2	1	3	2	3
Liatti	-	1	2	-	-	-
Sainz	-	-	4	3	3	2

FRANCE

For three days on the Tour of Corsica there was a titanic struggle fought out between Colin McRae in the role of the hunted and Francois Delecour in that of the hunter. On a course that was alternately greasy, dry or soaked, the pure talent of these two drivers set the stages alight. A touch lucky, disqualified then reinstated and a stage cancelled at just the right moment, the Scotsman managed to get the better of the

Frenchman and take the lead in the championship. However, the talent of Delecour and Panizzi was enough to stifle the performance of the three Citroens, which were not as commanding as they had been in Catalunya. As for Auriol, who had been favourite after his performance in Spain, he was ill at ease and endured mechanical problems which left him languishing in sixth place.

no cause to fear the pack..."

86.1

The McRae-Delecour duel

It was a rally with a capital "R;" a majestic event from the word go; a monument to motor sport with all the elements in place from sporting excellence to tactical trickery. It began with a great time from Philippe Bugalski. Thanks to his skill behind the wheel, but also to the soft tyres fitted to his Citroen Xsara, he set a fantastic time on the first stage, behind McRae who was keen to remind everyone he had won this event last year. But in the next stage, his tyres were suffering and "Bug" lost any advantage of his early pace. "I followed the instructions of my course openers," he explained, "but as they go through the stages two hours before us...." At that point, at least it was only a case of choosing between different options for dry tarmac. Later, the rains arrived and it would become a finely balanced choice between slicks and rain tyres. It was a very thin line choosing between them, finer than the slices of salsiccia, the local spicy sausage which is notoriously hard to cut. So, in the initial stages of the event, Makinen and then Sainz were in seventh heaven as they led the rally. "Making the right tyre choice is not easy," the Spaniard calmly related in the middle of the day. Dry roads, wet roads, it keeps changing." It would not be changeable for long as the heavens opened on the valleys.

When it comes to swimming through it, to braving the flooded roads without lifting off and to fearlessly tackle the aquaplaning, none do it better than McRae, Liatti and Magaud. Sadly for Makinen, the electronic control unit on his Mitsubishi drowns in the deluge, preventing the Finn from joining in the fun. The star of the aquatic conditions is Delecour and his little two wheel drive car. Still on slicks, he dances through the puddles to keep in touch with the front runners. His team mate Gilles Panizzi is gutted: "I've gone straight on twice with these tyres." Although freezing with the cold, Delecour goes further still, refusing a Michelin recommended evolution tyre choice for a product he knows better and keeps his hard fought second place in the wake of McRae. On this great day for motor sport, where no less than four crews took the lead over six stages, the most amazing aspect of the day was how tightly bunched was the pack (the first eight in less than 58.6!) and still the Peugeots and Citroens are in the leading group.

At the start of the second leg, the Tour of Corsica is draped in those dull grey colours, usually found in Wales and Scotland in winter on the RAC rally. It might well give McRae a fleeting memory of his native Highlands. And as usual, the

86.2

86.1
Revenge is sweet for the Peugeot 306 Maxi with Panizzi and Delecour unbeatable on the tarmac of the "Isle of Beauty."

86.2
Isolde Holderied, assisted by Anne-Chantal Pauwels was making her comeback on the world stage with a WRC Toyota Corolla.

87.1
Colin McRae had to face the FIA after being disqualified and then reinstated over dark deeds with tyres.

87.2
Spain's Carlos Sainz found it hard to match the pace of the Subarus.

Scottish warrior arose ready to repulse the attacks of his rivals. Right away, he kicks off with two fastest times. These confirm that on intermediate tyres on greasy tarmac, the Subarus, the deer if you will, have nothing to fear from the chasing pack. But, as if to prove this theory wrong, Carlos Sainz storms through to second ahead of McRae's team mate, Piero Liatti. However, it did not come easy for "His Emminence." "At the start of the day on a link section, the engine died," explained the Spaniard, standing alongside his now fully operational Toyota. "Then it cut out again after the stages." Coming out of the next service area, Sainz finds himself behind the wheel of a fully restored Corolla and puts in two quickest times. If McRae is to be challenged then the Spaniard is the man to do it. Auriol cannot be counted on, having problems firstly with his driving and then

going at the beginning of the leg. "These are the worst possible conditions for us," moaned Delecour. The roads are just greasy, not wet, nor totally dry." The sun would be required to do its job of completely drying the roads, for Delecour to move up towards the front again, despite brake problems. His will to win would stamp its mark on the final leg as he mounts an attack on the leaders. Taking advantage of a Sainz puncture, the Spaniard having omitted to use ATS mousse, "Latebrake" as Delecour is known, takes second place. McRae is in his sights. Stage after stage, the 306 closes in and McRae can do nothing about it. It looks like it will be a great fight to the finish, but it was not to be. A decision from the clerk of the course, taken a touch hastily in the opinion of the drivers, results in the cancellation of stage 16. Despite a final stage where the four remaining Kit Cars take the top four places, Delecour has missed out. McRae emerges the happy victor, Liatti is third, just ahead of Panizzi, which is good news for Subaru. It had been a close call for them.

A timely cancellation

Why exactly was special stage 16 cancelled? Too many spectators, according to rally officials. Very few people

confirmed that it was perfectly safe for the cars to pass. However, that day, the Tour of Corsica had an important visitor in the shape of FIA President, Max Mosley. And Mosley, the oh so white knight of safety appreciated this cancellation. Often in the bad books, the Corsican event thus became a paragon of virtue. At the end of the rally, Mosley confirmed the event's appearance on the 1999 calendar. Valid or not, this cancellation arrived at precisely the right time. Nevertheless, it deprived the event of a photo finish what with Delecour climbing all over McRae. Luckily the final gap (27.2) seemed too big for Delecour to have bridged it in the 22.63 kilometres clipped off the event. The sport emerged unblemished if not exactly head held high.

McRae had a close call

Accused of tyre torture and of having used his Pirellis beyond the legal limits on the abrasive Corsican tarmac, Colin McRae was in trouble when he reached Ajaccio at the end of the first leg of the rally. He was deemed to have contravened article 4.2 of the regulations, which carried the penalty of immediate exclusion from the rally. Having won this leg of the event, he would therefore be handing his lead to Francois Delecour, somewhat embarrassed, as was his team to have inherited a rubbery lead. But reason prevailed and McRae was finally reinstated once the incorrect nature of this decision had been shown up by the efficient Subaru boss David Richards, who for once had left his Benetton F1 obligations behind him. Of course the punishment was too severe, but many drivers were muttering along the lines of "rules is rules." McRae thus left Corsica with a second consecutive win on the Island of Beauty. Under the microscope, he emerged as the title contender with the least to reproach himself for. Makinen had a fine collection of accidents; Sainz was also guilty with an off in Catalunya and a puncture but no ATS in Corsica; Kankkunen was no more than a shadow of his former self; Auriol, unlucky or not was alternately either in a state of grace or simply in a state. McRae on the other

with his gearbox and turbocharger. The Fords and Citroens are not capable of doing anything either, generally off the pace. Even less able to mount a challenge are the Mitsubishis, now gone completely with the departure of Burns. The Peugeots are making hard work of it on the greasy

would agree to this, beginning with the course openers who confirmed that around the place in question, there were a lot less people on this third stage than on the first one, when the rally had already embarked on the section known as Filitosa-Bicchisano. On site, Yves Loubet

hand, had always done the best he could with the equipment he was given. Suddenly, he found himself the only man to have won two events this season and leading a Championship rich in uncertainty, which until then had seen Carlos Sainz at the top of the pile.

88.1

FRANCE
"The deer have no cause to fear the pack..."

88.1
Richard Burns' first visit to Corsica was interrupted by a crash.

88.2
Bruno Thiry had second place in his sights, but it was not to be after a spin on the final stage.

88.3
Manfred Stohl dominated Group N at the wheel of a Mitsubishi Ev. 5.

88.2

88.3

88.4

88.5

89.1

88.4

Even the talents of Alister McRae were not enough to make the Hyundai competitive.

88.5 - 89.1

An impressive display from the 2 litres in the rain.
Francois Delecour finished second.

88.6

Do not ask Didier Auriol if he is superstitious.
His troubles started at 13h13 and continued on stage 13.

89.2

Tapio Laukkanen brought his Megane Maxi from Finland to learn the twisty roads of the Corsican mountains.

89.2

42ND RALLY OF FRANCE

TOP ENTRIES

1. Tommi Makinen
   Risto Mannisenmaki
   MITSUBISHI LANCER EV.5

2. Richard Burns
   Robert Reid
   MITSUBISHI CARISMA GT

3. Colin McRae
   Nicky Grist
   SUBARU IMPREZA WRC

4. Piero Liatti
   Fabrizia Pons
   SUBARU IMPREZA WRC

5. Carlos Sainz
   Luis Moya
   TOYOTA COROLLA WRC

6. Didier Auriol
   Denis Giraudet
   TOYOTA COROLLA WRC

7. Juha Kankkunen
   Juha Repo
   FORD ESCORT WRC

8. Bruno Thiry
   Stéphane Prévot
   FORD ESCORT WRC

9. Philippe Bugalski
   Jean-Paul Chiaroni
   CITROËN XSARA KIT CAR

10. Gilles Panizzi
    Hervé Panizzi
    PEUGEOT 306 MAXI

11. Martin Rowe
    Derek Ringer
    RENAULT MAXI MÉGANE

12. Patrick Magaud
    Michel Périn
    CITROËN XSARA KIT CAR

14. François Delecour
    Daniel Grataloup
    PEUGEOT 306 MAXI

15. Tapio Laukkanen
    Tapio Jarvi
    RENAULT MEGANE MAXI

16. Fabien Doenlen
    Jean-Marc Andrié
    CITROËN XSARA KIT CAR

17. Volkan Isik
    Ilham Dokumcu
    TOYOTA CELICA GT-FOUR

18. Abdullah Bakhashab
    Arne Hertz
    TOYOTA CELICA GT-FOUR

19. Isolde Holderied
    Anne-Chantal Pauwels
    TOYOTA COROLLA WRC

20. Pavel Sibera
    Petr Gross
    SKODA OCTAVIA KIT CAR

21. Alister McRae
    Christopher Patterson
    HYUNDAI COUPÉ KIT CAR

22. Luis Climent
    Alex Romani
    MITSUBISHI LANCER EV.4

23. Gustavo Trelles
    Martin Christie
    MITSUBISHI LANCER EV.5

24. Manfred Stohl
    Peter Muller
    MITSUBISHI LANCER EV.5

25. Jean-Marie Santoni
    Jean-Marc Casamatta
    MITSUBISHI LANCER EV.5

26. Francis Mariani
    Bruno Brissart
    SUBARU IMPREZA

28. Jean-Pierre Manzagol
    Dominique Savignoni
    PEUGEOT 306 MAXI

6th leg of the 1998 world rally championships for constructors and drivers
6th leg of the constructors' "2 litre", production car drivers' and teams' world cups

Date: *4 - 6 May 1998*

Route: *1 145.69 km divided into three legs with 18 stages run on tarmac roads (399.18 km)*
1st leg: Monday 4th may, Ajaccio-Propriano-Ajaccio, 6 stages (134.65 km)
2nd leg: Tuesday 5th may, Ajaccio-Corte-Ajaccio, 6 stages (129.88 km)
3rd leg: Wednesday 6th may, Ajaccio-Propriano-Ajaccio, 6 stages (134.65 km)

Starters: *80 (44 Group A + 36 Group N)*

Finishers: *45 (25 Group A + 20 Group N)*

All sorts of mechanical problems stopped Didier Auriol from fighting for second place.

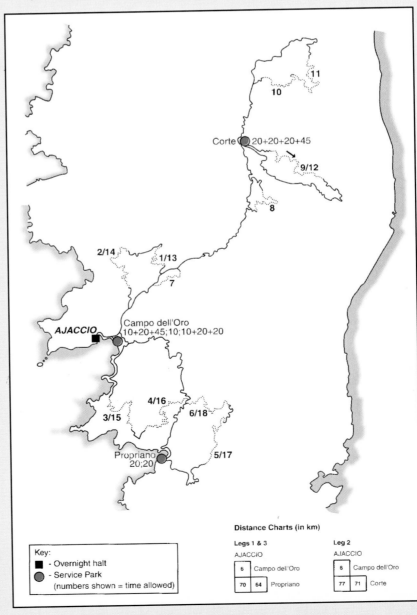

SPECIAL STAGE TIMES

ES.1 Vero-Pont d'Azzana 1 (18,22 km)
1. McRae 13'31"9; 2. Sainz 13'34"2; 3. Bugalski 13'34"7; 4. Makinen 13'41"6; 5. Auriol 13'55"5; Gr.N Stohl 1''18"7

ES.2 Lopigna-Sarrola 1 (25,77 km)
1. Thiry 17'06"9; 2. Panizzi 17'07"3; 3. Delecour 17'14"6; 4. Auriol 17'15"4; 5. Makinen 17'17"1; Gr.N Stohl 18'40'

ES.3 Verghia-Pietra Rossa 1 (26,55 km)
1. Sainz 17'29"8; 2. Panizzi 17'37"6; 3. Delecour 17'41"2; 4. Burns 17'41"6; 5. Auriol 17'42"; Gr.N Rognoni 19'28"3

ES.4 Filitosa-Bicchisano 1 (22,63 km)
1. Liatti 15'12"9; 2. Magaud 15'19"7; 3. Makinen 15'24"1; 4. Auriol 15'24"8; 5. Sainz 15'27"5; Gr.N Vericel 16'41"2

ES.5 Pont d'Acoravo-Zerubia 1 (20,94 km)
1. Liatti et McRae 13'28"7; 3. Magaud 13'37"3; 4. Delecour 13'38"4; 5. Thiry 13'49"7; Gr.N Rognoni 14'34"5

ES.6 Aullène-Petreto 1 (20,54 km)
1. Liatti 13'46"0; 2. Magaud 1''50"4; 3. McRae 13'52"3; 4. Thiry 14'00"3; 5. Delecour 14'08"8; Gr.N Vericel 15'25"3

ES.7 Gare de Carbuccia-Gare d'Ucciani (11,11 km)
1. McRae 7'59"0; 2. Sainz 8'04"; 3. Liatti 8'06"1; 4. Auriol 8'07"8; 5. Thiry 8'08"5; Gr.N Stohl 8'46"3; F2 Panizzi 8'09"3

ES.8 Muracciole-Noceta (16,48 km)
1. McRae 10'30"6; 2. Sainz 10'39"; 3. Liatti 10'39"4; 4. Bugalski 10'42"; 5. Auriol 10'42"3; Gr.N Stohl 11'34"9

ES.9 Feo-Pancheraccia 1 (20,59 km)
1. Sainz 13'13"7; 2. McRae 13'17"4; 3. Panizzi 13'18"4; 4. Delecour 13'18"7; 5. Bugalski 13'19"3; Gr.N Rognoni 14'19"

ES.10 Pont Saint-Laurent-Morosaglia (17,84 km)
1. Sainz 11'24"7; 2. Panizzi 11'26"4; 3. Bugalski et Delecour 11'26"7; 5. Auriol 11'29"3; Gr.N Trelles 12'27"

ES.11 Morosaglia-Campile (31,91 km)
1. McRae 20'40"4; 2. Sainz 20'42"4; 3. Liatti 20'44"8; 4. Delecour 20'45"2; 5. Bugalski 20'48"; Gr.N Stohl 22'48"4

ES.12 Feo-Pancheraccia 2 (20,59 km)
1. Liatti 13'36"1; 2. McRae 13'37"8; 3. Auriol 13'43"7; 4. Bugalski 13'44"5; 5. Sainz 13'45"7; Gr.N Vericel 14'51"6

ES.13 Vero-Pont d'Azzana 2 (18,22 km)
1. Thiry 12'58"9; 2. Panizzi 13'01"2; 3. McRae 13'04"; 4. Liatti 13'08"2; 5. Sainz 13'09"6; Gr.N Santoni 14'05"3

ES.14 Lopigna-Sarrola 2 (25,77 km)
1. Delecour et Thiry 17'01"1; 3. Panizzi 17'01"9; 4. Liatti 17'09"6; 5. McRae 17'09"8; Gr.N Trelles 18'26"5

ES.15 Verghia-Pietra Rossa 2 (26,55 km)
1. Delecour 16'49"7; 2. Auriol 16'52"; 3. Panizzi 16'52"6; 4. Thiry 16'56"3; 5. Liatti 17'01"3; Gr.N Stohl 18'13"5

ES.16 Filitosa-Bicchisano 2 (22,63 km)
annulée pour raisons de sécurité

ES.17 Pont d'Acoravo-Zerubia 2 (20,94 km)
1. Thiry 12'33"5; 2. Panizzi 12'34"8; 3. Magaud 12'35"7; 4. Doenlen 12'36"8; 5. Delecour 12'38"8; Gr.N Trelles 13'39"5

ES.18 Aullène-Petreto (20,54 km)
1. Panizzi 12'49"5; 2. Delecour 12'51"7; 3. Magaud 12'51"9; 4. Doenlen 12'56"8; 5. Liatti 13'02"9; Gr.N Trelles 13'57"1

RESULTS AND RETIREMENTS

Driver/Co-Driver	Car	N°	Gr	Total Time
1 Colin McRae - Nicky Grist	Subaru Impreza WRC	3	A	4h02m46,9s
2 François Delecour - Daniel Grataloup	Peugeot 306 Maxi	14	A	4h03m14,1s
3 Piero Liatti - Fabrizia Pons	Subaru Impreza WRC	4	A	4h03m16,9s
4 Gilles Panizzi - Hervé Panizzi	Peugeot 306 Maxi	10	A	4h03m23s
5 Bruno Thiry - Stéphane Prévot	Ford Escort WRC	8	A	4h03m32,7s
6 Didier Auriol - Denis Giraudet	Toyota Corolla WRC	6	A	4h05m26,2s
7 Fabien Doenlen - Jean-Marc Andrié	Citroën Xsara Kit Car	16	A	4h06m48s
8 Carlos Sainz - Luis Moya	Toyota Corolla WRC	8	A	4h06m50,4s
9 Juha Kankkunen - Juha Repo	Ford Escort WRC	7	A	4h07m34,5s
10 Patrick Magaud - Michel Périn	Citroën Xsara Kit Car	12	A	4h10m59,1s
ES.3 Luis Climent - Alex Romani	Mitsubishi Lancer Ev.5	22	N	Engine
ES.4 Tommi Makinen - Risto Manisenmaki	Mitsubishi Lancer Ev.5	1	A	Electrical
ES.9 Isolde Holderied - Anne-Chantal Pauwels	Toyota Corolla WRC	19	A	Accident
ES.10 Richard Burns - Robert Reid	Mitsubishi Carisma GT	2	A	Suspension
ES.12 Pavel Sibera - Petr Gross	Skoda Octavia Kit Car	20	A	Engine
ES.12 Philippe Bugalski - Jean-Paul Chiaroni	Citroën Xsara Kit Car	9	A	Suspension

GOSSIP

• PEUGEOT

The 1998 event was the last Tour of Corsica for the 306 Maxi. In 1999 it would be replaced by the 206 WRC which would make its debut here. It would be exactly fifteen years since the first appearance, actually in Corsica, of the mythical 205 Turbo 16.

• DELECOUR

A dirty rumour was doing the rounds in Corsica, fuelled by the Spanish press, that François Delecour had carried out an illegal recce before the Catalunya Rally. It turned out that, just like the Czech Sibera team in fact, he had been reprimanded by the Civil Guard for having cut across the corners too much on the public road. The date of this verbal proceeding proved that Delecour was running on a day when the recce was permitted, which was proven by Peugeot managers to the FIA.

• CITROEN

At the start there were three Xsaras for Bugalski, Magaud and Doenlen. Only the last two made it to the finish in Ajaccio. What with an occasional poor tyre choice, a crash from Magaud in the first stage which disconnected the battery, before he mounted a good rush to the front, spins from both Magaud and Doenlen and, broken suspension for Bugalski and punctures, it was a more than fraught event for Citroen. After the show they had put on in Catalunya, the red army finished less well here with Doenlen seventh and Magaud tenth, when at the same time, the Peugeots shone.

• HOLDERIED

The outing for the ladies team of Holderied-Pauwels came to a premature end in the second leg. "We pranged it," explained the co-driving brunette. "We were on slicks and Isolde locked the wheels on a damp patch and then we went up a small step." It was enough of an impact to damage the front right corner of the car and force the blonde driver to retire. "That's the first time in five years she has been off," whinged Pauwels.

• FRANCE

Once again, Citroen had a hot time on the Tour of Corsica. Counting towards the French Championship, the rally was notable for the absence of Simon Jean-Joseph, the main opponent for Citroen. However, with the double chevron performing badly, "Jean-Jo" was able to maintain his championship lead, just ahead of Doenlen.

PREVIOUS WINNERS

1973	Nicolas - Vial	ALPINE RENAULT A 110
1974	Andruet - "Biche"	LANCIA STRATOS
1975	Darniche - Mahé	LANCIA STRATOS
1976	Munari - Maiga	LANCIA STRATOS
1977	Darniche - Mahé	FIAT 131 ABARTH
1978	Darniche Mahé	FIAT 131 ABARTH
1979	Darniche - Mahé	LANCIA STRATOS
1980	Thérier - Vial	PORSCHE 911SC
1981	Darniche - Mahé	LANCIA STRATOS
1982	Ragnotti - Andrié	RENAULT 5 TURBO
1983	Alen - Kivimaki	LANCIA RALLY 037
1984	Alen - Kivimaki	LANCIA RALLY 037
1985	Ragnotti - Andrié	RENAULT 5 TURBO
1986	Saby - Fauchille	PEUGEOT 205 T16
1987	Béguin - Lenne	BMW M3
1988	Auriol - Occelli	FORD SIERRA RS COSWORTH
1989	Auriol - Occelli	LANCIA DELTA INTEGRALE
1990	Auriol - Occelli	LANCIA DELTA INTEGRALE
1991	Sainz - Moya	TOYOTA CELICA GT-FOUR
1992	Auriol - Occelli	LANCIA DELTA HF INTEGRALE
1993	Delecour - Grataloup	FORD ESCORT RS COSWORTH
1994	Auriol - Occelli	TOYOTA CELICA TURBO 4WD
1995	Auriol - Giraudet	TOYOTA CELICA GT-FOUR
1996	Bugalski - Chiaroní	RENAULT MAXI MEGANE
1997	McRae - Grist	SUBARU IMPREZA WRC

EVENT LEADERS

ES.1: McRae
ES.2: Makinen
ES.3 - ES.4: Sainz
ES.5 - ES.18: McRae

BEST PERFORMANCES

	1	2	3	4	5	6
McRae	5	2	2	-	1	3
Liatti	4	-	3	2	2	2
Thiry	4	-	-	2	2	-
Sainz	3	4	-	-	3	2
Delecour	2	1	2	4	2	3
Panizzi	1	5	3	-	-	3
Magaud	-	2	3	-	-	-
Auriol	-	1	1	3	4	1
Makinen	-	1	1	1	-	-
Bugalski	-	-	2	2	2	-
Burns	-	-	1	-	-	-
Doenlen	-	-	-	2	-	3

CHAMPIONSHIP CLASSIFICATIONS

Drivers:
1. Colin McRae 24
2. Carlos Sainz 22
3. Richard Burns 18
4. Juha Kankkunen 16
5. Didier Auriol 15

Constructors:
1. Subaru 35
2. Mitsubishi 32
3. Toyota 32
4. Ford 25

Group N:
1. Manfred Stohl 50
2. Gustavo Trelles 34
3. Luis Climent 24

Two Litres:
1. Peugeot 50
2. Seat 33
3. VW 17

Teams' Cup:
1. Scuderia Grifone 30
2. Sawfish Racing 10
2. Stomil Mobil 1 Rally Team 10
2. Toyota Marlboro Middle East 10

ARGENTINA

T he first time he came across the Argentinian
mountain tracks, Tommi Makinen won the
event showing an ability to adapt which revea-
led a rare talent. It is logical therefore that as the
years go by, so the world champion seems ever
more inaccessible. This time his win was possibly
even more remarkable, as the Flying Finn had to
cope with the advances of two drivers, Colin McRae
and Didier Auriol. These two were certainly not
there to make up the numbers and with a bit of
luck, either one of them might have emerged victorious. Until McRae had a mechanical failure that is
and so did Auriol, but until then they had both put
on a great show which ended all too early.

where only pebbles seem to grow..."

94.1
After the tarmac rally interlude, Oriol Gomez got Seat back into the winners' enclosure in the two litre class.

94.2
The ever enthusiastic Argentinian spectators turned up in droves to cheer on their favourite drivers.

95.1
Do not think for a moment that Tommi Makinen had any time for sightseeing over the three days of the event.

95.2
Toyota Team Europe's decision to temporarily abandon the joystick did not affect the performance of the WRC Corollas.

He will have proved that on this terrain, two crazies, himself and Tommi of course, are a cut above the rest. He will have also rescued a few championship points, the two on offer for fifth place. Not enough to prevent Sainz from taking the lead in the championship but enough to keep in touch.

However, it would not be fair to limit this Argentinian Rally to the Makinen-McRae duel. Because a third man had looked capable of interrupting their duel: Didier Auriol: "I was completely on the pace," he said. He was indeed the only one to nick the lead away from these two (after stage 3.) He finished the first evening sandwiched between them and them came the 13th page of the 13th stage. "I was going round a corner in third, I tried to select fourth and bang." Nothing- a dead engine, something of a rarity for a Toyota with a broken big end.

In the mountains of Argentina, where the tracks reach an altitude of 2000 metres, the other drivers were never to reach these heights. It did not prevent some of them from putting on a great show for the enthusiastic spectators. Worthy of note, Sainz and Kankkunen were fighting as though the most beautiful woman in the country was up for grabs, as the battled for second place. Sainz did it in the final stage. "I could not have gone one tenth quicker," confessed the redoubtable finisher. And the gap between them came down to tenths; Sainz ahead of Kankkunen by seven of them.

Makinen was now out on his own in front. Once Auriol and McRae were no longer bothering him he cruised to a trouble free finish apart from one non-threatening spin. This was his third win from three starts. What is the Finnish for hat-trick?

Makinen does as he pleases

They both wear the blue uniform, but the rows of advertising badges sewn on in yellow make it look as though they bear the stripes of a prison detail, even if it is only a two man chain gang. They hammer and hammer in this desolate universe where only pebbles seem to grow. There is tension in the air and in the energy Nicky Grist applies in his efforts to escape, while a silent Colin McRae seems almost indifferent to his fate. But both men want to break free of this cursed place and so they try and repair the damned and bent suspension arm and straighten the wheel which makes their Subaru's forward progress a painful crab-like sideways motion. "We were on the crest of a bump," admits McRae. "In a left hander there was a huge rock at the side of the road. It was impossible to see it in time and I was completely sideways, so I hit it very hard." The shock is a double one, physical and mental. Colin was leading by 15 seconds over Makinen, the master of the pampas. So, in order to vent their rage on something, McRae and Grist continue to fettle, with the jack, with stones, with a wrench and an adjustable spanner, with their feet. It seems to be in vain but it works in the end. The Subaru finally gets going again after twenty five minutes of forced labour and avoids exclusion by two seconds. They had not hammered in vain.

In the next stage, number 16, the El Condor, with this bodged car that looks as though it came out of a backstreet garage, McRae would fly ahead of all his opponents and would do it again in the following one, before going to bed, exhausted but not so unhappy after all.

Finnish century

Who knows what the real figure is, as believe it or not, men were rallying long before the world championship was officially created in 1973. But, as one has to make statistics official, it is worth recording that Makinen's Argentina victory was the one hundredth world championship rally to be won by a Finnish passport holder. Twenty one of those wins were on home turf in the Thousand Lakes and the first winner was Timo Makinen, spiritual father but no blood relative to Tommi.

Heading this list is Juha Kankkunen, still going strong, but these days more likely to be found lower down the order than first place since his Portugal win in 1994. Kankkunen, four times world champion, a cigarillo dangling from his lips has 21 wins to his credit. He is not yet forty and he has probably not finished yet.

In the current runner-up position comes Markku Alen on 19. Inventor of the "maximum attack" method, he was stuck like glue to the best Italy could provide, be it Fiat or Lancia and as was as twitchy as Kankkunen is laid back. It is one of the sport's injustices that he was never world champion, although he was provisionally, if one recalls the 1986 San Remo incident. On the evening of the third and penultimate leg, the Peugeots were excluded as they did not conform to the regulations. The Lancias were therefore free to win as they please. Cesare Fiorio ordered Biasion and Cerrato to let Alen through. The points gleaned from these events would be enough to give him the world championship a few months later. But Peugeot did not let the matter drop and continued the rally in the courts. The FIA cancelled the results of the San Remo Rally and Alen handed his title

to Kankkunen and that 20th rally win was also taken from him.

Third in the Finnish hit parade is Hannu Mikkola with 18 wins. Before taking the title with the revolutionary Audi Quattro in 1983, he was the king of the exotic event, winning the 1979 London to Mexico Rally and the 1972 East African Safari. He then took an early retirement in Florida but came home so his children would be brought up in their native land. Behind this legendary trio we have: Tommi Makinen, 12 wins and no doubt more in the pipeline, the less calm than he looked Timo Salonen on 11, Ari Vatanen the over impetuous with 10 wins, Timo Makinen, the original with 4 wins, Henri Toivonen, killed in action and far too young, 3 wins, and finally Pentti Airikkala and Kyosti Hamalainen on one apiece.

Flat out in the pampas

That part of the Argentinian government which controls the state of all forms of motorised transport does not seem to take its responsibilities too seriously. One only has to look at the hire cars on offer, where brakes appear to be an option or glance at the cars competing in the national rally which attempt to follow the world championship event. The top dog is the R18GTX. But those of us who come from Europe should not laugh and compare these to the Ford Escorts, Toyota Corollas, the 306, the Meganes and other pretty little cars which we see on rallies. The South Americans make do with what they have and what their economic climate dictates.

Rally historian Martin Holmes has unearthed traces of a rally in Brazil back in 1979, but he

cites 1980 as year zero for South American rallying when Argentina staged a world championship round for the first time. Before that it was the days of the wild and lawless road races, essentially the preserve of rich young things with money, life and petrol to burn.

As rallies became more organised, a few South Americans started to make names for themselves. Let us gloss over Fangio and Reutemann, who rapidly made the transition from road racing to circuits (Peugeot gave Reutemann cause for nostalgia, putting him behind the wheel of a 205 in the Argentina Rally.) First of the rest to get a reputation was Jorge Recalde, winner in Argentina in 1988 ahead of Biasion. His international career got off the ground thanks to a recommendation from Fangio. He was given a works Mercedes for the 1980 Ivory Coast Rally and justified the faith placed in him, by finishing second. He also drove for Lancia and Audi and led a Safari Rally for a long time. Recalde, comes from Mina Clavero, a frequent landmark on the Rally of Argentina and to this day he greets all those who are not in too much of a hurry during their recce.

Gustavo Trelles, from Uruguay, but based in Spain is the natural heir to Recalde. But for the most part, he is happy to run in Group N, a category he has won on two occasions. Carlos Menem Junior, the son of the Argentinian president, was killed in a helicopter accident, Rail Sufan, Marco Galanti have all chanced their arm in the Group A category. But too often, the distance from home and the lack of funds gets in the way of South American talent. It is not surprising the Europeans have virtually monopolised the world championship.

95.1

95.2

96.1

96.1

Before his engine let go, Didier Auriol was the only one to match Makinen and McRae.

96.2

Finally the Subaru was competitive again.

96.3

Following a pre-established plan, identical to the one used in previous years, Tommi Makinen took his third consecutive win in this event.

96.2

96.3

ARGENTINA

"A desolate universe where only pebbles seem to grow..."

97.1-3

Juha Kankkunen gave his all up to the penultimate stage, but Sainz beat him by seven tenths of a second at the line.

97.4-6

Would Richard Burns and Bruno Thiry be impressed by the performance of Finnish four times world champion and legendary cigarillo smoker.

97.1

97.2

97.3

97.4

97.5

97.6

18TH RALLY OF ARGENTINA

TOP ENTRIES

1 Tommi Makinen
Risto Mannisenmaki
MITSUBISHI LANCER EV.5

2 Richard Burns
Robert Reid
MITSUBISHI CARISMA GT

3 Colin McRae
Nicky Grist
SUBARU IMPREZA WRC

4 Piero Liatti
Fabrizia Pons
SUBARU IMPREZA WRC

5 Carlos Sainz
Luis Moya
TOYOTA COROLLA WRC

6 Didier Auriol
Denis Giraudet
TOYOTA COROLLA WRC

7 Juha Kankkunen
Juha Repo
FORD ESCORT WRC

8 Bruno Thiry
Stéphane Prévot
FORD ESCORT WRC

9 Krzystof Holowczyc
Maciej Wislawski
SUBARU IMPREZA WRC

10 Frédéric Dor
Kevin Gormley
SUBARU IMPREZA

11 Marco Galanti
Victor H. Zucchini
TOYOTA COROLLA WRC

12 Kenneth Eriksson
Staffan Parmander
HYUNDAI COUPÉ KIT CAR

14 Harri Rovanpera
Risto Pietilainen
SEAT IBIZA 16V KIT CAR

15 Kris Rosenberger
Per Carlsson
VW GOLF GTI KIT CAR

16 Oriol Gomez
Marc Marti
SEAT IBIZA 16V KIT CAR

17 Alister McRae
David Senior
VW GOLF GTI KIT CAR

19 Manfred Stohl
Peter Muller
MITSUBISHI LANCER EV.3

18 Gustavo Trelles
Martin Christie
MITSUBISHI LANCER EV.4

20 Jorge Recalde
José Garcia
MITSUBISHI LANCER EV.4

21 Hamed Al Wahaibi
Terry Harryman
MITSUBISHI LANCER EV.4

23 Gabriel Raies
José M. Volta
RENAULT CLIO WILLIAMS

7th leg of the 1998 world rally championships for constructors and drivers
7th leg of the constructors' "2 litre", production car drivers' and teams' world cups

Date: *20 - 23 May 1998*

Route: *1451.72 km divided into three legs with 23 stages run on loose surface roads.*
1st leg: Wednesday 20th and Thursday 21st May, Cordoba - La Cumbre, 9 stages (134.79 km)
2nd leg: Friday 22nd May, Cordoba - Mina Clavero - Cordoba, 8 stages (137.40 km)
3rd leg: Saturday 23rd May, Cordoba - Santa Rosa de Calamuchita, 6 stages (132.42 km)

Starters: *61 (34 Group A + 27 Group N)*

Finishers: *30 (16 Group A + 14 Group N)*

Best result of the season for Frederic Dor, tenth place.

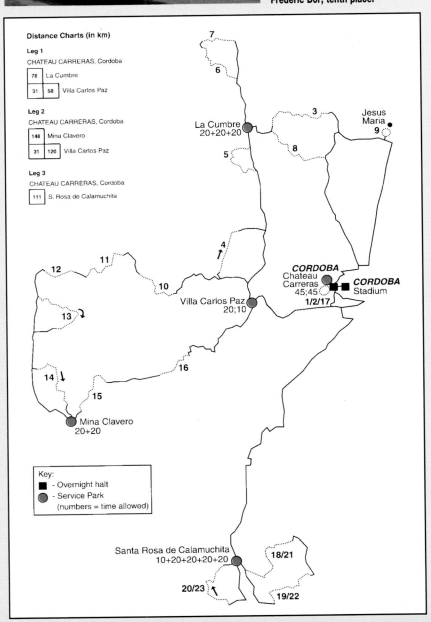

SPECIAL STAGE TIMES

ES.1 Camping San Martin (3,97 km)
1. McRae 3'06"5; 2. Makinen 3'08"1; 3. Kankkunen 3'08"2; 4. Auriol 3'10"2; 5. Liatti 3'10"7; Gr.N Trelles 3'20"7; F2 Eriksson 3'28"3

ES.2 Camping San Martin 1 (4,10 km)
1. Kankkunen 2'41"7; 2. Auriol 2'42"; 3. McRae 2'42"5; 4. Liatti 2'42"9; 5. Makinen 2'43"2; Gr.N Trelles 2'50"8; F2 Rovanpera 2'52"4

ES.3 Ascochinga - La Cumbre (28,93 km)
1. Auriol 18'54"; 2. Makinen 18'55"9; 3. Thiry 18'59"4; 4. Sainz 19'05"4; 5. Burns 19'06"9; Gr.N Trelles 20'08"1; F2 Rovanpera 20'08"1

ES.4 Tanti Cosquin (16,14 km)
1. Makinen 8'37"9; 2. Sainz 8'40"6; 3. Auriol 8'40"7; 4. Burns 8'41"7; 5. Kankkunen 8'42"4; Gr.N Trelles 9'97"7; F2 A.McRae 9'16"2

ES.5 Villa Giardino - La Falda (22,53 km)
1. McRae 16'18"7; 2. Makinen 16'28"9; 3. Kankkunen 16'30"4; 4. Auriol 16'32"2; 5. Burns 16'33"1; Gr.N Trelles 18'20"9; F2 A.McRae 18'19"5

ES.6 Capilla del Monte - San Marcos Sierras (17,40 km)
1. McRae 13'11"7; 2. Auriol 13'15"1; 3. Makinen 13'16"3; 4. Kankkunen 13'19"4; 5. Sainz 13'21"5; Gr.N Trelles 14'23"7; F2 A.McRae 14'23"2

ES.7 San Marcos Sierras - Charbonier (9,80 km)
1. McRae 6'42"8; 2. Makinen 6'44"3; 3. Burns 6'46"6; 4. Kankkunen 6'46"8; 5. Auriol 6'47"9; Gr.N Recalde 7'33"9; F2 Gomez 7'32"6

ES.8 La Cumbre - Agua de Oro (23,67 km)
1. Makinen 20'38"5; 2. Auriol 20'41"8; 3. McRae 20'49"5; 4. Kankkunen 20'51"5; 5. Liatti 20'57"5; Gr.N Trelles 22'29"8; F2 McRae 22'33"1

ES.9 Colonia Caroya (3,40 km)
1. Makinen 2'25"6; 2. Sainz 2'26"2; 3. Kankkunen 2'26"3; 4. Burns 2'26"6; 5. McRae 2'26"8; Gr.N Trelles 2'34"4; F2 A.McRae 2'36"9

ES.10 Mataderos - El Mirador (14,45 km)
1. McRae 8'33"7; 2. Sainz 8'36"7; 3. Auriol 8'37"2; 4. Burns 8'38"7; 5. Makinen 8'40"5; Gr.N Trelles 9'23"6; F2 Gomez 9'19"6

ES.11 Agua Fria - Tala Canada (22,31 km)
1. McRae 13'54"4; 2. Sainz 13'58"9; 3. Auriol 14'00"3; 4. Kankkunen 14'03"1; 5. Burns 14'03"7; Gr.N Trelles 15'17"1; F2 Gomez 14'59"3

ES.12 Tala Canada - Taninga (11,21 km)
1. Burns 5'41"6; 2 McRae 5'42"6; 3. Sainz 5'43"; 4. Auriol 5'44"1; 5. Kankkunen 5'44"8; Gr.N Trelles 6'14"3; F2 Gomez 6'07"9

ES.13 Chamico - Ambul (25,37 km)
1. McRae 18'21"5; 2. Makinen 18'23"8; 3. Sainz 18'34"9; 4. Kankkunen 18'36"3; 5. Burns 18'41"8; Gr.N Trelles 20'38"1; F2 A.McRae 20'29"7

ES.14 El Mirador - San Lorenzo (20,70 km)
1. McRae 11'39"9; 2. Burns 11'43"1; 3. Kankkunen 11'47"8; 4. Makinen 11'48"5; 5. Sainz 11'53"5; Gr.N Trelles 12'44"7; F2 Gomez 12'42"2

ES.15 Latoma - Giulio Cesare (22,26 km)
1. Makinen 18'24"3; 2. Kankkunen 18'30"8; 3. Sainz 18'34"; 4. Burns 18'40"; 5. McRae 18'41"7; Gr.N Trelles 20'52"5; F2 Gomez 20'21"8

ES.16 El Condor - Copina (16,98 km)
1. McRae 14'01"3; 2. Sainz 14'06"6; 3. Makinen 14'06"7; 4. Kankkunen 14'08"1; 5. Burns 14'12"7; Gr.N Trelles 15'16"1; F2 A.McRae

ES.17 Camping San Martin 2 (4,10 km)
1. McRae 2'40"5; 2. Burns 2'41"9; 3. Kankkunen 2'42"3; 4. Makinen 2'42"6; 5. Sainz 2'43"3; Gr.N Trelles 2'51"4; F2 A.McRae 2'53"4

ES.18 Santa Rosa de Calamuchita - San Agustin 1 (26,16 km)
1. McRae 15'25"8; 2. Burns 15'32"6; 3. Sainz 15'34"4; 4. Kankkunen 15'36"5; 5. Makinen 15'39"7; Gr.N Trelles 16'57"8; F2 Gomez 17'20"

ES.19 Las Bajadas - Villa Del Dique 1 (18,72 km)
1. Burns 10'13"3; 2. McRae 10'13"6; 3. Sainz 10'16"8; 4. Kankkunen 10'20"6; 5. Makinen 10'23"3; Gr.N Trelles 11'16"2; F2 Gomez 11'20"2

ES.20 Amboy - Santa Rosa de Calamuchita (21,33 km)
1. McRae 11'22"6; 2. Burns 11'23"8; 3. Kankkunen 11'31"7; 4. Sainz 11'32"6; 5. Makinen 11'34"; Gr.N Trelles 12'57"8; F2 Gomez 12'59"8

ES.21 Santa Rosa de Calamuchita - San Agustin 2 (26,16 km)
1. McRae 15'27"8; 2. Sainz 15'31"6; 3. Burns 15'34"7; 4. Kankkunen 15'34"8; 5. Makinen 15'37"2; Gr.N Trelles 17'12"2; F2 Gomez 17'26'6

ES.22 Las Bajadas - Villa del Dique 2 (18,72 km)
1. McRae 10'14"3; 2. Burns 10'14"4; 3. Sainz 10'15"1; 4. Kankkunen 10'18"3; 5. Makinen 10'20"6; Gr.N Trelles 11'15"8; F2 Gomez 11'25"

ES.23 Amboy - Santa Rosa de Calamuchita (21,33 km)
1. McRae 11'19"8; 2. Kankkunen 11'20"7; 3. Sainz 11'21"8; 4. Burns 11'25"1; 5. Makinen 11'36"3; Gr.N Trelles 12'59"6; F2 Gomez 12'53"3

RESULTS AND RETIREMENTS

	Driver/Co-Driver	Car	N°	Gr	Total Time
1	Tommi Makinen - Risto Mannisenmaki	Mitsubishi Lancer Ev.5	1	A	4h22m07,4s
2	Carlos Sainz - Luis Moya	Toyota Corolla WRC	5	A	4h22m34,2s
3	Juha Kankkunen - Juha Repo	Ford Escort WRC	7	A	4h22m34,9s
4	Richard Burns - Robert Reid	Mitsubishi Carisma GT	2	A	4h23m02,3s
5	Colin McRae - Nicky Grist	Subaru Impreza WRC	3	A	4h23m25s
6	Piero Liatti - Fabrizia Pons	Subaru Impreza WRC	4	A	4h27m14,9s
7	Krystof Holowczyc - Maciej Wislawski	Subaru Impreza WRC	9	A	4h33m46s
8	Marco Galanti - Victor Zucchini	Toyota Corolla WRC	11	A	4h44m23,5s
9	Gustavo Trelles - Martin Christie	Mitsubishi Lancer Ev.4	18	N	4h46m52,1s
10	Oriol Gomez - Marc Marti	Seat Ibiza 16v Kit Car	16	A	4h47m48,5s

ES.4	Manfred Stohl - Peter Muller	Mitsubishi Lancer Ev.3	19	N	Steering arm
ES.5	Harri Rovanpera - Risto Pietilainen	Seat Ibiza 16v Kit Car	14	A	Engine
ES.7	Bruno Thiry - Stéphane Prévost	Ford Escort WRC	8	A	Engine
ES.8	Jorge Recalde - José Garcia	Mitsubishi Lancer Ev.4	20	N	Steering arm
ES.10	Gabriel Raies - José Volta	Renault Clio Williams	23	A	Electrical
ES.12	Kenneth Eriksson - Staffan Parmander	Hyundai Coupé Kit Car	12	A	Engine
ES.13	Didier Auriol - Denis Giraudet	Toyota Corolla WRC	6	A	Engine
ES.17	Alister McRae - David Senior	VW Golf GTI Kit Car	17	A	Engine

GOSSIP

• IT'S BETTER WITH THREE

The super-stages never cease to evolve. Tiziano Siviero, former co-driver for Biasion and now organiser of the rally, instituted starts with three cars on the line at the same time. An original idea, even if an extra eye would come in handy to follow all the action.

• SUBARU IS SULKING

McRae, Grist, Liatti and Pons snubbed all official engagements, such as the shake down, or the now traditional photo, wedged between gauchos and pretty girls in national dress. Officially the Subaru team was involved in last minute testing. To tell the truth and nothing but the truth, David Richards, boss of Prodrive, who prepare the Subarus, is sulking because he is pushing for a reduction in the length of time between recce and rally, while Toyota and Mitsubishi are not.

• ERIKSSON IN FRONT

It was only for one stage and only in the two litre class, but Eriksson well and truly led, before his Hyundai ran out of puff and resumed its position behind the Seats. But for once, Rovanpera is out with engine problems and it is Gomez who wins, having fought off McRae the younger and his Golf GTI. It is Seat's third win of the season, the same number as Peugeot which is still leading this other championship.

• MAKINEN BREATHES EASY

"I hope the bad luck is behind me," sighs Tommi Makinen a happy winner. Four no scores from six events was beginning to be beyond a joke as it was putting the championship out of reach. This year for Makinen it was all or nothing.

• ANNIVERSARY

This Rally of Argentina is the 300th rally in the history of the world championship. It was set up in 1973 (for constructors only) and the drivers version was added in 1979.

PREVIOUS WINNERS

1980	Rohrl - Geistdorfer	FIAT 131 ABARTH
1981	Fréquelin - Todt	TALBOT SUNBEAM LOTUS
1983	Mikkola - Hertz	AUDI QUATTRO
1984	Blomqvist - Cederberg	AUDI QUATTRO
1985	Salonen - Harjanne	PEUGEOT 205 T16
1986	Biasion - Siviero	LANCIA DELTA S4
1987	Biasion - Siviero	LANCIA DELTA HF TURBO
1988	Recalde - Del Buono	LANCIA DELTA INTEGRALE
1989	Ericsson - Billstam	LANCIA DELTA INTEGRALE
1990	Biasion - Siviero	LANCIA DELTA INTEGRALE 16v
1991	Sainz - Moya	TOYOTA CELICA GT4
1992	Auriol - Occelli	LANCIA DELTA HF INTEGRALE
1993	Kankkunen - Grist	TOYOTA CELICA TURBO 4WD
1994	Auriol - Occelli	TOYOTA CELICA TURBO 4WD
1995	Recalde - Christie	LANCIA DELTA HF INTEGRALE
1996	Makinen Harjanne	MITSUBISHI LANCER EV.3
1997	Makinen Harjanne	MITSUBISHI LANCER EV.4

EVENT LEADERS

ES.1 - ES. 2: McRae
ES.3: Auriol
ES.4 - ES.10: Makinen
ES.11 - ES.14: McRae
ES.15 - ES.23: Makinen

BEST PERFORMANCES

	1	2	3	4	5	6
McRae	15	2	2	-	2	-
Makinen	4	6	2	2	8	1
Burns	2	5	2	5	4	3
Auriol	1	3	3	3	1	1
Kankkunen	1	2	6	10	2	2
Sainz	-	5	7	2	4	4
Thiry	-	-	1	-	-	1
Liatti	-	-	-	1	2	11

CHAMPIONSHIP CLASSIFICATIONS

Drivers:
1. Carlos Sainz 28
2. Colin McRae 26
3. Tommi Makinen 24
4. Richard Burns 21
5. Juha Kankkunen 20

Constructors:
1. Mitsubishi 45
2. Subaru 38
2. Toyota 38
4. Ford 29

Group N:
1. Manfred Stohl 50
2. Gustavo Trelles 47
3. Luis Climent 24

Two Litres:
1. Peugeot 55
2. Seat 40
3. VW 23

Teams'Cup:
1. Scuderia Grifone 30
2. Stomil Mobil 1 Rally Team 20
3. Uruguay en Carrera 15

"Pythia does not take pity on

everyone..."

ACROPOLIS

There was a stage on which Colin McRae was in the superb habit of clobbering his "favourite" rivals by a whopping number of seconds. There was none of that this year. The inaccessible dominator who used to come out fighting on one of his favourite events now had to make do with the weapon at his disposal, namely an ageing Subaru. The Scotsman did

not go mad this time, but bided his time and won it once again. He was assisted on his way by the kind help of some of his unlucky opponents, like Tommi Makinen and most of all Didier Auriol, who came in for very little help from the Greek Gods.

102.1

A gift for McRae

Rally drivers are men in a hurry. Even when they pass the ruins of history, they never have time to stop. Surely that is not right, especially at Delphi. Because the ruins set in cypress trees with a sea view are a beautiful sight. Because even centuries later, a consultation with a statue named Pythia deserves a stop. You have to watch your step with the Gods. A quick visit for the sake of good luck would do no harm. Surely the beautiful statue would have warned Makinen and Auriol. They simply drove on by and Pythia does not take pity on everyone and she promptly blew their fuses.

In Makinen's case it happened in the very first stage. A broken spring in the wiring loom. An impossible problem to solve in a hurry. It took Tommi half an hour to get going again. It was too late to take any road except the one which leads straight to Athens. In Auriol's case it was at the very end or almost, on stage 16. He had a 15 second lead over McRae who was concentrating on keeping his second place. And then..."we were hand braking round a hairpin, the car jumped and the engine died." Auriol and Giraudet soon traced the problem to the fuel pump fuse on the dashboard, just as happened in testing in Argentina. That's what irritated Auriol most of all: "we should not have had this sort of problem. It is so stupid." They would never make up the thirty or forty seconds lost for such a silly reason. In the last 27 kilometre stage, McRae, on one of his favourite sections takes on Auriol and beats him by 20 seconds.

"I made the most of the circumstances," he remarked. "But I did not steal this win, I made no mistakes and I was consistent."

He was among the four drivers who shared the lead before the final conclusion. First there was Thiry, before the pistons of his decidedly ageing Ford let him down on stage 5. Then came Burns, who had already led last year, which confirmed his ascendancy except that he suffered as first car on the stages because of all the unruly spectators and then his suspension failed. Of course, Auriol took his turn and once his Corolla was set up as he liked it, ran the perfect rally, easing the pace in the most car-breaking stages, attacking when he wanted. And to round it off along came McRae.

A collector of troubles

How do you judge a driver? Perhaps by simply looking at how many points he has accumulated. That would be too simple. It is important, indeed it is imperative to translate what the figures do not tell. You cannot account for mechanical problems and bad luck. Didier Auriol's 1998 season (Bruno

Thiry's would be equally interesting) is a good example. "We could have a 30 point lead in the championship," reckoned Denis Giraudet. If bad luck had passed him by, he would have won three times from four starts, in Catalunya, Argentina and Greece. But instead of looking after a 30 point lead, he is 15 points down. "I am not in the running for the championship," confirms Auriol. "But seeing these wins slip through my fingers gets me mad."

This is a resume of a tale of woe:

Monte Carlo. He is in full swing but makes an incorrect tyre choice, gets it wrong and crashes to finish 14th. Team mate Sainz also has an off, but wins.

Sweden. Second stage, the engine dies and he is out of the running for the win. At the end of the rally, the engine starts to miss again, just as he is fighting Eriksson for 4th place. He finishes 6th.

Safari. Electrical problems, endless punctures, a slow speed roll. 4th.

Portugal. Best time in the first stage. Gearbox not working well drops him to 12th, before forcing him to retire.

Catalunya. Ove Andersson decides to nominate Loix rather than Auriol as the constructors' championship points scorer. Auriol wins.

Corsica. He is not at one with his car, but reckons he is driving well anyway. But minor problems accumulate, he picks up a penalty and only finishes 6th in his favourite rally.

Argentina. Fighting for first place up to the 13th page of the road book in the 13th stage. The engine dies on him. Its enough for him to beat the car to death with his fists.

Greece. A fuse blows and victory blows away with it. Auriol is livid as he comes 2nd. Missed again.

And all of this carries no guarantees of a brighter future. There are times when he would do better to stay in a castle on the heights of Millau, watching the sun set and telling himself that is all he needs to be happy.

Auriol-Sainz, the same battle

Even with these little problems, Didier Auriol is back. After a year and half's "holiday" thanks to Toyota's little tricky turbo problem, the former world champion has bounced back, even if it took some time coming. Entrenched in his beautiful home in Millau, at first Didier had enjoyed being at home. He had made the most of it, watching his little family growing up, playing golf and feeding his donkeys. In short, he had enjoyed life. And then the world champion began to notice that his telephone was not ringing very much. Those little jobs for Subaru, Toyota or Mitsubishi did not really fill the hole. Then finally, Toyota remembered there is no substitute for experience when it comes to fine tuning a car. Auriol therefore got behind the wheel again, at first to set up the Corolla and then to drive it to victory. Here is an interview which focusses on him and his relationship with Carlos Sainz.

103.1

-When you signed for Toyota, did you ask for equal treatment?

-I did not need to ask and I had no worries about that with a team like Toyota. With the level of competitiveness that now exists at world championship level, a team cannot allow itself not to line up two cars at the highest level. I therefore knew my car would be as good as Carlos.'

-Carlos is reckoned to be difficult to live with. Is it true?

-How can I put it. Partly from his education and partly from his way of seeing things, he has always tended to want everything for himself, which is not the way I do things. But Carlos has matured and evolved. In any case the team knows how to deal with it. So overall, we get on very well with Carlos. There is no tension, We work together for the good of the team and for Toyota. We play the game and when the rally starts, that's it. Okay, seven or eight years ago I would not have said the same thing.

-You certainly do not suffer in comparison with Carlos.

-Apart perhaps from Sweden, but not by a lot. In all the rallies where I had no problems, I was at the same level as Carlos, even a bit ahead of him. That is always good for morale.

-He is ahead of you in the championship. Is that just down to your bad luck?

-Obviously. I have missed out on success, yet again here in Greece. The gap is down to that and nothing else. There is no favouritism.

102.1
In the dust and rock strewn Greek tracks, Colin McRae took an unexpected victory.

103.1
Various mechanical problems delayed the progress of Freddy Loix.

103.2
Victory slipped through Didier Auriol's fingers, all the for the sake of a fifty pence fuse.

103.3
Two stages from the finish, the engine died in Isolde Holdereid's WRC Corolla, forcing her to retire.

103.3

ACROPOLIS
"Pythia does not take pity on everyone..."

104.1
In the lead after the first stage, Richard Burns would be considerably handicapped by his position on the road, the following day.

104.2
Carlos Sainz was delayed on several occasions by the unreliability of his mount.

104.3
Juha Kankkunen's consistency took him to third place on the podium.

104.1

104.2

104.3

105.1

105.4

105.1
Once the WRC Corolla started to run reliably,
Didier Auriol once again demonstrated that he had
to be in the running for victory.

105.2
With this third win, the most famous of the Flying
Scotsmen took the championship lead.

105.3
Mixed fortunes for Tommi Makinen and Colin McRae.

105.4
On two occasions, Pavel Sibera and his Skoda Octavia
was the quickest of the two litre runners.

45TH ACROPOLIS RALLY

TOP ENTRIES

1 Tommi Makinen - Risto Mannisenmaki
MITSUBISHI LANCER EV.5

2 Richard Burns - Robert Reid
MITSUBISHI CARISMA GT

3 Colin McRae - Nicky Grist
SUBARU IMPREZA WRC

4 Piero Liatti - Fabrizia Pons
SUBARU IMPREZA WRC

5 Carlos Sainz - Luis Moya
TOYOTA COROLLA WRC

6 Didier Auriol - Denis Giraudet
TOYOTA COROLLA WRC

7 Juha Kankkunen - Juha Repo
FORD ESCORT WRC

8 Bruno Thiry - Stéphane Prévot
FORD ESCORT WRC

9 Freddy Loix - Sven Smeets
TOYOTA COROLLA WRC

10 Uwe Nittel - Tina Thorner
MITSUBISHI CARISMA GT

11 Thomas Radstrom - Gunnar Barth
TOYOTA COROLLA WRC

12 Aris Vovos - John Alvanos
SUBARU IMPREZA WRC

14 Rui Madeira - Nuno da Silva
TOYOTA COROLLA WRC

15 Leonidas Kirkos - John Stravropoulos
FORD ESCORT WRC

17 Jean-Pierre Richelmi - Freddy Delorme
SUBARU IMPREZA

18 Isolde Holderied - Anne-Chantal Pauwels
TOYOTA COROLLA WRC

19 Volkan Isik - Iham Documcu
TOYOTA CELICA GT-FOUR

20 Frederic Dor - Didier Breton
SUBARU IMPREZA WRC

21 Abdullah Bakhashab - Arne Hertz
TOYOTA CELICA GT-FOUR

22 Alexander Nikonenko - Victor Timkovsky
FORD ESCORT WRC

23 Gustavo Trelles - Martin Christie
MITSUBISHI LANCER EV.5

24 Manfred Stohl - Peter Muller
MITSUBISHI LANCER EV.3

25 Harri Rovanpera - Risto Pietilanen
SEAT IBIZA 16V KIT CAR

26 Kenneth Eriksson - Staffan Parmander
HYUNDAI COUPÉ KIT CAR

27 Luis Climent - Alex Romani
PROTON WIRA EV.3

28 Hamed Al Wahaibi - Terry Harryman
Mitsubishi Lancer Ev.4

29 Pavel Sibera - Petr Gross
SKODA OCTAVIA KIT CAR

30 Oriol Gomez - Marc Marti
SEAT IBIZA 16V KIT CAR

31 Mark Higgins - Philip Mills
NISSAN ALMERA GTI KIT CAR

34 Wayne Bell - Ian Stewart
HYUNDAI COUPÉ KIT CAR

8th leg of the 1998 world rally championships for constructors and drivers
8th leg of the constructors' "2 litre", production car drivers' and teams' world cups

Date: *7 - 9 June 1998*

Route: *1036.49 km divided into three legs with 17 stages run on loose surface roads.*
1st leg: Sunday 7th June, Athens - Delphi, 7 stages (132.18 km)
2nd leg: Monday 8th June, Delphi - Gravia - Delphi, 5 stages (128.29 km)
3rd leg: Tuesday 9th June, Delphi - Gravia - Delphi, 5 stages (128 .29 km)

Starters: *103 (87 Group A + 16 Group N)*

Finishers: *59 (52 Group A + 7 Group N)*

Gustavo Trelles inherited the Group N victory after the retirement of Manfred Stohl.

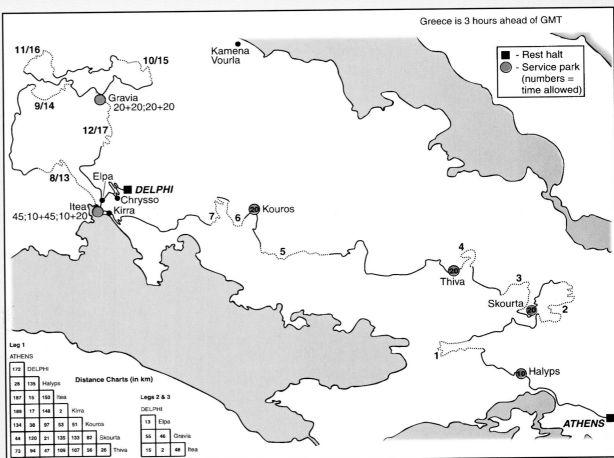

SPECIAL STAGE TIMES

ES.1 Pateras (22,29 km)
1.Thiry 14'02"6; 2. McRae 14'07"5; 3. Liatti 14'12"; 4. Burns 14'12"6; 5. Nittel 14'13"7; Gr.N Stohl 15'37"8; F2 Eriksson 15'19"9

ES.2 Skourta (18,94 km)
Annulée

ES.3 Pili (20,11 km)
1. Kankkunen 12'43"1; 2. Liatti 12'47"; 3. Burns 12'47"2; 4. Auriol 12'47"9; 5. Sainz 12'47"9; Gr.N Al Wahaibi 13'52"8; F2 Rovanpera 13'39"2

ES.4 Thiva (18,29 km)
1. Thiry 14'49"8; 2. Sainz 14'50"5; 3. Burns 14'50"8; 4. Liatti 14'57"; 5. Auriol 14'57"6; Gr.N Travaglia 15'41"3; F2 Rovanpera 15'44"1

ES.5 Evangelistria (22,74 km)
1. McRae 17'04"; 2. Kankkunen 17'05"8; 3. Burns 17'10"; 4. Loix 17'11"8; 5. Auriol 17'14"1; Gr.N Stohl 18'49"; F2 Gomez 18'41"4

ES.6 Livadia (11,40 km)
1. Auriol 9'20"9; 2. Loix 9'25"; 3. McRae 9'30"5; 4. Kankkunen 9'31"8; 5. Burns 9'34"9; Gr.N Trelles 10'06"6; F2 Rovanpera 9'57"

ES.7 Karakolithos (16,70 km)
1. Burns 9'52"7; 2. Auriol 9'53"; 3. Loix 9'53"7; 4. McRae 9'55"; 5. Liatti 9'59"3; Gr.N Trelles 10'51"2; F2 Sibera 10'53"8

ES.8 Bauxites-Karoutes 1 (28,61 km)
1. McRae 17'48"2; 2. Liatti 17'51"2; 3. Sainz 17'52"4; 4.Auriol 17'55"5; 5. Kankkunen 17'59"2; Gr.N Trelles 18'57"5; F2 Gomez 19'02"8

ES.9 Stromi-Inohori 1 (22,49 km)
1. Loix 18'14"6; 2. Auriol 18'25"5; 3. Sainz 18'26"; 4. Liatti 18'26"6; 5. McRae 18'27"5; Gr.N Stohl 19'23"2; F2 Gomez 19'31"8

ES.10 Drimea 1 (25,14 km)
1. Sainz 17'08"1; 2. Kankkunen 17'10"7; 3. Auriol 17'15"7; 4. Burns 17'20"9; 5. Liatti 17'23"4; Gr.N Trelles 19'05"2; F2 Gomez 19'13"6

ES.11 Pavliani 1 (24,83 km)
1. Sainz 20'48"2; 2. Kankkunen 20'51"4; 3. Auriol 20'51"8; 4. McRae 21'00"6; 5. Burns 21'04"9; Gr.N Trelles 22'34"6; F2 Gomez 22'54"5

ES.12 Gravia 1 (27,22 km)
1. Sainz 19'36"8; 2. Kankkunen 19'39"1; 3. McRae 19'43"; 4. Auriol 19'43"9; 5. Liatti 19'47"7; Gr.N Trelles 21'57"3; F2 Rovanpera 21'12"

ES.13 Bauxites-Karoutes (28,61 km)
1. Auriol 17'28"6; 2. McRae 17'30"; 3. Sainz 17'31"1; 4. Burns 17'31"1; 5. Loix 17'35"; Gr.N Al Wahaibi 19'32"6; F2 Rovanpera 19'16"7

ES.14 Stromi-Inohori 2 (22,49 km)
1. Auriol 18'02"1; 2. Loix 18'08"6; 3. McRae 18'08"8; 4. Burns 18'14"7; 5. Liatti 18'15"5; Gr.N Trelles 19'49"4; F2 Rovanpera 19'43"3

ES.15 Drimea 2 (25,14 km)
1. McRae 17'00"6; 2. Kankkunen 17'04"3; 3. Auriol 17'06"9; 4. Sainz 17'09"8; 5. Liatti 17'12"4; Gr.N Trelles 19'45"; F2 Rovanpera 20'09"4

ES.16 Pavliani 2 (24,83 km)
1. McRae 20'43"7; 2. Kankkunen 20'46"7; 3. Sainz 20'47"6; 4. Auriol 21'17"8; 5. Loix 21'24"7; Gr.N Trelles 23'40"9; F2 Rovanpera 22'45"8

ES.17 Gravia 2 (27,22 km)
1. Sainz 20'00"3; 2. McRae 20'03"4; 3. Auriol 20'03"9; 4. Liatti 20'05"7; 5. Kankkunen 20'10"8; Gr.N Al Wahaibi 22'51"6; F2 Rovanpera 22'35"1

RESULTS AND RETIREMENTS

	Driver/Co-Driver	Car	N°	Gr	Total Time
1	Colin McRae - Nicky Grist	Subaru Impreza WRC	3	A	4h26m31,6s
2	Didier Auriol - Denis Giraudet	Toyota Corolla WRC	6	A	4h26m51,6s
3	Juha Kankkunen - Juha Repo	Ford Escort WRC	7	A	4h27m15,9s
4	Carlos Sainz - Luis Moya	Toyota Corolla WRC	5	A	4h28m09,3s
5	Freddy Loix - Sven Smeets	Toyota Corolla WRC	9	A	4h29m20s
6	Piero Liatti - Fabrizia Pons	Subaru Impreza WRC	4	A	4h37m18s
7	Rui Madeira - Nuno da Silva	Toyota Corolla WRC	14	A	4h39m01,8s
8	Leonidas Kirkos - John Stavropoulos	Ford Escort WRC	15	A	4h40m33,5s
9	Jean-Pierre Richelmi - Freddy Delorme	Subaru Impreza	17	A	4h41m52,5s
10	Volkan Isik - Iham Documcu	Toyota Celica GT-Four	19	A	4h43m38,3s

ES.1	Tommi Makinen - Risto Mannisenmaki	Mitsubishi Lancer Ev.5	1	A	Electrical
ES.1	Wayne Bell - Ian Stewart	Hyundai Coupé Kit Car	34	A	Gearbox
ES.4	Thomas Radstrom - Gunnar Barth	Toyota Corolla WRC	11	A	Transmission
ES.5	Bruno Thiry - Stéphane Prévot	Ford Escort WRC	8	A	Engine
ES.6	Kenneth Eriksson - Staffan Parmander	Hyundai Coupé Kit Car	26	A	Electrical
ES.9	Mark Higgins - Philip Mills	Nissan Almera GTI Kit Car	31	A	Transmission
ES.11	Uwe Nittel - Tina Thorner	Mitsubishi Lancer Ev.5	10	A	Accident
ES.15	Isolde Holderied - Anne-Chantal Pauwels	Toyota Corolla WRC	18	A	Engine
ES.15	Richard Burns - Robert Reid	Mitsubishi Carisma GT	2	A	Suspension

PREVIOUS WINNERS

1973	Thérier - Delferrier ALPINE RENAULT A110
1975	Rohrl - Berger OPEL ASCONA
1976	Kallstrom - Andersson DATSUN 160J
1977	Waldegaard - Thorszelius FORD ESCORT RS
1978	Rohrl - Geistdorfer FIAT 131 ABARTH
1979	Waldegaard - Thorszelius FORD ESCORT RS
1980	Vatanen - Richards FORD ESCORT RS
1981	Vatanen - Richards FORD ESCORT RS
1982	Mouton - Pons AUDI QUATTRO
1983	Rohrl - Geistdorfer LANCIA RALLY 037
1984	Blomqvist - Cederberg AUDI QUATTRO
1985	Salonen - Harjanne PEUGEOT 205 T16
1986	Kankkunen - Piironen PEUGEOT 205 T16
1987	Alen - Kivimaki LANCIA DELTA HF TURBO
1988	Biasion - Siviero LANCA DELTA INTEGRALE
1989	Biasion - Siviero LANCA DELTA INTEGRALE
1990	Sainz - Moya TOYOTA CELICA GT4
1991	Kankkunen - Piironen LANCIA DELTA INTEGRALE 16v
1992	Auriol - Occelli LANCIA DELTA INTEGRALE
1993	Biasion - Siviero FORT ESCORT RS COSWORTH
1994	Sainz - Moya SUBARU IMPREZA
1995	Vovos - Stefanis LANCIA DELTA INTEGRALE
1996	McRae - Ringer SUBARU IMPREZA
1997	Sainz - Moya FORD ESCORT WRC

MICHELIN

EVENT LEADERS

ES.1 - ES.4: Thiry
ES.5 - ES.7: Burns
ES.8 - ES.10: McRae
ES.11 - ES.15: Auriol
ES.16 - ES.17: McRae

BEST PERFORMANCES

	1	2	3	4	5	6
McRae	4	2	3	2	1	3
Sainz	4	2	3	1	1	-
Auriol	3	2	4	4	2	-
Thiry	2	-	-	-	-	-
Kankkunen	1	6	-	1	3	4
Burns	1	-	4	3	2	1
Loix	1	2	1	2	2	4
Liatti	-	2	1	3	4	2
Nittel	-	-	-	-	1	1
Richelmi	-	-	-	-	-	1

CHAMPIONSHIP CLASSIFICATIONS

Drivers:
1. Colin McRae 36
2. Carlos Sainz 31
3. Juha Kankkunen 24
4. Tommi Makinen 24
5. Richard Burns 21

Constructors:
1. Subaru 49
2. Toyota 47
3. Mitsubishi 45
4. Ford 33

Group N:
1. Gustavo Trelles 60
2. Manfred Stohl 50
3. Luis Climent 29

Two Litres:
1. Seat 56
2. Peugeot 55
3. VW 23

Teams'Cup:
1. Scuderia Grifone 40
2. Stomil Mobil 1 Rally Team 20
3. Uruguay en Carrera 17

GOSSIP

• NO MORE JOYSTICKS?
The little lever which smacks of the game console but is used to change gear in the cockpit of the Toyota Corolla might well be one of those gadgets which is more fun than useful. Or maybe not. Although the joystick was not seen in Argentina, not in Greece, it might well appear on smoother roads.

• PEUGEOT ON A VISIT
Nothing is official yet, even if everything is decided. Xavier Carlotti and Vincent Laverne, the men from Peugeot Sport appear to be on holiday in Greece and surprisingly, their sightseeing route follows that of the rally to the letter. Obviously they are here to study the logistics of a modern rally. The days of the 205 are long gone, but life looks simpler today with its common service points and a reduced and more concentrated route.

• LIATTI IS CAREFUL
For the works teams, the Acropolis is the rally where they are least likely to be disturbed by the privateers as the gaps per kilometre are so big. Liatti went off towards the end of the rally and lost ten minutes, but he only dropped two places.

• STOHL IS CARELESS
You have to have your heart well strapped in when you sit in a rally car. Even on the road sections. Manfred Stohl was leading in Group N, but he drove off a cliff on a link section between two stages. Clever boy.

• SEAT IS WORRIED ABOUT PEUGEOT
Jaime Puig, the Seat boss, who still remembers the demonstration drives put on by Peugeot (and even the Citroens) in Monte Carlo, Catalunya and Corsica, has given a piece of advice to his drivers, telling them to make sure they get a one-two finish. "It is our only chance up against the Peugeots." The factory Peugeots will be back for San Remo.

"No tears left in heaven..."

NEW ZEALAND

There are days like that, when Didier Auriol is at one with his car, forgetting he is on earth, flying over obstacles in his way and past even his strongest rivals. He is in total symbiosis with the elements and nobody can disturb his pace and rhythm. That was the situation when it rained in New Zealand. But the engine cut out, unjustly depriving the Frenchman of a richly deserved win. Victory would also have served to put an end to

any doubts his employer might have been harbouring about his talents. Destiny caught up with him within sight of the podium. Sainz of course was waiting in the wings and he did not need to be asked twice to take centre stage.

Auriol is badly paid

He could have asked the sky if it had any more rain-filled clouds in stock, just to provide a dab of damp to wet his eyes. But Didier Auriol has long since passed the age of crying over wins that escaped him, no matter how well deserved, even when they slipped from his hands like a bar of soap that is squeezed too tightly. "That's the way it goes. There is nothing I can do about it," he said, down-hearted but not desperate.

For those who might not have realised what had just happened, as they huddled under their umbrellas and their raincoats, the winner, Carlos Sainz spelt it out: "Didier deserved to win. He drove a fantastic rally. Winning against a team-mate who runs into problems is not the nicest way to win." At the end of it all, they celebrated together with champagne. But for Auriol it was a cold shower.

The irony of this story which involved showers, either with or without bubbles, is that the rain suddenly stopped on the third day, drowning out Auriol's plans. Up until then, the Frenchman had been the master of the situation, just like the rams which lead the packs of sheep around the neighbouring countryside. Auriol did not care about the rain. He did not, for example, copy McRae's old trick of slowing visibly in the final corner of a super-stage in order not to be first on the road and have to open the stages on the second day of the rally. Auriol just put his foot down, picking up the fastest times. He did not ask himself any questions but just

kept going in that trance-like state of his, indicating he is on top form. Behind him, Sainz kept running into trouble. "The points for second place are not so bad," he admitted at half distance. The others had all gradually fallen by the wayside. Thiry had rolled his Escort, McRae, who had been quite close for a while, punctured when he did not have a spare on board, Makinen taking on the style of a Sunday driver as he shot off the road in a repeat of past performances in New Zealand. As the third day dawned, Auriol could take comfort from a 30 second lead over Sainz and even if the rain gradually stopped there was no need to worry too much about his slight advantage in opening the stages turning to a big disadvantage. Because, just like snails come out with the first shower, so too, the tiny pebbles which turn the road into a rolling road reappear once the layer of mud has cleared away. "I have taken the gravel off for the others," was how Auriol summed it up. The thirty seconds would have been enough if, on stage 19, the Toyota's engine had not suffered a fit of apoplexy. "I had already noticed the engine had a tendency to cut out when I locked the wheels under braking," said the poor victim. "At one point it happened again in a corner, when I was on full lock. I found I had no power steering and when I went to re-start the car - nothing. I managed to stop, but one wheel was in the ditch. Then I got the engine to fire, selected reverse, but we were still stuck. Spectators pulled us out but we had lost over a minute."

Auriol thus handed a 10.8 second lead to Sainz, but tough fighter that he is, he retook

the lead by 4.5 seconds after another two stages. But the skies had no more to offer, there were no tears left in heaven and Auriol had to settle for second.

Come in Number 22

Carlos likes numbers, especially those that swell his bank balance in recognition of his talents. But he also likes those which bestow legendary status on a driver. This win in New Zealand was not simply one more victory, it was his 22nd and he is the one and only driver to have won so many in the world rally championship.

"I am happy to have done it," commented Sainz. "It's nice, but it is not an end in itself. I still want to win more rallies and championships."

This glorious title is a modern phenomenon. The great drivers of the past, Alen for example, did not systematically compete in the whole championship, with many of the Finns hardly ever bothering with tarmac events. It should be pointed out that the championship has only been in existence since 1973 for the constructors and 1979 for the drivers. Sainz (22 wins) now precedes Kankkunen (21 wins.) The irony of this situation is that, as the two men were team-mates the previous season at Ford, Juha occasionally had to back off, as he did in Indonesia, to let Carlos through. One can understand why his apparent willingness did not always hide his true feelings as he was contributing to his own demise at the top of the wins list. Behind Sainz and Kankkunen come Auriol and

Mikkola 18, Biasion 17, McRae and Waldegaard 16 and so on.

As Kankkunen, Auriol and McRae are still hard at work, Sainz has not exactly entered the history books yet. But he has proved he can win in all conditions. To make it even more perfect and complete, he needs to win Sweden, San Remo and Australia, the only events where victory has so far eluded him. It would be the best way to go for another record, for the number of championships, where once again he would find Kankkunen on his path to glory.

The calendar needs another look

The principle of rallying is that is carried out in Mr. Everybody's car, or almost, on roads used by Mr. Everybody, but not with everybody on them. One can observe that of course, it snows, it rains, it hails, it gets windy and that it gets dark on route, but somehow the cars more often than not "rally" to their destination. But why make matters worse? July in the upside down world of the kiwi is winter and the month of November for the Brits. is winter. So, why not switch dates so that instead of

111.1

110.1
Once again, Auriol was in a class of his own, but it was not to end in a win.

111.1
Harri Rovanpera took his very last two litre win. From the Finnish Rally he would pilot a WRC car.

111.2
Colin McRae gave his all and then some, but he complained of a car that was nervous and hard to master.

111.3
Juha Kangas was entrusted with a works Subaru, but he was a disappointment.

two rainy and cold rallies, we have two more summer events? It would avoid drowning out the New Zealand rally where two stages had to be cancelled with bridges and roads being washed away. It would avoid holding the RAC on a skating rink, running outside the world championship, won by Schwarz, with cars going off everywhere on the ice and Kankkunen and so many others out of the running. The point should be pushed home with the RAC organisers, who usually put

their fingers in their ears when the question is raised. Obviously, they do not want to lose their place as last rally of the year, where the championship is often decided and when next year's cars sometimes appear for the first time. It is called the weight of tradition, but that is a privilege which could be shared. Spain, Indonesia, Kenya and Australia have all changed the date of their event and have benefited from it.

111.2

111.3

112.1

NEW ZEALAND
"No tears left in heaven..."

112.1

Tommi Makinen had but one aim; to finish the rally after falling off the road for the past three years.

112.2-3 / 113.3

Despite this spin on the Tasmanian coast road did not stop Finland's Tommi Makinen from scoring points and an unexpected third place.

112.4

Yoshio Fujimoto had a very quiet race.

112.2
112.3

112.4

113.1

113.2

113.3

113.4

113.1

Improvements to the Evolution 2 Hyundai allowed Kenneth Eriksson to get up to the level of the Seats.

113.2

Thomas Radstrom won the teams' cup despite an off-road excursion.

113.4

Carlos Sainz fought like made to add a 22nd victory to his name (a new record.)

TOP ENTRIES

1 Tommi Makinen - Risto Mannisenmaki
MITSUBISHI LANCER EV.5

2 Richard Burns - Robert Reid
MITSUBISHI CARISMA GT

3 Colin McRae - Nicky Grist
SUBARU IMPREZA WRC

4 Piero Liatti - Fabrizia Pons
SUBARU IMPREZA WRC

5 Carlos Sainz - Luis Moya
TOYOTA COROLLA WRC

6 Didier Auriol - Denis Giraudet
TOYOTA COROLLA WRC

7 Juha Kankkunen - Juha Repo
FORD ESCORT WRC

8 Bruno Thiry - Stéphane Prévot
FORD ESCORT WRC

10 Marcus Gronholm - Timo Rautianen
TOYOTA COROLLA WRC

11 Possum Bourne - Craig Vincent
SUBARU IMPREZA

14 Thomas Radstrom - Gunnar Barth
TOYOTA COROLLA WRC

15 Juha Kangas - Pentti Kukkala
SUBARU IMPREZA WRC

16 Yoshihiro Kataoka - Satoshi Hayashi
MITSUBISHI LANCER EV.3

17 Ed Ordynsky - Mark Stacey
MITSUBISHI LANCER EV.3

18 Yoshio Fujimoto - Tony Sircombe
TOYOTA COROLLA WRC

19 Harri Rovanpera - Risto Pietilainen
SEAT IBIZA 16V KIT CAR

20 Frédéric Dor - Kevin Gormley
SUBARU IMPREZA

22 Gustavo Trelles - Martin Christie
MITSUBISHI LANCER EV.4

24 Kenneth Eriksson - Staffan Parmander
HYUNDAI COUPÉ KIT CAR

25 Kris Rosenberger - Per Carlsson
VW GOLF GTI KIT CAR

27 Hideaki Miyoshi - Damien Long
SUBARU IMPREZA

29 Toni Gardemeister - Paavo Lukkander
SEAT IBIZA 16V KIT CAR

30 Nobuhiro Tajima - Glenn MacNeall
SUZUKI BALENO

31 Wayne Bell - Iain Stewart
HYUNDAI COUPÉ KIT CAR

34 Manfred Stohl - Iika Petrasko
MITSUBISHI LANCER EV.3

35 Hamed Al Wahaibi - Terry Harryman
MITSUBISHI LANCER EV.4

28TH NEW ZEALAND RALLY

9th leg of the 1998 world rally championships for constructors and drivers
9th leg of the constructors' "2 litre", production car drivers' and teams' world cups

Date: *24 - 27 July 1998*

Route: *1466.12 km divided into 3 legs with 25 stages on loose surface roads (388.39 km)*
1st leg: Friday 24th and Saturday 25th July, Auckland - Maramarua - Auckland, 8 stages (48.10 km)
2nd leg: Sunday 26th July, Auckland - Maungaturoto - Auckland, 10 stages (157.91 km)
3rd leg: Monday 27th July, Auckland - Otorohanga - Auckland, 6 stages (182.38 km)

Starters: *79 (50 Group A + 29 Group N)*

Finishers: *50 (32 Group A + 18 Group N)*

Richard Burns went off in the last stage, losing over 15 minutes.

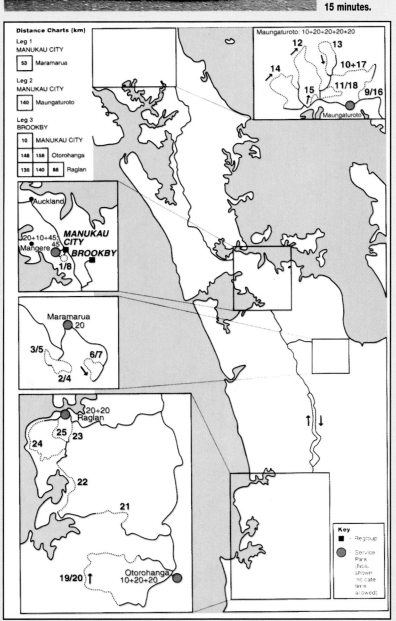

SPECIAL STAGE TIMES

ES.1 Manukau Super 1 (2,10 km)
1. Sainz 1"39"6; 2. McRae 1'40"5; 3. Taguchi 1'41"2; 4. Gronholm 1'41"9; 5. Arai 1'42"3; F2 Eriksson 1'49"8

ES.2 West 1 (6,26 km)
1. McRae 3'26"2; 2. Sainz 3'28"1; 3. Auriol 3'30"3; 4. Makinen 3'30"4; 5. Burns 3'30"6; Gr.N Trelles 3'47"; F2 Eriksson 3'50"5

ES.3 Fyfe 1 (6,81 km)
1. Sainz 3'02"4; 2. McRae 3'04"4; 3. Auriol 3'06"4; 4. Burns 3'06"8; 5. Makinen et Kankkunen 3'07"4; Gr.N Holmes 3'25"9; F2 Eriksson 3'27"7

ES.4 West 2 (6,26 km)
1. Auriol 3'26"9; 2. McRae 3'28"6; 3. Kankkunen 3'30"1; 4. Burns et Sainz 3'30"2; Gr.N Trelles 3'44"9; F2 Rovanpera 3'48"4

ES.5 Fyfe 2 (6,81 km)
1.Auriol 3'00"4; 2. Makinen et Gronholm 3'02"6; 4. Sainz 3'02"8; 5. McRae 3'03"5; Gr.N Trelles 3'25"1; F2 Rovanpera 3'25"1

ES.6 Quarry 1 (8,88 km)
1. McRae 5'17"1; 2. Sainz 5'19"6; 3. Auriol 5'20"3; 4. Kankkunen 5'21"9; 5. Burns 5'22"4; Gr.N Trelles 5'47"1; F2 Rosenberger 5'50"6

ES.7 Quarry 2 (8,88 km)
1. Auriol 5'15"2; 2. Burns 5'17"1; 3. Makinen 5'17"8; 4. Kankkunen 5'19"3; 5. Sainz 5'19"7; Gr.N Meekings 5'42"8; F2 Rovanpera 5'46"4

ES.8 Manukau Super 2 (2,10 km)
1. Auriol 1'40"7; 2. Burns 1'41"6; 3. Kataoka 1'41"9; 4. Makinen 1'42"3; 5. Kankkunen 1'42"4; Gr.N Taguchi 1'42"6; F2 Tajima 1'51"1

ES.9 Waipu Gorge 1 (11,24 km)
1. Sainz 6'40"8; 2. Auriol 6'42"; 3. McRae 6'44"1; 4. Burns 6'45"3; 5. Kankkunen 6'47"6; Gr.N Herbert 7'11"5; F2 Rovanpera 7'23"1

ES.10 Brooks (16,15 km)
Annulée (inondations)

ES.11 Paparoa Station 1 (11,66 km)
Annulée (inondations)

ES.12 Ararua (31,95 km)
1. Auriol 20'12"9; 2. Burns 20'22"3; 3. Sainz 20'28"4; 4. Makinen 20'31"8; 5. McRae et Kankkunen 20'32"9; Gr.N Guest 22'08"5; F2 Eriksson 22'25"

ES.13 Cassidy (20,06 km)
1. Burns et Sainz 11'30"; 3. McRae 11'30"5; 4. Auriol 11'31"; 5. Kankkunen 11'38"7; Gr.N Holmes; F2 Rovanpera 12'36"1

ES.14 Parahi (24 km)
1. Auriol 12'36"9; 2. Burns 12'41"8; 3. Sainz 12'43"8; 4. McRae 12'44"7; 5. Kankkunen 12'52"9; Gr.N Trelles 14'03"7; F2 Eriksson 14'13"7

ES.15 Sterling (3,80 km)
1. Sainz 2'05"3; 2. Auriol 2'06"7; 3. Burns et Kankkunen 2'08"1; 5. McRae 2'08"5; Gr.N Guest 2'21"1; F2 Eriksson 2'21"1

ES.16 Waipu Gorge 2 (11,24 km)
1. Auriol 6'41"2; 2. Sainz 6'45"5; 3. McRae 6'45"8; 4. Makinen 6'46"3; 5. Burns 6'47"3; Gr.N Trelles 7'13"5; F2 Rovanpera 7'21"3

ES.17 Brooks 2 (16,15 km)
1. Auriol 10'04"7; 2. Sainz 10'08"5; 3. Burns 10'09"1; 4. Makinen 10'12"; 5. McRae 10'14"; Gr.N Trelles 11'02"1; F2 Rovanpera 11'13"8

ES.18 Paparoa Station 2 (11,66 km)
1. Auriol 6'25"5; 2. Sainz 6'26"8; 3. Makinen 6'27"6; 4. Burns 6'28"9; 5. McRae 6'30"4; Gr.N Trelles 7'05"6; F2 Rovanpera 7'24"4

ES.19 Te Koraha 1 (47,43 km)
1. McRae 34'16"1; 2. Sainz 34'21"6; 3. Makinen 34'31"1; 4. Kankkunen 34'38"2; 5. Liatti 34'50"2; Gr.N Trelles 36'25"9; F2 Rovanpera 37'19"5

ES.20 Te Koraha 2 (47,43 km)
1. Makinen 35'09"; 2. Burns 35'18"6; 3. Auriol et Kankkunen 35'18"6; 5. Sainz 35'28"; Gr.N Trelles 37'00"5; F2 Rovanpera 37'31"1

ES.21 Pekanui (16,50 km)
1. Auriol 10'18"5; 2. Burns 10'19"8; 3. Sainz 10'24"4; 4. Makinen 10'25"2; 5. McRae et Kankkunen 10'27"5; Gr.N Guest 11'05"4; F2 Gardemeister 11'06"9

ES.22 Bridal Veil (23,48 km)
1. Sainz 16'45"8; 2. Auriol 16'49"4; 3. Burns 16'55"3; 4. Makinen 16'58"4; 5. McRae 17'00"2; Gr.N Guest 17'53"1; F2 Rovanpera 17'59"2

ES.23 Mangatawhiri (6,63 km)
1. Burns 3'51"4; 2. Sainz 3'51"7; 3. Auriol 3'53"2; 4. Radstrom 3'53"5; 5. McRae 3'54"4; Gr.N Guest 4'04"; F2 Gardemeister 4'05"9

ES.24 Whaanga Coast (29,52 km)
1. Burns 21'49"9; 2. Sainz 21'52"3; 3. Auriol 21'53"8; 4. Liatti 21'58"6; 5. McRae 22'08"3; Gr.N Stohl 23'00"5; F2 Gardemeister 23'12"8

ES.25 Te Hutewai (11,39 km)
1. Burns 8'18"; 2. Sainz 8'19"3; 3. Auriol 8'21"3; 4. Kankkunen 8'25"8; 5. Liatti 8'25"9; Gr.N Stohl 8'49"1; F2 Gardemeister 8'57"8

RESULTS AND RETIREMENTS

	Driver/Co-Driver	Car	N°	Gr	Total Time
1	Carlos Sainz - Luis Moya	Toyota Corolla WRC	5	A	3h54m57,1s
2	Didier Auriol - Denis Giraudet	Toyota Corolla WRC	6	A	3h55m01,2s
3	Tommi Makinen - Risto Mannisenmaki	Mitsubishi Lancer Ev.5	1	A	3h56m40,8s
4	Juha Kankkunen - Juha Repo	Ford Escort WRC	7	A	3h57m03,8s
5	Colin McRae - Nicky Grist	Subaru Impreza WRC	3	A	3h58m47,5s
6	Piero Liatti - Fabrizia Pons	Subaru Impreza WRC	4	A	3h59m25,2s
7	Thomas Radstrom - Gunnar Barth	Toyota Corolla WRC	14	A	4h02m28,6s
8	Yoshio Kataoka - Satoshi Hayashi	Mitsubishi Lancer Ev.3	16	A	4h10m11,7s
9	Richard Burns - Robert Reid	Mitsubishi Carisma GT	2	A	4h10m26,6s
10	Yoshio Fujimoto - Tony Sircombe	Toyota Corolla WRC	18	A	4h10m27,6s
ES.7	Bruno Thiry - Stéphane Prévot	Ford Escort WRC	8	A	Accident
ES.9	Marcus Gronholm - Timo Rautiainen	Toyota Corolla WRC	10	A	Engine
ES.12	Juha Kangas - Pentti Kukkala	Subaru Impreza WRC	15	A	Accident
ES.18	Possum Bourne - Craig Vincent	Subaru Impreza	11	A	Engine
ES.19	Wayne Bell - Iain Stewart	Hyundai Coupé Kit Car	31	A	Accident

GOSSIP

• SUBARU BROUGHT OUT

the casting couch in the shape of a third car. Up for audition was the Finn, Juha Kangas. But he broke his lovely blue works car on stage twelve, when he was lying 13th.

• ABSENT

Oriol Gomez, the usual works driver in one of the Seats gave up his seat for Finland's Toni Gardemeister. Officially, Gomez was testing the Seat Cordoba due to be used in Finland. Off the record, Gomez, regularly outpaced by Harri Rovanpera, is losing credit with the Spaniards. Coincidence or not, Seat's one - two finish finally took them to the lead of the two litre class.

• HYUNDAI IS TRYING HARD

The first outing for Evolution 2 of the kit Car coupe from the Korean company, prepared by English specialists MSD, did

Kenneth Eriksson the world of good. He had begun to find time going by rather slowly, especially in the stages, but Eriksson, winner here last year with Subaru, was delighted to find he was often the quickest of the two litre bunch. But for a few minor problems, Hyundai could have threatened the Seat.

• SMOKE JOKE

The mechanics from the Subaru team, sponsored by 555 cigarettes, all donned T-shirts with the legend "Better a tobacco sponsor, than no sponsor at all." The background to this tale is that last year's event was supported by the anti- smoking lobby and the cars had to carry "Smoking kills" stickers. This year the antis left and the mechanics thus took their verbal revenge.

PREVIOUS WINNERS

1977	Bacchelli - Rosetti	Fiat 131 Abarth
1978	Brookes - Porter	Ford Escort RS
1979	Mikkola - Hertz	Ford Escort RS
1980	Salonen - Harjanne	Datsun 160J
1982	Waldegaard - Thorzelius	Toyota Celica GT
1983	Rohrl - Geistdorfer	Opel Ascona 400
1984	Blomqvist - Cederberg	Audi Quattro A2
1985	Salonen - Harjanne	Peugeot 205 T16
1986	Kankkunen - Piironen	Peugeot 205 T16
1987	Wittmann - Patermann	Lancia Delta HF 4WD
1988	Haider - Hinterleitner	Opel Kadett GSI
1989	Carlsson - Carlsson	Mazda 323 Turbo
1990	Sainz - Moya	Toyota Celica GT-Four
1991	Sainz - Moya	Toyota Celica GT-Four
1992	Sainz - Moya	Toyota Celica Turbo 4WD
1993	McRae - Ringer	Subaru Legacy RS
1994	McRae - Ringer	Subaru Impreza
1995	McRae - Ringer	Subaru Impreza
1996	Burns - Reid	Mitsubishi Lancer Ev.3
1997	Eriksson - Parmander	Subaru Impreza WRC

EVENT LEADERS

ES.1: Sainz
ES.2: McRae
ES.3: Sainz
ES.4: McRae
ES.5: Sainz
ES.6 - ES.7: McRae
ES.8 - ES.18: Auriol
ES.19 - ES.20: Sainz
ES.21 - ES.22: Auriol
ES.23 - ES.25: Sainz

BEST PERFORMANCES

	1	2	3	4	5	6
Auriol	10	3	7	1	-	1
Sainz	6	9	3	2	2	1
Burns	4	6	3	4	3	1
McRae	3	3	3	1	9	-
Makinen	1	1	3	7	1	7
Gronholm	-	1	-	1	-	2
Kankkunen	-	-	3	4	7	6
Liatti	-	-	-	1	2	3
Taguchi	-	-	1	-	-	-
Kataoka	-	-	1	-	-	-
Radstrom	-	-	-	1	-	-
Arai	-	-	-	-	1	-

CHAMPIONSHIP CLASSIFICATIONS

Drivers:
1. Carlos Sainz 41
2. Colin McRae 38
3. Tommi Makinen 28
4. Juha Kankkunen 27
4. Didier Auriol...................... 27

Constructors:
1. Toyota 63
2. Subaru 52
3. Mitsubishi 49
4. Ford 36

Group N:
1. Gustavo Trelles 68
2. Manfred Stohl 55
3. Luis Climent 29

Two Litres:
1. Seat 75
2. Peugeot 55
3. VW 26

Teams'Cup:
1. Scuderia Grifone 50
2. Uruguay en Carrera 23
3. Stomil Mobil 1 Rally Team 20

"The hyppy* where the sky is

the horizon..."

And four and one makes five. Another victory for Tommi Makinen in Finland, where he feels so at home, which is quite natural as the rally never misses the chance to go right past the farm where he was brought up as a child. No other dri-

ver, had ever won a single rally so many times. Makinen thus passed Shekhar Mehta, who "only" managed to win the Safari on four occasions. Only Sainz, a driver happy on every sort of surface and one who has never lost his motivation despite years competing at the top, allowed himself the illusion that he might be capable of winning this year. But true to form, Makinen won pretty much as he pleased.

* *yump in Finnish*

118.1-3
Carlos Sainz seemed impressed by Tommi Makinen's performance. The Finn had just won "his" rally for an amazing fifth time in a row. It was a historic record!

rid of that image and takes some lessons.
He chose Juha Kankkunen as his master, following the baton of the world champion who showed him the ropes on a few stages. "In Monte-Carlo it will be Gilles who shows me how to go quickly." Panizzi, his usual works 306 Maxi transformed for this event into a modest 106 Group N found in Denmark, tried to follow from not too far behind. Obviously, once the rally was underway, more than one car had been through and covered all trace of Juha when it was his turn to race the clock. "It was not a problem," claimed Gilles. "I could have got my hands on a big Japanese four wheel drive, but I did not want to be unfaithful to Peugeot and I might have got carried away. I was not there to end up in a tree on the third stage. I was there to learn."
The double French champion, on tarmac, was not put off by all the sliding required, nor by the jumps which often have nothing but sky for a horizon, but his little 106 certainly deprived him of some of the more extreme sensations of rallying in Finland. With no trace of sweaty fear on his face he was keen to get going. "I think I am going to like this. It was a good idea to come here. The notes and the changes in surface are all in my head."
This little tale has an end, but you will have to turn over a page of the results to find the Panizzi - Panizzi duo down in 35th place, almost an hour down on Makinen. That is not far off a difference of 9 seconds per kilometre. Things will no doubt be different when the 106 grows into a 206.

Makinen of course

Finland and its dismal plains, Finland and its dismal forests. Timo Salonen, who hides his hilarity under a stern exterior summed it up. "Here, you either leave, drink or drive," and Tommi Makinen fits that bill. He is the master here, flying further and faster than all the others and claiming his fifth win in Finland, something never seen here or anywhere else. He has now overtaken Shekhar Mehta and his four Safari wins.
Did Tommi ever doubt he would win again here? His right hand man Mannisenmaki has the answer: "It is all very relaxed in the car." Makinen had been nice. He let Sainz lead for 19 kilometres and then it was a case of catch me if you can and of course no one could, as he piled on the pressure taking huge chunks of time off the others in his favourite stages, as has become something of a habit recently. "I like the twisty stages with lots of gullies," commented Makinen. "You have to be able to switch rhythm there to make the difference. I love it and go flat out and it pays off."
Although never far away and already a winner in Finland, Sainz seemed to be more calculating than attacking; a world championship obviously in his thoughts. McRae was once again McCrash, starting with a Subaru that was "fantastic" and quickly transforming it into a mangled arty mobile on the very first morning. Auriol, still at the mercy of his confidence, bothered by noises in his transmission and spongy suspension was biding

his time. Kankkunen could do little with a Ford which should have been pensioned off and thanked for services rendered at least two years ago. Gronholm was busy racking up fastest times, even more than Makinen, but a puncture followed by an off cooled his ardour, even more than the incessant rain.
Anyway, Makinen was out on his own. "People talk to me about statistics and records," he recounted. "But that is not the important part of it. I have got maximum points and I am back in the race." P1 WRC is the number plate on his road car, a Mitsubishi 3000 GT. Position One, World Rally Championship is what he wants and P2 is of no use to him.

A beginner called Panizzi

Show Gilles Panizzi the door and he will come back through the key hole. Peugeot had given serious consideration to coming to the land of the trolls and thousand jumps, but changed their minds after working out the bill. But Panizzi himself was so keen on the idea, he turned up anyway with an anonymous 71 for a start number, with a few stickers, advertising sponsors who had thrown in a few quid and some money he found for himself and with the help of Mouton-Johnson, who now look after him and his destiny. "I thought it would be a good idea to try out the dirt." Panizzi is one of those Latin characters who is an expert on asphalt but considered a bit of a clumsy oaf once off the smooth surfaces. So, why not get

Seat finally sees big

A lot of water has passed under the bridge. It was not so many months ago, that Seat was tossing up between traditional rallies and the rally raid variety. They had a crack at the Baja, entrusting Cyril Neveu, a multiple Dakar winner on two wheels, with a pretty little prototype. But then they suddenly called off a test session in Tunisia to reappear in Monte-Carlo with the little Ibiza, notably with Erwin Weber. In short, it seemed like a half-hearted approach, as if Seat, suffocated by Audi and embarrassed by Skoda (all cars from the same group,) could not make up their minds.
So it took a very long and winding road before the WRC version of the Cordoba finally arrived here to confirm the Spanish company's firm resolve to go down this route. Naturally, this long and winding road is going to take some time before straightening itself out and heading for victory and even the giant Jaime Puig, team boss admits it. His technical director, Frenchman Benoît Bagur (ex Citroen ZX on rally raids) was looking downcast as the first stage times filtered through. "One and a half seconds per kilometre is huge and very disappointing." The second and third days brought a little consolation for the car's father. "The basis is good," Oriol Gomez felt confident enough to announce, even though he was out of the final classification because an error in the notes led to a rock and no further. "We managed to finish and that has been good for the development of the car," added Harri

Rovanpera, an honest ninth. On the commiseration note handed to Bagur: the lack of engine power, poor high speed balance and the differentials. Anything else? If only Seat had not wasted so much time in choosing its programme.

Financial jackpot for McRae

Motoring News, the English weekly which knows every last detail about every last nut and bolt of all the cars and every last penny of every salary, ran it as the lead story. "A six million pound gamble." McRae appeared to have his bottom glued to the seat of a Subaru for ever, but here he was changing cars, switching to Ford and picking up a packet on the way. On top of the king's ransom of a salary, there was more icing on the cake in as much as he would be allowed to bulk up the income by selling space on his overalls to personal sponsors.

Extract of the Motoring News interview.

-They say you will pick up six million pounds?
-Yes, that's about right. The deal is for ten million dollars. Ten sounds better. You have to say it in dollars.
-Why leave a team which has been world

champion three times in a row?
-Good question. I think there comes a point when you just need a change. Maybe I could have waited one more year, but the development of the Focus would have been a long way down the road and maybe going in the wrong direction. So I think it is better to be in on the start of it. If it works and I am sure it will, then it will have increased my credibility.
-Are any of the Subaru people going with you?
-No, for the moment, Ford has all the right people in all the right places.
-Is it a gamble?
-A new car means at least one year's work, so it has to be a gamble, which will mean missing out on at least one championship.
-And at the end of the first year?
-There is a get-out clause for both parties after one year.
-Will this put extra pressure on you?
-No, on the contrary, if a win is a long time coming, it will logically be down to the car still needing development. Pressure will come later.
-Any regrets about leaving Subaru?
-It is an exciting time in my life, but sad at the same time. I am

leaving the team that took me from nothing and made me world champion.

119.1
"Flat absolute" was Juha Kankkunen's plan for keeping up.

119.2
Toni Gardemeister's frightening accident handed two litre victory to Alister McRae.

FINLAND
"The hyppy* where the sky is the horizon..."

120.1
Carlos Sainz was unable to challenge the Finn's superiority.

120.2
Tommi Makinen's brilliant performance was run on rain soaked roads after torrential storms.

120.3
Thomas Radstrom proved to be quite at home in his Finnish cousins' backyard.

120.4
Tommi Makinen's son never misses an opportunity to copy his world champion father.

120.1

120.2

120.3

120.4

121.1
Although this was his first attempt at the famous "yumps," Richard Burns was the revelation of the event, finishing much higher than he expected and in the points.

121.2
Marcus Gronholm threw it all away with an accident which dropped him to seventh place.

121.3
Still paralysed from his New Zealand Rally accident, Bruno Thiry was never on the pace.

121.4
Oriol Gomez' performance in the new WRC Seat Cordoba ended with a crash.

121.1

121.2

121.4

48TH RALLY OF FINLAND

TOP ENTRIES

1 Tommi Makinen - Risto Mannisenmaki
MITSUBISHI LANCER EV.5

2 Richard Burns - Robert Reid
MITSUBISHI CARISMA GT

3 Colin McRae - Nicky Grist
SUBARU IMPREZA WRC

4 Jarmo Kytolehto - Arto Kapanen
SUBARU IMPREZA WRC

5 Carlos Sainz - Luis Moya
TOYOTA COROLLA WRC

6 Didier Auriol - Denis Giraudet
TOYOTA COROLLA WRC

7 Juha Kankkunen - Juha Repo
FORD ESCORT WRC

8 Bruno Thiry - Stéphane Prévot
FORD ESCORT WRC

9 Harri Rovanpera - Risto Pietilainen
SEAT CORDOBA WRC

10 Oriol Gomez - Marc Marti
SEAT CORDOBA WRC

11 Ari Vatanen - Fred Gallagher
FORD ESCORT WRC

12 Marcus Gronholm - Timo Rautiainen
TOYOTA COROLLA WRC

14 Sebastian Lindholm - Timo Hantunen
FORD ESCORT WRC

15 Thomas Radstrom - Gunnar Barth
TOYOTA COROLLA WRC

16 Uwe Nittel - Tina Thorner
MITSUBISHI CARISMA GT

17 Rui Madeira - Nuno da Silva
TOYOTA COROLLA WRC

18 Pasi Hagstrom - Tero Gardemeister
TOYOTA CELICA GT-FOUR

20 Volkan Isik - Iiham Dokumcu
TOYOTA CELICA GT-FOUR

21 Abdullah Bakhashab - Arne Hertz
TOYOTA CELICA GT-FOUR

22 Jouko Puhakka - Mika Ovaskainen
MITSUBISHI CARISMA GT

23 Gustavo Trelles - Martin Christie
MITSUBISHI LANCER EV.5

24 Kenneth Eriksson - Staffan Parmander
HYUNDAI COUPÉ KIT CAR

25 Alister McRae - David Senior
VW GOLF GTI KIT CAR

26 Tapio Laukkanen - Tapio Jarvi
RENAULT MEGANE MAXI

27 Gwyndaf Evans - Howard Davies
SEAT IBIZA GTI 16V KIT CAR

28 Mark Higgins - Philip Mills
NISSAN ALMERA GTI KIT CAR

29 Pavel Sibera - Jiratko Karel
SKODA OCTAVIA KIT CAR

30 Toni Gardemeister - Paavo Lukander
SEAT IBIZA GTI 16V KIT CAR

31 Wayne Bell - Iain Stewart
HYUNDAI COUPÉ KIT CAR

36 Luis Climent - Alex Romani
MITSUBISHI LANCER EV.5

37 Juuso Pykalisto - Esko Mertsalmi
MITSUBISHI CARISMA GT

38 Juha Kangas - Jani Laaksonen
MITSUBISHI CARISMA GT

41 Frédéric Dor - Didier Breton
SUBARU IMPREZA WRC

71 Gilles Panizzi - Hervé Panizzi
PEUGEOT 106 RALLYE

10th leg of the 1998 world rally championships for constructors and drivers
10th leg of the constructors' "2 litre", production car drivers' and teams' world cups

Date: *21 - 23 August 1998*

Route: *1271.10 km divided into three legs with 24 stages on loose surface roads (384.10 km)*
1st leg: Friday 21st August, Jyvaskyla - Jyvaskyla, 9 stages (90.08 km)
2nd leg: Saturday 22nd August, Jyvaskyla - Orivesi - Jyvaskyla, 9 stages (194.58 km)
3rd leg: Sunday 23rd August, Jyvaskyla - Josemora - Jyvaskyla, 6 stages (99.44 km)

Starters: *116 (70 Group A + 46 Group N)*

Finishers: *62 (37 Group A + 25 Group N)*

The Panizzi brothers chose Finland for their first foray on dirt roads. They finished in an encouraging 35th place.

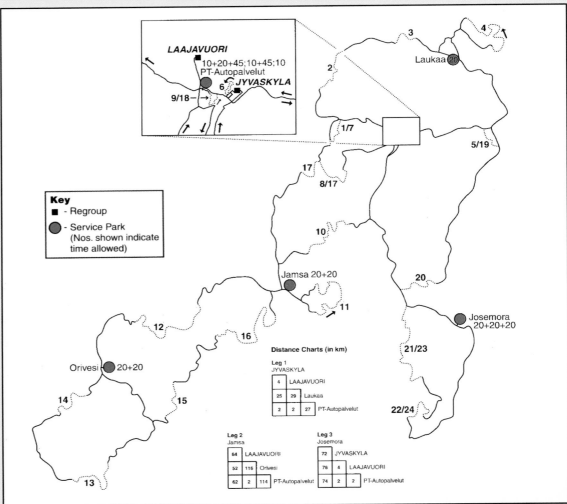

SPECIAL STAGE TIMES

ES.1 Kuohu 1 (6,34 km)
1. Sainz et Kankkunen 3'03"6; 3. Makinen 3'06"7; 4. Burns 3'07"; 5. Gronholm 3'07"4; Gr.N Puhakka 3'19"5; F2 Gardemeister 3'27"2

ES.2 Mokkipera (13,43 km)
1. McRae 6'52"7; 2. Sainz 6'53"1; 3. Makinen 6'54"5; 4. Kankkunen 6'57"6; 5. Auriol 7'02"6; Gr.N Ahvenlammi 7'48"7; F2 Eriksson 7'57"

ES.3 Valkola (8,46 km)
1. McRae 4'38"6; 2. Makinen 4'39"1; 3. Gronholm 4'40"9; 4. Burns 4'43"1; 5. Kankkunen 4'43"2; Gr.N Puhakka 5'08"1; F2 Laukkanen 5'19"5

ES.4 Lankamaa (26,20 km)
1. Gronholm 13'33"3; 2. Sainz 13'35"2; 3. Makinen 13'36"2; 4. Kankkunen 13'38"4; 5. Auriol 13'43"1; Gr.N Kangas 14'42"4; F2 Eriksson 14'57"6

ES.5 Ruuhimaki 1 (7,34 km)
1. Auriol 3'53"7; 2. Makinen 3'54"7; 3. Gronholm 3'54"9; 4. Kankkunen 3'55"4; 5. Burns 3'55"4; Gr.N Trelles 4'15"4; F2 Eriksson 4'18"2

ES.6 Harju (2,57 km)
1. Sainz 1'59"2; 2. Makinen 1'59"9; 3. Kytoletho 2'00"6; 4. Auriol 2'01"6; 5. Burns et Kankkunen 2'01"4; Gr.N Trelles 2'09"2; F2 Higgins 2'14"4

ES.7 Kuohu 2 (7,74 km)
1. Gronholm 3'54"8; 2. Kankkunen 3'55"2; 3. Makinen et Sainz 3'55"4; 5. Auriol 3'56"4; Gr.N Kangas 4'19"; F2 Gardemeister 4'24"7

ES.8 Parkkola (16,31 km)
1. Makinen 8'16"3; 2. Auriol 8'16"9; 3. Kankkunen 8'18"8; 4. Gronholm 8'19"6; 5. Sainz 8'22"4; Gr.N Kangas 9'12"1; F2 Gardemeister 9'15"8

ES.9 Hippos 1 (1,69 km)
1. Radstrom 1'40"5; 2. Auriol et Gronholm 1'40"8; 4. Burns et Sainz 1'40"9; Gr.N Trelles 1'48"1; F2 Higgins 1'50"9

ES.10 Leustu (23,57 km)
1. Makinen 12'02"; 2. Gronholm 12'03"6; 3. Sainz 12'07"9; 4. Kankkunen 12'11"7; 5. Auriol 12'13"2; Gr.N Kangas 13'44"; F2 Higgins 14'01"9

ES.11 Vaheri (31,32 km)
1. Makinen 15'41"1; 2. Sainz 15'52"4; 3. Kankkunen 15'52"7; 4. Gronholm 16'01"7; 5. Radstrom 16'07"8; Gr.N Kangas 17'41"8; F2 Gardemeister 18'07"6

ES.12 Juupajoki (30,94 km)
1. Gronholm 15'45"9; 2. Sainz 15'54"8; 3. Makinen 15'55"4; 4. Auriol 15'57"1; 5. Kankkunen 15'58"8; Gr.N Jokinen 17'17"4; F2 A.McRae 17'13"4

ES.13 Sahalahti (20,50 km)
1. Kankkunen 9'58"2; 2. Makinen 9'59"; 3. Sainz et Gronholm 10'00"9; 5. Auriol 10'04"2; Gr.N Jokinen 10'43"6; F2 Gardemeister 10'38"1

ES.14 Siitama (14,70 km)
1. Makinen 7'30"7; 2. Kankkunen 7'30"8; 3. Sainz 7'31"; 4. Gronholm 7'31"3; 5. Auriol 7'34"3; Gr.N Jokinen 8'01"9; F2 A.McRae 8'12"

ES.15 Vastila (12,42 km)
1. Sainz 5'58"7; 2. Gronholm 5'59"6; 3. Makinen 6'01"8; 4. Auriol 6'02"8; 5. Kankkunen 6'02"9; Gr.N Jokinen 6'28"1; F2 Gardemeister 6'25"7

ES.16 Ouninpohja (34,55 km)
1. Sainz 16'42"4; 2. Makinen 16'42"7; 3. Kankkunen 16'47"6; 4. Radstrom 16'50"2; 5. Kytoletho 16'58"1; Gr.N Jokinen 17'52"4; F2 Gardemeister 18'11"4

ES.17 Surkee (24,91 km)
1. Makinen 12'57"9; 2. Kankkunen 13'08"1; 3. Sainz 13'10"2; 4. Burns 13'12"; 5. Gronholm 13'14"; Gr.N Jokinen 14'53"6; F2 A.McRae 15'02"9

ES.18 Hippos 2 (1,69 km)
1. Radstrom 1'39"2; 2. Auriol 1'40"; 3. Sainz 1'40"5; 4. Burns 1'40"7; 5. Makinen et Gronholm 1'40"8; Gr.N Climent 1'46"9; F2 A.McRae 1'51"3

ES.19 Ruuhimaki 2 (7,34 km)
1. Burns 3'52"9; 2. Auriol 3'53"1; 3. Gronholm 3'53"8; 4. Sainz 3'54"1; 5. Kankkunen 3'54"2; Gr.N Trelles 4'16"4; F2 Gardemeister 4'17"9

ES.20 Hauhanpohja (11,34 km)
1. Gronholm 5'44"5; 2. Kankkunen 5'44"9; 3. Burns 5'46"1; 4. Makinen 5'47"1; 5. Kytoletho 5'47"3; Gr.N Luis Climent 6'30"5; F2 Gardemeister 6'15"

ES.21 Lempaa 1 (28,47 km)
1. Gronholm 13'45"2; 2. Kankkunen 13'50"2; 3. Sainz 13'51"5; 4. Auriol 13'52"7; 5. Makinen 13'55"6; Gr.N Climent 15'36"6; F2 Gardemeister 14'54"4

ES.22 Ylemmainen 1 (11,91 km)
1. Gronholm 6'25"2; 2. Makinen 6'27"2; 3. Kankkunen 6'28"3; 4. Sainz 6'29"3; 5. Auriol 6'31"1; Gr.N Kuzaj 7'12"7; F2 A.McRae 6'52"2

ES.23 Lempaa 2 (28,47 km)
1. Gronholm 13'45"1; 2. Makinen 13'49"3; 3. Auriol 13'50"; 4. Sainz 13'50"5; 5. Kankkunen 13'50"9; Gr.N Kuzaj 15'39"1; F2 Gardemeister 14'52"8

ES.24 Ylemmainen 2 (11,91 km)
1. Gronholm 6'20"8; 2. Radstrom 6'25"8; 3. Makinen et Kankkunen 6'26"; 5. Sainz 6'27"8; Gr.N Walfridsson 7'11"2; F2 Gardemeister 6'55"6

RESULTS AND RETIREMENTS

	Driver/Co-Driver	Car	N°	Gr	Total Time
1	Tommi Makinen - Risto Mannisenmaki	Mitsubishi Lancer Ev.5	1	A	3h16m56,1s
2	Carlos Sainz - Luis Moya	Toyota Corolla WRC	5	A	3h17m31,7s
3	Juha Kankkunen - Juha Repo	Ford Escort WRC	7	A	3h17m41,3s
4	Didier Auriol - Denis Giraudet	Toyota Corolla WRC	6	A	3h19m25,3s
5	Richard Burns - Robert Reid	Mitsubishi Carisma GT	2	A	3h19m52,9s
6	Thomas Radstrom - Gunnar Barth	Toyota Corolla WRC	15	A	3h20m07s
7	Marcus Gronholm -Timo Rautiainen	Toyota Corolla WRC	12	A	3h21m02s
8	Jarmo Kytoletho - Arto Kapanen	Subaru Impreza WRC	4	A	3h23m46,4s
9	Pasi Hagstrom - Tero Gardemeister	Toyota Celica GT-Four	18	A	3h28m11,4s
10	Bruno Thiry - Stéphane Prévot	Ford Escort WRC	8	A	3h30m05,5s

	Driver/Co-Driver	Car	N°	Gr	
ES.2	Sebastian Lindholm - Timo Hantunen	Ford Escort WRC	14	A	Accident
ES.4	Colin McRae - Nicky Grist	Subaru Impreza WRC	3	A	Accident
ES.4	Tapio Laukkanen - Tapio Jarvi	Renaut Megane Maxi	26	A	Accident
ES.4	Jouko Puhakka - Mika Ovaskainen	Mitsubishi Carisma GT	22	N	Accident
ES.5	Gwyndaf Evans - Howard Davies	Seat Ibiza GTI 16v Kit Car	27	A	Electrical
ES.6	Kenneth Eriksson - Staffan Parmander	Hyundai Coupé Kit Car	24	A	Electrical
ES.7	Uwe Nittel - Tina Thorner	Mitsubishi Carisma GT	16	A	Accident
ES.21	Oriol Gomez - Marc Marti	Seat Cordoba WRC	10	A	Accident
ES.22	Ari Vatanen - Fred Gallagher	Ford Escort WRC	11	A	Engine
ES.22	Wayne Bell - Iain Stewart	Hyundai Coupé Kit Car	31	A	Engine

LES ECHOS

• THE GRIFFON IS CHAMPION

The first year of the Teams' Cup, a championship for the privateer teams, has already been decided before the end of the season, in favour of the scuderia HF Grifone, run by the famous Tabaton family (the Griffon is the emblem of Genoa, the town where the team is based.) The Griffon, for a long time linked to Lancia is now a common sight on Toyotas, having run the Celicas while Toyota was suspended because of the illegal turbo affair.

• COLIN'S BROTHER ALISTER

Yes, you have guessed it, the McRae boys, whose rallying genes can be traced back to father Jimmy. Alister finished, winning the two litre class ahead of the local Gardemeister, therefore making it a major achievement. Alister did think for a moment that his win was going out the window when his power assisted steering packed up at dawn on the final day. The mechanics produced the usual miracles.

• GUSTAVO TRELLES

Gustavo in not Finnish, he even comes from the other side of the Atlantic on a diagonal crossing to boot. This did not prevent him from walking off with the Group N honours in his Mitsubishi. Quite a rarity.

• VATANEN IS BACK

Or maybe he never went away. Ari does not settle for coming back for regular family holidays somewhere near the Russian border. Instead he got behind the wheel of a not too bad but very old Escort, to jump for the joy of it once again. If the overheating engine had been up to the job, Ari would surely have finished in the top ten. Next year for sure.

PREVIOUS WINNERS

1973	Makinen - Liddon FORD ESCORT RS 1600
1974	Mikkola - Davenport FORD ESCORT RS 1600
1975	Mikkola - Aho TOYOTA COROLLA
1976	Alen - Kivimaki FIAT 131 ABARTH
1977	Hamalaiinen - Tiukkanen FORD ESCORT RS
1978	Alen - Kivimaki FIAT 131 ABARTH
1979	Alen - Kivimaki FIAT 131 ABARTH
1980	Alen - Kivimaki FIAT 131 ABARTH
1981	Vatanen - Richards FORD ESCORT RS
1982	Mikkola - Hertz AUDI QUATTRO
1983	Mikkola - Hertz AUDI QUATTRO
1984	Vatanen - Harryman PEUGEOT 205 T16
1985	Salonen - Harjanne PEUGEOT 205 T16
1986	Salonen - Harjanne PEUGEOT 205 T16
1987	Alen - Kivimaki LANCIA DELTA HF TURBO
1988	Alen - Kivimaki LANCIA DELTA INTEGRALE
1989	Ericsson - Billstam MITSUBISHI GALANT VR4
1990	Sainz - Moya TOYOTA CELICA GT-FOUR
1991	Kankkunen - Piironen LANCIA DELTA INTEGRALE 16v
1992	Auriol - Occelli LANCIA DELTA INTEGRALE
1993	Kankkunen - Giraudet TOYOTA CELICA TURBO 4WD
1994	Makinen - Harjanne FORD ESCORT RS COSWORTH
1995	Makinen - Harjanne MITSUBISHI LANCER EV.3
1996	Makinen - Harjanne MITSUBISHI LANCER EV.3
1997	Makinen - Harjanne MITSUBISHI LANCER EV.4

EVENT LEADERS

ES.1: Sainz et Kankkunen
ES.2: Sainz
ES.3 - ES.24: Makinen

BEST PERFORMANCES

	1	2	3	4	5	6
Gronholm	8	2	4	4	3	-
Makinen	5	7	7	1	2	-
Sainz	4	4	7	4	2	1
Kankkunen	2	5	4	5	6	1
Radstrom	2	1	-	1	1	5
McRae	2	-	-	-	-	-
Auriol	1	4	1	4	7	3
Burns	1	-	1	5	2	8
Kytolehto	-	-	1	-	2	4

CHAMPIONSHIP CLASSIFICATIONS

Drivers:
1. Carlos Sainz 47
2. Colin McRae 38
3. Tommi Makinen 38
4. Juha Kankkunen 31
5. Didier Auriol 30

Constructors:
1. Toyota 72
2. Mitsubishi 61
3. Subaru 52
4. Ford 40

Group N:
1. Gustavo Trelles 81
2. Manfred Stohl 55
3. Luis Climent 37

Teams'Cup:
1. Scuderia Grifone 56
   (vainqueur de la coupe)
2. Uruguay en Carrera 23
3. Stomil Mobil 1 Rally Team ...20

"*The flash of pure diamond on*

patched up tarmac..."

Makinen took his second ever tarmac rally win with a class performance. "I'm a tarmac expert!" laughed the world champion who thus put himself ever more firmly in the frame for this year's title race, closing to within two points of Sainz. In Italy, only Liatti came anywhere near giving him a hard time, something his team mate Burns could not manage, after an inconsistent performance which nevertheless netted him third place. Sainz was having set-up problems, Auriol

was fed up after yet another retirement and the Fords and Seats were off the pace. As for the kit cars, their crews were able to see that, even on this their preferred surface, the gap in performance to the WRC was growing ever bigger.

The infernal trio

In the 1998 SanRemo rally, the winning combination was Makinen, Mitsubishi, Lancer Evo. V. Outside this hand of aces, this infernal trio, any team thinking of putting up a fight, would have done better to go down to the rococo Casino in the city of flowers and gambled away the money that would be spent on the twisty roads around the heights of San Remo on day one and in south Piedmont on day two. The Finn was quickest from the second stage of the event and he would never be knocked off his perch, even if Piero Liatti was up with him on the fifth stage, as both men set equal times. In fact,

Makinen was toying with the Italian, filling him with false hopes. Consistent and quick, the Subaru man was perfectly at home on his favourite stages and was doing well compared to team-mate McRae, a winner here in '97. Although it has to be said the Scotsman was heavily handicapped after a puncture in stage four. But the world champion was under pressure. It was at the end of the Ponzone stage, in the middle of the second leg, that Makinen definitively shattered any illusions his opposition might have been nursing. Just like a big cat which can kill its prey with one well-timed blow, Makinen killed the rally with his talent. Up there, 22 kilometres of patched up tarmac awaited them. It was damp and slippery under the

trees, covered in parts with dirt and dust, treacherous, narrow, tortuous and twisty. It is a slow and difficult stage where one pretty much gets by with just the first three gears. The sort of stage where the flash of a pure diamond can sparkle. Makinen is rich in carat and as they come out of Ponzone, he had 8 seconds on McRae, 12 on Liatti, thus increasing his lead over the Italian five fold. The second time through this section, he improved his own time by 18 seconds, stuffing Liatti by 15 this time! The competition was over. Not only was Makinen in total control on tarmac, his "weak point" back in the past, but his hard working team had also given him an Evo. V which was perfectly adapted to the task in hand. Conceived partly to overcome its predecessor's slight disadvantage on this surface, this remarkable car had undergone over ten days of specific testing. And some people dare say that hard work does not pay off! Of the crumbs left behind, Liatti took the biggest share, while McRae, not on absolute top form, clawed his way back from 14th to 3rd place, just keeping a flat out Sainz under control towards the end.

Kit Cars in the shadows and light

Once again and once more the party poopers were back. Those spoil sports who got in the way and stopped others from winning and generally upset the form book, neatly established over the course of the season. Here they came, swarming across

126.1
In the final days of its career, the Ford Escort was not good enough for Bruno Thiry to fight for victory.

126.2
Back in the world championship, Marc Duez replaced Oriol Gomez to continue the development of the WRC Cordoba.

127.1
Always very comfortable on his home turf, Piero Liatti had no trouble dominating his team-mate.

the border from France in their usual whites and reds, making their first appearance since the Corsica rally. There were two works 306 Maxis for Delecour and Panizzi, three Xsara kit cars, also the full works, entrusted to Bugalski and Magaud, with heavy back up from Spain's Puras. Nevertheless, although they were far from bad, the roads on the first leg had enough traps to destroy the hopes of these drivers. "The first stages were damp and treacherous in parts. We managed to break away from the other kit cars," explained Daniel Grataloup, evidently impressed with his driver, Delecour's explosive start. But overall, the roads were all too slippery to allow these lively, spectacular and noisy cars to trouble the 4 x 4 brigade, who made the most of their traction to open the stages in style. "We have to face the fact that these stages do not suit us as well as those in Catalunya or Corsica," admitted Delecour. "On top of that, the others have made a lot of progress. Makinen's Mitsubishi...wow!" But while they could not beat the big boys, the kit cars were breathing down their exhaust pipes. Jesus Puras proved how good they could be. Taking it easy at first, the Citroen wild card made the most of the drying roads on the fourth stage, to be the only two wheel driver car to set a fastest time. The Spaniard would not go much further, after an oil pipe came adrift and the engine instantly blew all its oil out. Back in San Remo therefore there was not much to be downhearted about among their ranks. Francois Delecour was the best of their bunch in fifth place, a logical result. "I am happy. We are where

we should be." But the next day held nothing but torment for him. Not only were the roads of Monferatto narrow, twisty and tricky and occasionally wet, but his 306 started to play up as well. At the end of the day, he had a difficult task bringing home his kit car with a crumbling clutch and dodgy electrics. "Dust from the carbon disc brakes caused the problem," explained the boss, Jean-Pierre Nicholas. Despite the best efforts of the mechanics, Delecour would go no further thanks to a loss of fuel pressure. With Magaud out of the running, the best of the kit cars was now Bugalski, as incisive as ever and Panizzi (who set a fastest time) as he slowly recovered from a crippling stomach bug which had affected his performance the day before. The two of them were separated by just seven seconds and were waiting impatiently for the final stage to clinch it one way or the other. It all went pear shaped for "Bug." "Fourteen kilometres into the stage on a right hander, the back end of the Xsara got away from me; the bumper hit the mountainside, before it lost balance, hit off the rock and started to slide. I had lost all control. As there was a left just after, it fell down a drop, stopping with the back just level with the road. It was a bit difficult to drive as the front tyres were over pressured because of the heat, but I have to say I was going a bit quickly. We were having a fight and I was having fun." Panizzi did not ease off and set four fastest times on perfectly dry roads, which saw him move up to fifth. Quickest in the final stage and second overall behind Makinen, Gilles and Herve Panizzi brought the 306 Maxi's

career to a great conclusion, as this was its final official outing. There would soon be new challenges to confront.

Another crown for Trelles

Come to collect the 1998 Group N World Cup, Gustavo Trelles, ably abetted as usual by the Argentinian Martin Christie, did not have to fight for long. The driver from the Uruguay, who once again dominated this season at the wheel of his efficient Mitsubishi Lancer Evo IV then V, was crowned right from the second stage. It was here that the engine in the Mitsubishi of Austria's Manfred Stohl, gave up the ghost. He had been the only man who could still have challenged Trelles in the world ranking. The title was now as good as in the bag. All he had to do was enjoy a pleasant drive on the Italian roads, leaving the locals to fight over the win, which eventually went to Galli after a great tussle with Stagni.

Gustavo Trelles finished third in class and was free to celebrate with his financial backer who had made the trip from South America for this third consecutive title. This jovial driver is in fact the only one who can put together a real world cup programme as his main rivals like Stohl and Spain's Climent do not enter as many events. Nevertheless, Trelles is head and shoulders above the rest in the production car category. Now it is up to him to prove he can cut it in the upper category, if he can find the money.

SANREMO

"The flash of pure diamond on patched up tarmac..."

128.1
According to the drivers, the huge number of fans were better
behaved than in the past.

128.2
Just as in the Tour of Corsica, the battle between Peugeot
and Citroen was settled in favour of the Lions.

128.3
Juha Kankkunen lacked motivation and ended up
crashing out of the rally.

129.1
This was the last time a Peugeot 306 Maxi would cross
the finish line of a world championship rally.

129.2
A pace note error led to Didier Auriol's retirement.

128.1

128.2

128.3

129.1

129.2

TOP ENTRIES

1. **Tommi Makinen**
   Risto Mannisenmaki
   MITSUBISHI LANCER EV.5
2. **Richard Burns - Robert Reid**
   MITSUBISHI CARISMA GT
3. **Colin McRae - Nicky Grist**
   SUBARU IMPREZA WRC
4. **Piero Liatti - Fabrizia Pons**
   SUBARU IMPREZA WRC
5. **Carlos Sainz - Luis Moya**
   TOYOTA COROLLA WRC
6. **Didier Auriol - Denis Giraudet**
   TOYOTA COROLLA WRC
7. **Juha Kankkunen - Juha Repo**
   FORD ESCORT WRC
8. **Bruno Thiry - Stéphane Prévot**
   FORD ESCORT WRC
9. **Harri Rovanpera - Risto Piitilainen**
   SEAT CORDOBA WRC
10. **Marc Duez - Luc Manset**
    SEAT CORDOBA WRC
11. **François Delecour - Daniel Grataloup**
    PEUGEOT 306 MAXI
12. **Philippe Bugalski - Jean-Paul Chiaroni**
    CITROËN XSARA KIT CAR
14. **Gilles Panizzi - Hervé Panizzi**
    PEUGEOT 306 MAXI
15. **Andrea Aghini - Loris Roggia**
    TOYOTA COROLLA WRC
16. **Jesus Puras - Carlos Del Barrio**
    CITROËN XSARA KIT CAR
18. **Franco Cunico - Luigi Pirollo**
    FORD ESCORT WRC
19. **Patrick Magaud - Michel Perrin**
    CITROËN XSARA KIT CAR
20. **Andrea Dallavilla - Danilo Fappani**
    SUBARU IMPREZA WRC
21. **Andrea Navarra - Renzo Casazza**
    SUBARU IMPREZA
22. **Angelo Medeghini - Barbara Medeghini**
    FORD ESCORT WRC
23. **Patrick Snijers - Dany Colbunders**
    FORD ESCORT WRC
24. **Paolo Andreucci - Simona Fedeli**
    RENAULT MEGANE MAXI
25. **Alister McRae - David Senior**
    VW GOLF GTI KIT CAR
26. **Rui Madeira - Nuno da Silva**
    TOYOTA COROLLA WRC
27. **Grégoire de Mevius - Jean-Marc Fortin**
    SUBARU IMPREZA WRC
28. **Krzysztof Holowczyc - Maciej Wislawski**
    SUBARU IMPREZA WRC
29. **Toni Gardemeister - Paavo Lukander**
    SEAT IBIZA 16V KIT CAR
30. **Kenneth Eriksson - Staffan Parmander**
    HYUNDAI COUPÉ KIT CAR
31. **Pavel Sibera - Petr Gross**
    SKODA OCTAVIA KIT CAR
32. **Wayne Bell - Iain Stewart**
    HYUNDAI COUPÉ KIT CAR
33. **Martin Rowe - Derek Ringer**
    RENAULT MAXI MEGANE
34. **Mark Higgins - Philip Mills**
    NISSAN ALMERA GTI KIT CAR
35. **Abdullah Bakhashab - Arne Hertz**
    TOYOTA CELICA GT-FOUR
36. **Tapio Laukkanen - Kaj Linstrom**
    RENAULT MEGANE MAXI
37. **Fabio Danti - Marcello Olivari**
    SKODA OCTAVIA KIT CAR
38. **Janos Toth - Ferenc Gergely**
    TOYOTA COROLLA WRC
40. **Volkan Isik - Ilham Dokumcu**
    TOYOTA CELICA GT-FOUR
41. **Gustavo Trelles - Martin Christie**
    MITSUBISHI LANCER EV.5
42. **Manfred Stohl - Peter Muller**
    MITSUBISHI CARISMA GT
53. **Renaud Verreydt - Jean-François Elst**
    SUBARU IMPREZA WRC

40TH SANREMO RALLY

11th leg of the 1998 world rally championships for constructors and drivers
11th leg of the constructors' "2 litre", production car drivers' and teams' world cups

Date: *12 - 14 October 1998*

Route: *1494.80 km divided into three legs with 24 stages on tarmac roads (400.30 km)*
1st leg: Monday 12th October, SanRemo - SanRemo, 8 stages (120.17 km)
2nd leg: Tuesday 13th October, SanRemo - Acqui Terme - SanRemo, 10 stages (173.72 km)
3rd leg: Wednesday 14th October, SanRemo - SanRemo, 6 stages (106.16 km)

Starters: *153 (94 Group A + 59 Group N)*

Finishers: *76 (44 Group A + 32 Group N)*

Newcomer Patrick Magaud was the only one of the Citroen clan to survive.

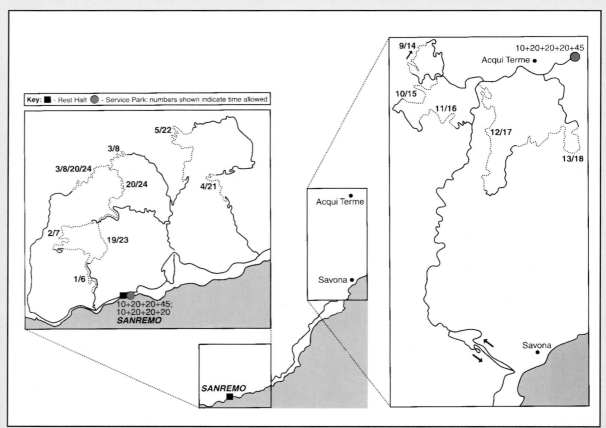

SPECIAL STAGE TIMES

ES.1 Coldirodi 1 (10,12 km)
1. Auriol 6'34"6; 2. Makinen 6'35"1; 3. Sainz 6'37"4; 4. Dallavilla 6'38"5; 5. Delecour 6'38"8

ES.2 Baiardo 1 (16,86 km)
1. Makinen 12'04"5; 2. Cunico 12'08"3; 3. Liatti 12'09"5; 4. Sainz 12'10"6; 5. Dallavilla 12'11"1; F2 Delecour 12'12"9

ES.3 Langan 1 (18,29 km)
1. Liatti 12'39"4; 2. Makinen 12'40"6; 3. Dallavilla 12'40"8; 4. Auriol 12'43"; 5. Sainz 12'44"; Gr.N Trelles 13'34"3; F2 Puras 12'48"2

ES.4 Pantasina 1 (9,28 km)
1. Puras 6'25"5; 2. Liatti 6'26"; 3. Bugalski 6'26"5; 4. Panizzi 6'26"7; 5. Makinen 6'27"3

ES.5 Colle d'Oggia 1 (20,35 km)
1. Liatti 13'53"5; 2. Cunico 13'54"4; 3. Auriol 13'55"4; 4. Makinen 13'55"5; 5. Panizzi 13'55"9

ES.6 Coldirodi 2 (10,12 km)
1. Makinen 6'27"7; 2. Liatti 6'28"6; 3. Bugalski 6'28"7; 4. Sainz 6'29"4; 5. Auriol 6'30"1

ES.7 Baiardo 2 (16,86 km)
1. Makinen 11'57"2; 2. Auriol 11'57"5; 3. Liatti 11'58"2; 4. Bugalski 12'00"9; 5. Delecour 12'02"4

ES.8 Langan 2 (18,29 km)
1. Makinen 12'37"7; 3. Liatti 12'39"5; 4. Sainz 12'41"5; Delecour 12'41"6

ES.9 Loazzolo 1 (10,80 km)
1. Burns 7'40"7; 2. Liatti 7'41"8; 3. Thiry 7'43"6; 4. Sainz 7'43"9; 5. Makinen 7'44"8; Gr.N Galli 8'04"4; F2 Panizzi 7'48"6

ES.10 Madonna Della Neve 1 (14,10 km)
1. Makinen 10'18"1; 2. Burns et McRae 10'18"5; 4. Liatti 10'19"7; 5. Sainz 10'20"5; F2 Panizzi 10'38"2

ES.11 Torre Del Vengore 1 (11,91 km)
1. Dallavilla 8'22"9; 2. Burns et McRae 8'23"1; 4. Liatti et Sainz 8'24"9; Gr.N Galli 8'50"4; F2 Panizzi 8'30"2

ES.12 Turpino 1 (24,45 km)
1. Panizzi 15'37"1; 2. Burns et McRae 15'40"8; 4. Makinen 15'42"1; 5. Sainz 15'42"5; Gr.N Stagni 16'35"2

ES.13 Ponzone 1 (22,68 km)
1. Makinen 17'39"3; 2. McRae 17'46"9; 3. Liatti 17'50"8; 4. Sainz 17'51"5; 5. Burns 17'55"8; Gr.N Stagni 18'36"4; F2 Panizzi 18'08"1

ES.14 Loazzolo 2 (10,80 km)
1. McRae 7'30"5; 2. Makinen 7'32"6; 3. Liatti 7'34"8; 4. Dallavilla 7'35"2; 5. Burns 7'37"9; Gr.N Galli 8'01"1; F2 Bugalski 7'42"8

ES.15 Madonna Della Neve 2 (14,10 km)
1. McRae 10'03"3; 2. Liatti 10'09"7; 3. Burns 10'10"8; 4. Dallavilla 10'10"9; 5. Sainz 10'14"; F2 Bugalski 10'26"8

ES.16 Torre Del Vengore 2 (11,91 km)
1. Makinen et Dalavilla 8'15"3; 3. McRae 8'16"2; 4. Burns et Liatti 8'20; F2 Bugalski 8'26"3

ES.17 Turpino 2 (24,45 km)
1. Makinen 15'31"; 2.McRae 15'33"1; 3. Liatti 15'34"; 4. Burns 15'35"5; 5. Bugalski 15'38"2; Gr.N Galli 16'26"

ES.18 Ponzone 2 (22,68 km)
1. Makinen 17'21"5; 2. McRae 17'35"4; 3. Liatti 17'36"8; 4. Sainz 17'43"5; 5. Dallavilla 17'48"4; Gr.N Stagni 19'13"8; F2 Bugalski 18'05"4

ES.19 Bignone 1 (10,31 km)
1. Panizzi 6'45"6; 2. Bugalski 6'45"7; 3. Liatti 6'45"9; 4. Makinen 6'47"1; 5. Sainz 6'47"4; Gr.N Stagni 7'15"7

ES.20 Monte Ceppo 1 (28,08 km)
1. Makinen 19'28"9; 2. Panizzi 19'31"3; 3. Burns 19'32"4; 4. Liatti et Thiry 19'34"; Gr.N Stagni 20'44"8

ES.21 Pantasina 2 (9,28 km)
1. Panizzi 6'25"2; 2. Liatti 6'26"; 3. Travaglia 6'27"2; 4. Magaud 6'27"3; 5. McRae 6'27"7

ES.22 Colle d'Oggia 2 (20,35 km)
1. Panizzi 13'44"1; 2. Liatti 13'49"7; 3. McRae 13'50"7; 4. Sainz 13'50"9; 5. Magaud 13'53"7; Gr.N Stagni 14'44"6

ES.23 Bignone 2 (10,31 km)
1. Panizzi 6'40"9; 2. Liatti 6'43"5; 3. Aghini 6'44"9; 4. Thiry 6'45"5; 5. McRae 6'45"8; Gr.N Galli 7'09"8

ES.24 Monte Ceppo 2 (28,08 km)
1. Liatti 19'24"7; 2. Sainz 19'26"1; 3. McRae 19'27"5; 4.Panizzi 19'27"9; 5. Makinen 19'29"2; Gr.N Stagni 21'00"1

RESULTS AND RETIREMENTS

	Driver/Co-Driver	Car	N°	Gr	Total Time
1	Tommi Makinen - Risto Mannisenmaki	Mitsubishi Lancer Ev.5	1	A	4h34m34,5s
2	Piero Liatti - Fabrizia Pons	Subaru Impreza WRC	4	A	4h34m50,3s
3	Colin McRae - Nicky Grist	Subaru Impreza WRC	3	A	4h36m04,7s
4	Carlos Sainz - Luis Moya	Toyota Corolla WRC	5	A	4h36m06,4s
5	Gilles Panizzi - Hervé Panizzi	Peugeot 306 Maxi	14	A	4h37m55,7s
6	Bruno Thiry - Stéphane Prévot	Ford Escort WRC	8	A	4h38m21,7s
7	Richard Burns - Robert Reid	Mitsubishi Carisma GT	2	A	4h39m15,8s
8	Andrea Dallavilla - Danilo Fappani	Subaru Impreza WRC	20	A	4h39m39,5s
9	Andrea Aghini - Loris Roggia	Toyota Corolla WRC	15	A	4h40m10,8s
10	Andrea Navarra - Renzo Casazza	Subaru Impreza	21	A	4h40m28,6s
ES.2	Manfred Stohl - Peter Muller	Mitsubishi Carisma GT	42	N	Engine
ES.3	Harri Rovanpera - Risto Pietilainen	Seat Cordoba WRC	9	A	Accident
ES.4	Toni Gardemeister - Paavo Lunkander	Seat Ibiza 16v Kit Car	29	A	Clutch
ES.6	Jesus Puras - Carlos Del Barrio	Citroën Xsara Kit Car	16	A	Engine
ES.9	Franco Cunico - Luigi Pirollo	Ford Escort WRC	18	A	Torn off
ES.11	Didier Auriol - Denis Giraudet	Toyota Corolla WRC	6	A	Suspension
ES.13	Juha Kankkunen - Juha Repo	Ford Escort WRC	7	A	Accident
ES.16	François Delecour - Daniel Grataloup	Peugeot 306 Maxi	11	A	Clutch
ES.20	Philippe Bugalski - Jean-Paul Chiaroni	Citroën Xsara Kit Car	12	A	Accident
ES.21	Rui Madeira - Nuno Da Silva	Toyota Corolla WRC	26	A	Fuel feed

PREVIOUS WINNERS

1973	Thérier - Jaubert	ALPINE RENAULT A110
1975	Waldegaard - Thorszelius	LANCIA STRATOS
1976	Waldegaard - Thorszelius	LANCIA STRATOS
1977	Andruet - Delferrier	FIAT 131 ABARTH
1978	Alen - Kivimaki	LANCIA STRATOS
1979	Fassina - Mannini	LANCIA STRATOS
1980	Rohrl - Geistdorfer	FIAT 131 ABARTH
1981	Mouton - Pons	AUDI QUATTRO
1982	Blomqvist - Cederberg	AUDI QUATTRO
1983	Alen - Kivimaki	LANCIA RALLY 037
1984	Vatanen - Harryman	PEUGEOT 205 T16
1985	Rohrl - Geistdorfer	AUDI SPORT QUATTRO S1
1986	Alen - Kivimaki	LANCIA DELTA S4
1987	Biasion - Siviero	LANCIA DELTA HF 4WD
1988	Biasion - Siviero	LANCIA DELTA INTEGRALE
1989	Biasion - Siviero	LANCIA DELTA INTEGRALE
1990	Auriol - Occelli	LANCIA DELTA INTEGRALE
1991	Auriol - Occelli	LANCIA DELTA INTEGRALE
1992	Aghini - Farnocchia	LANCIA DELTA HF INTEGRALE
1993	Cunico - Evangelisti	FORD ESCORT RS COSWORTH
1994	Auriol - Occelli	TOYOTA CELICA TURBO 4WD
1995	Liatti - Alessandrini	SUBARU IMPREZA
1996	McRae - Ringer	SUBARU IMPREZA
1997	McRae - Grist	SUBARU IMPREZA WRC

EVENT LEADERS

ES.1: Liatti
ES.2 - ES.4: Makinen
ES.5: Liatti et Makinen
ES.6 - ES.24: Makinen

BEST PERFORMANCES

	1	2	3	4	5	6
Makinen	9	4	-	3	3	2
Panizzi	5	1	-	2	1	-
Liatti	4	7	8	4	-	1
Dallavilla	2	-	1	3	2	1
McRae	2	6	3	-	2	3
Burns	1	3	2	2	2	1
Auriol	1	1	1	2	1	1
Puras	1	-	-	-	-	1
Cunico	-	2	-	-	-	-
Sainz	-	1	1	7	5	5
Bugalski	-	-	3	1	1	2
Thiry	-	-	1	2	-	3
Travaglia	-	-	1	-	-	-
Aghini	-	-	1	-	-	-
Magaud	-	-	-	1	1	-
Delecour	-	-	-	-	3	1

CHAMPIONSHIP CLASSIFICATIONS

Drivers:
1. Carlos Sainz 50
2. Tommi Makinen 48
3. Colin McRae 42
4. Juha Kankkunen 31
5. Didier Auriol 30

Constructors:
1. Toyota 75
2. Mitsubishi 71
3. Subaru 62
4. Ford 41

Group N:
1. Gustavo Trelles 86
   (vainqueur de la coupe)
2. Manfred Stohl 55
3. Luis Climent 37

Two Litres:
1. Seat 81
2. Peugeot 69
3. VW 39

Teams'Cup:
1. Scuderia Grifone 66
   (vainqueur de la coupe)
2. Uruguay en Carrera 29
3. Stomil Mobil 1 Rally Team 20

GOSSIP

• TWO LITRES

Victory in San Remo would have no effect on Peugeot's policy as regards the 1998 Two Litre title, even though they were now in with a chance of winning it. There would be no 306 Maxi on the RAC. "It is not our target," claimed Jean-Pierre Nicolas, the boss of the rally department. "If the opportunity had arisen to score points earlier in the season with our customers, we might have made the effort, but we currently have a huge job of work to do in developing the 206 WRC." What is more the 306 Maxi is specifically adapted for tarmac events. With this news, the title looked as though it would inevitably go to Seat.

• AURIOL

As he was stepping up the pace to catch the leaders, Didier Auriol retired at the start of the second leg. "It was a left hand corner and there was a big rock hidden in the grass. I hit it flat out and it suddenly threw the car into the air. The wheel came off, the suspension was broken and the track was gone, so it was impossible to continue. That stone had not been in the notes when we did the recce. The same thing happened to Liatti. The spectators told me he hit it hard but continued. Its a cock up in the notes." With this retirement, any hope of the 1998 title evaporated.

• SEAT

Harri Rovanpera had a big fright. The brakes on his Cordoba WRC were getting worse with every passing kilometre on stage three and he had to keep pumping the pedal to slow down. But 300 metres from the finish, the rear wheels locked, the car slid and crashed heavily at the right front, before a small fire under the bonnet was soon brought under control. The crew escaped unharmed. For his part, Marc Duez was driving slowly to bring to a successful conclusion what was in effect a major test session for the Cordoba WRC, making its first tarmac appearance.

"*Having to play road sweepers the*

following morning..."

AUSTRALIA

This event which wound its way around Perth was one of changing fortunes. In fact, the Australian stages saw the three pretenders to the 1998 championship crown all lead for a while. Finally, it was Tommi Makinen who took the spoils thanks not only to his speed, but also to a touch of luck, after a penalty was revoked and McRae's turbo broke. The Scot was the big loser on

this event; fourth overall, he was from then on kicked out of the title reckoning, as was Subaru. As for Sainz, second, he saved the day having come close to clinching the crown prematurely in Australia. The only certainty to come out of the Antipodes, was that it would all be decided on the RAC.

Makinen's luck

One thing has always held good on the Australian event which is that no one has ever wanted to be first on the road as it is more than just an inconvenience, it is a real disadvantage. It is a challenge that can knock a driver for six, having to sweep all those dashed little pebbles off the road so that the following hordes can get their grooved tyres to dig in even better. Therefore, a little game is often played out, whereby the odd second is dropped here and there, in order not to have to play road sweepers the following morning.

This is pretty much what happened to Richard Burns the morning after an opening super stage won jointly by Auriol and Makinen. Ready for action, the Mitsubishi Number Two showed a gritty determination throughout the first leg. "I am here to win the rally," explained the winner of seven of the ten stages run that day, "and I am concentrating on that objective." Attacking in such a generous fashion also suited his team leader, Tommi Makinen. However, on his favourite type of stage, the Finn hit a rock at a very brisk pace, breaking his suspension. By the time his mechanics had fixed it, a time penalty awaited the poor lad. While he just missed being out of time, Makinen still finished the leg over two minutes behind Burns. But Burns, with Auriol in brilliant form behind him had effectively blocked the road for the two other title

134.1

chasers, Sainz and McRae, who were respectively 1m 26.5 and 1m 36.1 behind. Finally, after being overshadowed on recent events, Juha Kankkunen was reborn on Australian soil for one of his favourite events, which he has won four times before. Third in the first leg, the mighty Juha described this position as: "ideal for tackling the third leg."

On the next day, neither Burns nor indeed Auriol could resist the advances of the Sainz-Makinen duo. Especially as the English redhead got it wrong. In the Bunnings forest, the Spaniard finally took the lead, even if the best performance came from the reigning world champion. Not only did he take six of that day's eight stages, but in five of these six fastest

times, he set new records. On that day he was in a different league to the rest. Having been 2m 22.8 behind Burns, he moved up to second, 22.8s behind Sainz! It was a superb performance. Of the three title chasers, only McRae was marking time: "The left rear drive shaft broke for no apparent reason, which cost me a good thirty seconds in the stage," the Subaru driver would explain later. One incident on this crazy day was to have serious consequences: the penalty inflicted on Makinen for a jumped start was cancelled. There followed some evil political shenanigans. Luckily for the Mitsubishi driver, he was not penalised a minute. He still had a long way to go to win on the third day, which was characterised by an absolutely wild charge from McRae. Delayed until then, the Scotsman took 53 seconds off Sainz, the then leader after the first three stage, with Makinen hanging onto his heels. McRae then took the lead and was heading for another victory when a turbo failed in the penultimate stage, dropping him to fourth place. With victory going to a majestic Makinen - he took 18 seconds off Sainz in the 25.2 km long Bunnings South stage - McRae was out of the title race. For Makinen however, everything was going his way with three wins from the last three rallies and he was now leading the championship for the first time this season, with only a two point lead over Sainz. In Australia, the RAC was beckoning.

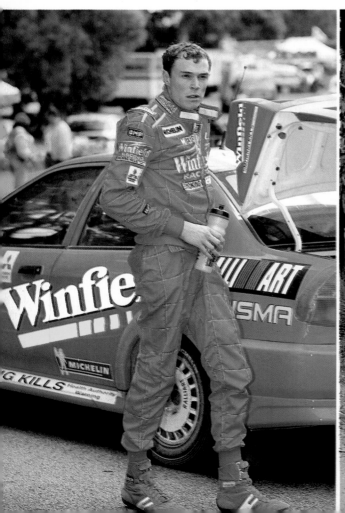

135.1

The politic

Sainz was adamant: "In these circum-stances, I only want one thing, to go home and see my family and shut myself away!" The Spaniard had good reason, it is true, to be annoyed when the stewards cancelled the one minute penalty imposed on Makinen, which thus freed the Finn to fly to victory. There was a lot of anger. But why? At the start of the Langley Park super stage on the second leg, Tommi Makinen impatiently tore off the line four hun-dredths of a second too soon. It should be noted that in Australia, the cars are sent on their way with a set of lights, but the watch only starts when the car flies past a pho-toelectric cell. So, although he was in the wrong, Makinen derived absolutely no benefit from his premature departure. But the law is the law and he was quite rightly given a one minute penalty. Mitsubishi appealed and won its case and the driver was cleared. "The start system does not appear in the FIA regulations," explained Mitsubishi's team manager Phil Short. That is why we made this appeal which the ste-wards have upheld." As for Toyota's appeal, it was rejected. With a one minute penalty, Makinen would have finished the event in sixth place, scoring only one point instead of ten. McRae would have been third, thus scoring four points. They would thus have had 49 and 46 points respectively while Sainz would have had 60 if he had won. It would have been enough to crown the Spaniard as '98 world champion.

The winning machine

From Finland to Australia, the Makinen-Mitsubishi tan-dem had proved to be unbea-table. On three very specific terrains, with two loose sur-face rallies with very diffe-rent characteristics and one entirely on tarmac (the third of his short career,) victory awaited the efforts expended by a fantastic team. The Lancer Evo. V for Makinen and the Carisma GT for Burns, having made its debut in Catalunya, certainly beca-me the most competent win-ning machine of the field. If proof is needed, in Australia, Makinen and Burns between them set 15 fastest times out of the 24 special stages. It is true that this car, developed by the French engineer Bernard Lindauer, had a lot

135.1
Juha Kankkunen likes the Australian rally. He did some remarkable times at the wheel of a Ford Escort long past its sell-by date.

135.2
Harri Rovanpera was the only Seat driver to make it to the finish. Marc Duez went off during the second leg of his first attempt at this event.

of work done on it by the men of Ralliart Europe, led by Andrew Cowan. Longer and bulkier than all the other cars in the field, this Group A machine, unlike its WRC adversaries, often proved to be the most agile. Makinen played a key role in its deve-lopment. He always wanted a car he could chuck around, as well as one with a lot of traction. The world champion himself, Burns and test driver Lasse Lampi did not stint in their efforts. The Evo V's handling is therefore exemplary. On the exit to corners it naturally swings back into a straight line, without a hint of oversteer, even though it is quite willing to get its tail out on the way into the corner. A lot of work was invested in the differentials and their programming, its ride height, suspension, anti-dive, trac-tion control and anti-roll. Before the San Remo, Mitsubishi was the only team to carry out ten days of specific testing to improve a car that was already quick on tarmac, thanks partly to its wider track, the one weak point of the Evo IV. It was also built to a very high standard and so the Mitsubishi was pretty much unbeatable. In Australia, not even a few offs could upset it. Going into the very important RAC rally, where the title would be decided, the Finn therefore had a distinct advantage over Sainz' Toyota. Furthermore, despite the siren song from Peugeot and even more so from Ford, Tommi Makinen certainly reaped the benefit of putting pen to paper with Cowan's team for 1999, when it came to contract renewal time. Burns' case however was another matter.

136.1

136.2

136.3

136.4

137.1

136.1
In only his second appearance here, Freddy Loix was more than capable of matching the pace of the best.

136.2
This third win put Tommi Makinen in the championship lead for the first time this season.

136.3
Having just taken the lead, Colin McRae lost any hope of victory and a world championship when his turbo blew in the penultimate stage.

136.4
The laid-back attitude of the Finnish drivers is no doubt one of the keys to their success.

136.5
Harri Rovanpera's position did not reflect the progress of the Cordoba WRC.

137.1-2
Carlos Sainz could have won the title in Australia, but various circumstances conspired to put him in a difficult position before the RAC.

API 12 1998 RALLY AUSTRALIA

11ST RALLY AUSTRALIA

TOP ENTRIES

1 Tommi Makinen - Risto Mannisenmaki
MITSUBISHI LANCER EV.5

2 Richard Burns - Rober Reid
MITSUBISHI CARISMA GT

3 Colin McRae - Nicky Grist
SUBARU IMPREZA WRC

4 Piero Liatti - Fabrizia Pons
SUBARU IMPREZA WRC

5 Carlos Sainz - Luis Moya
TOYOTA COROLLA WRC

6 Didier Auriol - Denis Giraudet
TOYOTA COROLLA WRC

7 Juha Kankkunen - Juha Repo
FORD ESCORT WRC

8 Bruno Thiry - Stéphane Prévot
FORD ESCORT WRC

9 Harri Rovanpera - Risto Pietilainen
SEAT CORDOBA WRC

10 Marc Duez - Luc Manset
SEAT CORDOBA WRC

11 Freddy Loix - Sven Smeets
TOYOTA COROLLA WRC

12 Neal Bates - Coral Taylor
TOYOTA COROLLA WRC

13 Possum Bourne - Craig Vincent
SUBARU IMPREZA

14 Sebastian Lindholm - Jukka Aho
FORD ESCORT WRC

15 Ed Ordynski - Mark Stacey
MITSUBISHI LANCER EV.3

16 Yoshio Fujimoto - Tony Sircombe
TOYOTA COROLLA WRC

17 Volkan Isik - Ilham Dokumcu
TOYOTA CELICA GT-FOUR

18 Abdullah Bakhashab - Arne Hertz
TOYOTA CELICA GT-FOUR

19 Kenneth Eriksson - Staffan Parmander
HYUNDAI COUPÉ KIT CAR

20 Alister McRae - David Senior
VW GOLF GTI 16V KIT CAR

21 Toni Gardemeister - Paavo Lukander
SEAT IBIZA GTI 16V KIT CAR

22 Wayne Bell - Iain Stewart
HYUNDAI COUPÉ KIT CAR

23 Nobuhiro Tajima - Glenn MacNeall
SUZUKI BALENO

24 Kris Rosenberger - Per Carlsson
VW GOLF GTI 16V KIT CAR

25 Gwyndaf Evans - Howard Davies
SEAT IBIZA GTI 16V KIT CAR

28 Gustavo Trelles - Martin Christie
MITSUBISHI LANCER EV.4

30 Manfred Stohl - Peter Muller
MITSUBISHI LANCER EV.3

31 Jean-Pierre Richelmi - Freddy Delorme
MITSUBISHI LANCER EV.4

32 Yoshihiro Kataoka - Satoshi Hayashi
MITSUBISHI LANCER EV.3

33 Hideaki Miyoshi - Damien Long
SUBARU IMPREZA

34 Hamed Al-Wahaibi - Terry Harryman
MITSUBISHI LANCER EV.4

35 Jorge Recalde - Jorge Del Buono
MITSUBISHI LANCER EV.5

36 Masao Kamioka - Hiroshi Suzuki
SUBARU IMPREZA

12th leg of the 1998 world rally championships for constructors and drivers
12th leg of the constructors' "2 litre", production car drivers' and teams' world cups

Date: *4 - 8 November 1998*

Route: *1408.22 km divided into three legs with 24 stages run on loose surface roads (404.69 km)*
1st leg: Thursday 4th and Vendredi 5th November, Perth - Mundaring - Perth, 11 stages (134.99 km)
2nd leg: Saturday 6th November, Perth - Collie - Perth, 8 stages (160.83 km)
3rd leg: Sunday 7th November, Perth - Bunnings - Perth, 5 stages (108.93 km)

Starters: *92 (48 Group A + 44 Group N)*

Finishers: *58 (35 Group A + 23 Group N)*

Yoshio Fujimoto wins the Asia-Pacific Championship.

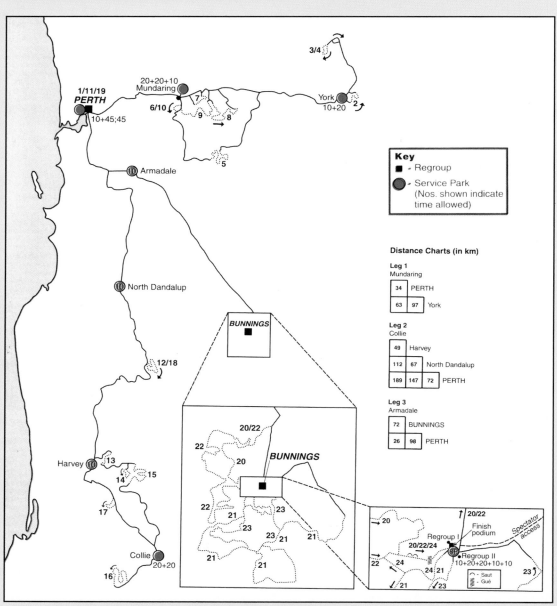

Key
■ - Regroup
● - Service Park
(Nos. shown indicate time allowed)

Distance Charts (in km)

Leg 1
Mundaring

34	PERTH	
63	97	York

Leg 2
Collie

49	Harvey	
112	67	North Dandalup
189	147	72	PERTH

Leg 3
Armadale

72	BUNNINGS	
26	98	PERTH

SPECIAL STAGE TIMES

ES.1 Langley Park 1 (2,20 km)
1. Makinen et Auriol 1'32"; 3. Sainz 1'32"3;
4. Kankkunen 1'32"8; 5. Loix 1'33"1; Gr.N Stohl 1'40"9; F2 Eriksson 1'44"2

ES.2 York Railway (5,30 km)
1. Makinen 2'37"9; 2. Burns 2'38"2; 4. Sainz 2'38"4; 5. Makinen 2'39"; Gr.N Trelles 2'50"3; F2 Eriksson 2'52"4

ES.3 Muresk 1 (6,81 km)
1. Burns 3'31"3; 2. Auriol 3'31"6; 3. McRae 3'33"5; 4. Makinen, Sainz et Thiry 3'33"7; Gr.N Taguchi 3'50"; F2 A.McRae 3'50"5

ES.4 Muresk 2 (6,81 km)
1. Auriol 3'27"1; 2. Burns 3'27"5; 3. Sainz 3'28"4; 4. Liatti 3'29"2; 5. McRae 3'29"; Gr.N Trelles 3'46"5; F2 Eriksson 3'48"7

ES.5 Beraking (28,59 km)
1. Burns 15'58"7; 2. Makinen 16'12"3; 3. Kankkunen 16'17"3; 4. McRae 16'18"5; 5. Auriol 16'23"9; Gr.N Guest 17'27"4; F2 Eriksson 17'27"2

ES.6 Atkins 1 (4,42 km)
1. Burns 3'02"7; 2. Sainz 3'05"; 3. Bourne 3'05"7; 4. Makinen 3'05"8; 5. Loix 3'06"; Gr.N Guest 3'16"2; F2 Eriksson 3'20"1

ES.7 Kev's (10,18 km)
1. Burns 5'52"9; 2. Makinen 5'53"4; 3. Kankkunen 4'51"6; 5. Loix 6'02"1; Gr.N Trelles 6'23"3; F2 Eriksson 6'18"2

ES.8 Flynns (34,01 km)
1. Burns 20'08"2; 2. Sainz 20'25"7; 3. Auriol 20'28"; 4. Loix 20'28"1; 5. McRae 20'29"; Gr.N Guest 22'07"3; F2 Evans 22'19"

ES.9 Helena (30,05 km)
1. Burns 16'44"9; 2. Makinen 16'46"2; 3. Loix 16'56"1; 4. Auriol 16'57"4; 5. Kankkunen 16'58"4; Gr.N Guest 18'04"9; F2 Bell 18'20"8

ES.10 Atkins 2 (4,42 km)
1. Burns 3'00"3; 2. Makinen 3'02"1; 3. Loix 3'02"7; 4. Auriol 3'02"8; 5. Kankkunen 3'03"5; Gr.N Guest 3'19"; F2 Bell 3'23"

ES.11 Langley Park 2 (2,20 km)
1. Auriol 1'32"1; 2. Makinen 1'32"5; 3. McRae 1'32"9; 4. Loix 1'33"; 5. Burns et Kankkunen 1'33"1; Gr.N Trelles 1'38"4; F2 Rosenberger et Evans 1'43"8

ES.12 Murray Pines 1 (18,53 km)
1. Makinen 10'52"8; 2. Sainz 11'00"3; 3. Burns 11'01"2; 4. Thiry 11'05"1; 5. Kankkunen 11'05"5; Gr.N Guest 11'44"2; F2 Eriksson 11'44"2

ES.13 Harvey Weir (8,19 km)
1. Sainz 4'47"6; 2. Makinen 4'47"9; 3. Burns 4'49"9; 4. Makinen 4'51"6; 5. Auriol 4'53"5; Gr.N Guest 5'12"2; F2 Eriksson 5'10"1

ES.14 Stirling West (15,89 km)
1. Makinen 9'36"6; 2. McRae 9'38"7; 3. Sainz 9'38"8; 4. Auriol 9'40"5; 5. Kankkunen 9'40"6; Gr.N Trelles 10'23"1; F2 Eriksson 10'16"6

ES.15 Stirling East (35,48 km)
1. Makinen 20'07"2; 2. Sainz 20'13"6; 3. Kankkunen 20'24"3; 4. Auriol et Loix 20'24"6; Gr.N Guest 21'50"4; F2 Eriksson 21'45"3

ES.16 Wellington Dam (45,38 km)
1. Makinen 25'51"; 2. McRae 25'53"3; 3. Sainz 25'57"2; 4. Auriol 26'12"5; 5. Loix 26'14"8; Gr.N Trelles 28'07"3; F2 A.McRae 27'58"6

ES.17 Brunswick (16,63 km)
1. Makinen 9'19"; 2. Sainz 9'19"1; 3. McRae 9'20"; 4. Kankkunen 9'23"4; 5. Burns 9'25"2; Gr.N Guest 10'03"5; F2 A.McRae 10'03"6

ES.18 Murray Pines 2 (18,53 km)
1. Makinen 10'45"9; 2. McRae 10'53"9; 3. Sainz 10'56"; 4. Kankkunen 10'57"1; 5. Burns 11'00"6; Gr.N Guest 11'42"1; F2 A.McRae 11'57"8

ES.19 Langley Park 3 (2,20 km)
1. Sainz et Auriol 1'32"; 3. Makinen 1'32"1; 4. McRae 1'33"3; 5. Kankkunen 1'33"8; Gr.N Stohl 1'38"2; F2 Eriksson 1'43"2

ES.20 Bunnings East (13,77 km)
1. McRae 7'27"9; 2. Burns 7'32"9; 3. Auriol 7'34"5; 4. Loix 7'36"3; 5. Kankkunen 7'39"2; Gr.N Trelles 8'06"9; F2 Eriksson 8'27"6

ES.21 Bunnings West (35,29 km)
1. McRae 17'38"; 2. Burns 17'41"1; 3. Makinen 17'52"9; 4. Loix 17'53"4; 5. Kankkunen 17'56"5; Gr.N Trelles 19'15"8; F2 A.McRae 19'32"8

ES.22 Bunnings North (31,92 km)
1. McRae 17'23"5; 2. Burns 17'33"; 3. Makinen 17'38"; 4. Auriol 17'41"; 5. Kankkunen 17'49"8; Gr.N Trelles 19'22"3; F2 A.McRae 19'44"3

ES.23 Bunnings South (25,16 km)
1. Makinen 15'15"4; 2. Auriol 15'20"9; 3. Kankkunen 15'29"3; 4. Sainz 15'33"; 5. Loix 15'47"6; Gr.N Stohl 16'35"4; F2 Eriksson 16'41"1

ES.24 API TV (2,73 km)
1. Sainz 1'36"1; 2. McRae 1'36"7; 3. Makinen 1'37"3; 4. Auriol 1'37"5; 5. Kankkunen 1'39"9; Gr.N Guest et Nishio1'46"6; F2 Avci 1'48"3

RESULTS AND RETIREMENTS

	Driver/Co-Driver	Car	N°	Gr	Total Time
1	Tommi Makinen - Risto Mannisenmaki	Mitsubishi Lancer Ev.5	1	A	3h52m48,7s
2	Carlos Sainz - Luis Moya	Toyota Corolla WRC	5	A	3h53m05,2s
3	Didier Auriol - Denis Giraudet	Toyota Corolla WRC	6	A	3h53m13,7s
4	Colin McRae - Nicky Grist	Subaru Impreza WRC	3	A	3h53m20,3s
5	Juha Kankkunen - Juha Repo	Ford Escort WRC	7	A	3h53m44,8s
6	Freddy Loix - Sven Smeets	Toyota Corolla WRC	11	A	3h56m42,9s
7	Bruno Thiry - Stéphane Prévot	Ford Escort WRC	8	A	3h57m03,6s
8	Possum Bourne - Craig Vincent	Subaru Impreza	13	A	3h59m30,2s
9	Sebastian Lindholm - Jukka Aho	Ford Escort WRC	14	A	4h02m50,1s
10	Ed Ordynski - Mark Stacey	Mitsubishi Lancer Ev.3	15	A	4h04m15,3s
ES.5	Piero Liatti - Fabrizia Pons	Subaru Impreza WRC	4	A	Accident
ES.8	Toni Gardemeister - Paavo Lukander	Seat Ibiza GTI 16v Kit Car	21	A	Clutch
ES.15	Marc Duez - Luc Manset	Seat Cordoba WRC	10	A	Accident
ES.16	Jean-Pierre Richelmi - Freddy Delorme	Mitsubishi Lancer Ev.4	31	N	Accident
ES.17	Wayne Bell - Iain Stewart	Hyundai Coupé Kit Car	22	A	Steering
ES.23	Richard Burns - Robert Reid	Mitsubishi Carisma GT	2	A	Accident

EVENT LEADERS

ES.1 Auriol et Makinen
ES.2 Sainz et Kankkunen
ES.3 Burns
ES.4 Auriol
ES.5 - ES.14: Burns
ES.15 - ES.21: Sainz
ES.22: McRae
ES.23 - ES.24: Makinen

BEST PERFORMANCES

	1	2	3	4	5	6
Makinen	8	6	4	2	1	2
Burns	7	4	3	-	3	-
McRae	4	4	3	2	2	2
Auriol	4	2	3	7	2	4
Sainz	3	5	5	4	-	3
Kankkunen	1	-	3	4	10	3
Loix	-	-	2	5	5	4
Bourne	-	-	1	-	-	-
Thiry	-	-	-	2	-	2
Liatti	-	-	-	1	-	1
Lindholm	-	-	-	-	-	1
Bates	-	-	-	-	-	1

GOSSIP

• LIATTI

The Rally of Australia signalled the end of the road for Piero Liatti at Subaru. The Italian did not go far in this event, hitting a tree very hard at the start of the first leg and having to retire. His time with the Anglo-Japanese team will be remembered for the single great exploit of taking victory in the 1997 Monte Carlo rally.

• GROUP N

In Australia, as in New Zealand earlier in the year, the Group N prize went to Subaru and not to the all conquering Mitsubishi Lancer. It was actually Australia's Michael Guest who, thanks to his Impreza, won yet again, thrashing Trelles by 31.5 seconds.

• SUBARU OUT

Liatti's accident and McRae's fourth place effectively put Subaru out of the running for the constructors' title. Before the RAC only Toyota and Mitsubishi stood a chance of taking the much wanted crown. Four points separated the two rivals, the former having 85 to the latter's 81.

• BURNS

The young Englishman, Richard Burns put on a fiery performance during a remarkable drive. A great winner of the first leg, he went off on the second and then came back again. Sadly, another error saw him out for good on the penultimate stage and Burns never got to the end of the event.

• WINDSCREEN

There was a strange epidemic at Toyota. At the end of one stage, all three works Corollas emerged with broken windscreens after a heavy landing following the same jump for Sainz, Auriol and Loix. As for the young Belgian, his second consecutive run on this course had been remarkable. He was only slowed by gearbox problems. Mitsubishi had a lot to thank Makinen and Burns for.

PREVIOUS WINNERS

1989	Kankkunen - Piironen TOYOTA CELICA GT-FOUR
1990	Kankkunen - Piironen LANCIA DELTA INTEGRALE
1991	Kankkunen - Piironen LANCIA DELTA INTEGRALE
1992	Auriol - Occelli LANCIA DELTA HF INTEGRALE
1993	Kankkunen - Grist TOYOTA CELICA TURBO 4WD
1994	McRae - Ringer SUBARU IMPREZA
1995	Eriksson - Parmander MITSUBISHI LANCER EV.2
1996	Makinen - Harjanne MITSUBISHI LANCER EV.3
1997	McRae - Grist SUBARU IMPREZA WRC

CHAMPIONSHIP CLASSIFICATIONS

Drivers:
1. Tommi Makinen 58
2. Carlos Sainz 56
3. Colin McRae 45
4. Didier Auriol 34
5. Juha Kankkunen 33

Constructors:
1. Toyota 85
2. Mitsubishi 81
3. Subaru 65
4. Ford 43

Group N:
1. Gustavo Trelles 94
   (vainqueur de la coupe)
2. Manfred Stohl 58
3. Luis Climent 37

Two Litres:
1. Seat 83
2. Peugeot 69
3. VW 49

Team's Cup :
1. Scuderia Grifone 66
   (vainqueur de la coupe)
2. Uruguay en Carrera 29
3. Toyota Team Sweden 22

GREAT BRITAIN

E Everything was still to play for on the final rally, with both constructors' and drivers' championships in the balance. While Tommi Makinen had a two point lead over Carlos Sainz, Toyota enjoyed a four point cushion over Mitsubishi. After Makinen's unbelievable retirement from the rally, the outcome looked perfectly clear: Sainz would make sure of the three points he needed for the crown, while Richard Burns, leading after Didier Auriol went out, would hand the manufacturers' cup to Mitsubishi. But the best laid plans of mice and men are no competition for the

rallying gods. With just a few hundred metres to go in the very last special stage, Sainz' engine expired in a cloud of flame and smoke. The mood in the Ralliart Europe camp was ecstatic after an amazing triple: Makinen's drivers' title, Mitsubishi's constructors' championship and Burns' rally win.

his gaunt face, streaked with tears..."

Richard, prince of wales

"Every year the organisers promise us that there will be less tarmac on the first day and every year there is more!" complains Bernard Lindauer, Mitsubishi's technical director. These days, the first leg of the Rally of Great Britain spends more time on race tracks like Silverstone and Donington than on the more traditional stately homes and parks. It gives the teams a major headache, because the cars are set up for the loose, on rain tyres adapted for tarmac. This delivers less than perfect handling on increasingly ridiculous spectator stages. However, this first day still managed to put a note in the history books. Two brothers set exactly the same time to lead a rally after the first stage. Of course it was the McRae brothers as Alister was replacing Piero Liatti at the wheel of the second Subaru. This entire first day was to be dominated by Colin, who was very motivated as he made his final 1998 appearance in front of his fans, even though no title awaited him.

On the subject of the title, Makinen was out of the rally on only the fifth stage, having skidded on a patch of oil. From then on, Sainz only had to finish no lower than fourth to take the championship. As the Radio Rally commentator so neatly put it: "this is a stage where there is nothing to win and everything to lose." Makinen clearly demonstrated that principle.

The next day brought a change of scene as the rally headed off into the Welsh forests. Delayed the previous day by problems with the electronic differential, Richard Burns began his pursuit of Colin McRae. On muddy stages, albeit in unexpected sunny conditions, the Englishman was catching the Scotsman like a rocket. McRae fought back later in the day, but then with absolutely no warning, his engine let go. What a gift for Burns, who returned to Cheltenham with a comfortable lead. Behind him, it seemed no one had been spared from some disaster or other. Auriol had been brilliant up until his clutch gave out at the end of the day, Alister McRae was slowed by turbo worries, while Carlos Sainz went straight on without any serious consequences. Burns totally dominated the final leg, setting fastest time on every stage. The other great drive on the last day came from Bruno Thiry, who climbed through the field to steal third place from Sainz, thus putting two Escorts on the podium for the car's world championship farewell, with Juha Kankkunen second. Richard Burns' second win was somewhat overshadowed by the terrible misfortune which befell Carlos Sainz, his engine expiring just 800 metres from the end of the last stage.

Makinen's last minute salvation

A crossroads in the middle of nowhere. Well, not quite anywhere; Church Farm, Lidlington to be precise. A few buildings, a shed and some "boys in blue" to keep the traffic moving. It was the point where the rally picked up the route book again after the first five stages. The service crews were gathering, because Radio Rally had been very vocal and everyone knew Makinen was nursing a winged Mitsubishi along the road.

Rocking and rolling along like a drunk

142.1-2
By winning his third consecutive world championship, Tommi Makinen allowed Finland to celebrate doing the double in Formula 1 and Rallying, something achieved by no other nation.

143.1-2
Richard Burns' superb win gave Mitsubishi its first ever constructors' title. As a thank you, the Englishman gave his Carisma a big kiss for all the satisfaction it gave him throughout the year.

coming home, with its head in the air and its back end scraping the deck, the Lancer suddenly got a second wind and hammered along a short straight. Not for long though, as the motorcycle cop indicated to Tommi Makinen that he was to pull over and get off the road. The Mitsu is stuck to the ground, its suspension hanging off and the right rear corner appears to have vanished into thin air. Makinen says a few words to his team over the radio, climbs out of his seat and slams the door shut and bashes on the roof of the stricken car. Rather more outspoken, his co-driver Risto Mannisenmaki lets out some juicy swear words. That was it as the Finnish duo are not exactly noted for exhibitionism, even though that is the end of their rally and their world championship hopes are in tatters. Crucified symbolically and literally as he had his arms out, Makinen could only say: "There was oil!" Then in a bitter speech, haltingly delivered, he continued: "There was oil on the first left hand corner of the stage. The road was black. I skidded and the car hit a concrete barrier." The impact bent the suspension and a few kilometres later, the wheel came off completely. The driver managed to get to the finish all the same and then tackled the next Millbrook stage, still on three wheels. The ultimate insult came when Carlos Sainz overtook him. As for the rally organisers, they kept a low profile: the course cars said nothing about the puddle of oil, although some, including the radio commentator, knew it was there and that the concrete barriers had not been there during the recce.

"It's out of our hands now," added Makinen as he sat on the bonnet of the stricken beast. Indeed, Sainz held rally destiny firmly in his safe hands.

Cut to forty eight hours later, while the rally is winding through the hills above Cardiff, Tommi Makinen is still in Cheltenham. "I was about to leave for the airport," recalls the Finn with a grin. "In fact I was just going out of the hotel but I agreed to do one more interview for a Finnish television station, when my brother called me on the phone. He was there at the end of the stage and he was saying, 'Carlos has stopped and his engine is on fire.' I could not believe it and I told him, stop kidding around, it's not funny. And he was screaming, it's true, it's true."

What a banal way to win or at least to retain a world title. However, Makinen would have preferred to go after it from behind the wheel. "It is nice of course, but I would rather have had to fight for it, than to get it like this. Remember, I was really unlucky at the start of the rally. Carlos was unlucky at the end of the event, breaking his engine. Anything can happen here! It must be terrible for him. He can't be feeling too good, given the circumstances. But I suffered as well." Then, letting slip a touch of Finnish fatalism: "In rallying, it seems that you always have to count on a bit of luck." For the past three years, Makinen has combined luck with his talent. Jackpot! Three titles in a row, which is a record.

Agony for Sainz

A few golden rays of afternoon sun lay on the park in Margam. It is a beautiful spot, with its manor house not far from the abbey and the orangery. The slopes are gentle, the fields are green and the trees are majestic. Sticking out like a sore thumb can be seen the figure of a man in red overalls. The man is walking with his head hung low, so that his cap hides his gaunt face, streaked with tears. A deer walks past but he does not notice anything. A few journalists run towards him. Carlos Sainz crouches for a moment before walking towards the pack, his eyes still wet. All he utters is: "the engine exploded. I cannot express what I feel in words." Then he is off. Out of nowhere comes a helicopter which belongs to Subaru-Prodrive boss David Richards. He waves at Sainz, who jumps in. Destination despair. He leaves behind him a dead and useless Corolla, whose engine gave up the ghost just 800 metres from the very last timing point on the rally. He also leaves behind a tearful Luis Moya, sitting in the stricken car. Most of all though, he leaves behind a world championship that seemed to be his for the taking, the third of his career.

Because, once Tommi Makinen was out, Sainz only had one target; to finish no lower than fourth to score the three points needed to beat the Finn. With his rival gone, Sainz was patient, avoiding all danger except on the second leg. "In the last but one stage, we missed a junction flat out in sixth!" By some miracle, no harm was done. The Spaniard did a U-turn and set off at a more sedate pace. His tyre choice, the new Michelin mud specification, his driving, nice and calm, his tactics, sensible; all these factors should have lead to success. All except for an engine and eight hundred metres.

144.1
Happy anniversary Ari! The Finn celebrated his 100th participation in a world championship rally.

144.2
After Makinen's retirement, Carlos Sainz kept up a quick pace without taking too many risks up to the point where it all turned to disaster.

145.1
For their world championship farewell both Escorts made it to the podium.

145.2
Throughout the event, Armin Schwarz was unable to match the pace of the front runners.

144.3 - 145.3
The battle between Colin McRae and Richard Burns ended far too early for the Scotsman on the second leg because of an engine problem.

144.1

144.2

144.3

145.1

145.2

GREAT BRITAIN

145.4
*Kytolehto and his Astra eventually had to give best in
the two litre class to Laukkanen's Renault Megane Maxi.*
145.5
*Always very competitive on the British stages, Gregoire
de Mevius finished a surprising fourth.*

145.3

145.4

145.5

54TH RALLY OF GREAT BRITAIN

TOP ENTRIES

1 Tommi Makinen - Risto Mannisenmaki
MITSUBISHI LANCER EV.5

2 Richard Burns - Robert Reid
MITSUBISHI CARISMA GT

3 Colin McRae - Nicky Grist
SUBARU IMPREZA WRC

4 Alister McRae - David Senior
SUBARU IMPREZA WRC

5 Carlos Sainz - Luis Moya
TOYOTA COROLLA WRC

6 Didier Auriol - Denis Giraudet
TOYOTA COROLLA WRC

7 Juha Kankkunen - Juha Repo
FORD ESCORT WRC

8 Bruno Thiry - Stéphane Prévot
FORD ESCORT WRC

9 Harri Rovanpera - Risto Pietiläinen
SEAT CORDOBA WRC

10 Gwyndaf Evans - Howard Davies
SEAT CORDOBA WRC

11 Marcus Gronholm - Timo Rautiainen
TOYOTA COROLLA WRC

12 Ari Vatanen - Fabrizia Pons
SUBARU IMPREZA WRC

14 Armin Schwarz - Manfred Hiemer
FORD ESCORT WRC

16 Gregoire De Mevius - Jean-Marc Fortin
SUBARU IMPREZA WRC

17 Krzysztof Holowczyc - Maciej Wislawski
SUBARU IMPREZA WRC

18 Jarmo Kytolehto - Arto Kapanen
OPEL ASTRA KIT CAR

19 Martin Rowe - Derek Ringer
RENAULT MAXI MEGANE

20 Kenneth Eriksson - Staffan Parmander
HYUNDAI COUPÉ KIT CAR

21 Gilles Panizzi - Hervé Panizzi
SUBARU IMPREZA

22 Pavel Sibera - Petr Gross
SKODA OCTAVIA KIT CAR

23 Mark Higgins - Philip Mills
NISSAN ALMERA KIT CAR

24 Sebastian Lindholm - Jukka Aho
FORD ESCORT WRC

25 Tapio Laukkanen - Kaj Lindstrom
RENAULT MAXI MEGANE

26 Marc Duez - Luc Manset
SEAT IBIZA GTI 16V KIT CAR

27 Henrik Lundgaard - Henrik Vestergaard
TOYOTA COROLLA WRC

28 Toni Gardemeister - Paavo Lukander
SEAT IBIZA GTI 16V KIT CAR

29 Wayne Bell - Iain Stewart
HYUNDAI COUPÉ KIT CAR

30 Abdullah Bakhashab - Arne Hertz
TOYOTA CELICA GT-FOUR

31 Raimund Baumschlager - Klaus Wicha
VW GOLF GTI 16V KIT CAR

32 Volkan Isik - Ilham Dokumcu
TOYOTA CELICA GT-FOUR

33 Markko Martin - Toomas Kitsing
TOYOTA CELICA GT-FOUR

34 Hamed Al-Wahaibi - Terry Harryman
MITSUBISHI LANCER EV.4

36 Frederic Dor - Didier Breton
SUBARU IMPREZA WRC

53 Manfred Stohl - Peter Muller
MITSUBISHI LANCER EV.5

63 Will Hoy - Sean Kelly
FORD ESCORT RS 2000

13th leg of the 1998 world rally championships for constructors and drivers
13th leg of the constructors' "2 litre", production car drivers' and teams' world cups

Date: 22 - 24 November 1998

Route: 1892.38 km divided into three legs with 24 stages run on loose surface roads (380.30 km)
1st leg: Sunday 22nd November, Cheltenham - Cheltenham, 13 stages (70.94 km)
2nd leg: Monday 23rd November, Cheltenham - Cheltenham, 8 stages (142.99 km)
3rd leg: Tuesday 24th November, Cheltenham - Cheltenham, 7 stages (166.37 km)

Starters: 159 (96 Group A + 63 Group N)

Finishers: 84 (44 Group A + 40 Group N)

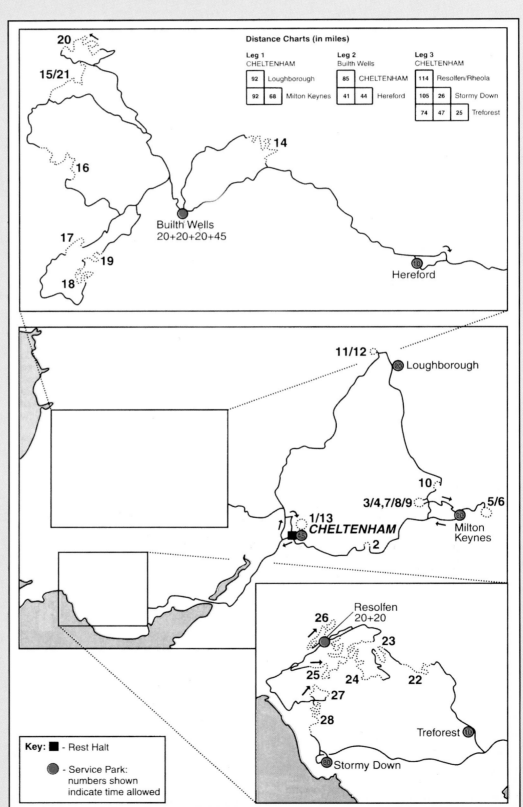

SPECIAL STAGE TIMES

ES.1 Cheltenham 1 (1,76 km)
1. McRae et A.McRae 1'29"4; 3. Auriol et Buckley 1'29"8; 5. Sainz 1'29"9; Gr.N Stohl 1'33"8; F2 Kytoletho 1'36"4

ES.2 Cornbury (4,16 km)
1. McRae 2'52"1; 2. Makinen et A.McRae 2'53"; 4. Gronholm 2'54"9; 5. Auriol 2'55"; Gr.N Al-Wahaibi 3'01"5; F2 Eriksson 3'10"4

ES.3 Silverstone 1 (8,69 km)
1. McRae 5'44"8; 2. Holowczyc 5'45"5; 3. Sainz 5'46"1; 4. Kankkunen 5'47"2; 5. Lundgaard 5'48"6; Gr.N Panizzi 6'07"; F2 Higgins 5'54"7

ES.4 Silverstone 2 (8,69 km)
1. McRae 5'41"6; 2. Holowczyc 5'43"4; 3. Lindholm 5'45"9; 4. Sainz 5'46"; 5. Makinen 5'46"4; Gr.N Stohl 6'05"2; F2 Kytoletho 5'51"3

ES.5 Millstone 1 (7,13 km)
1. McRae 4'38"8; 2. Auriol 4'40"9; 3. A.McRae 4'41"1; 4. Schwarz 4'42"3; 5. Burns 4'42"4; Gr.N Stohl 4'58"1; F2 Gardemeister 4'54"8

ES.6 Millbrook 2 (7,13 km)
1. McRae 4'35"5; 2. Auriol 4'37"3; 3. Gronholm 4'38"3; 4. A.McRae 4'38"5; 5. Thiry 4'39"1; Gr.N Stohl 4'53"9; F2 Gardemeister 4'50"7

ES.7 Silverstone Super Special (1,96 km)
1. Sainz 1'27"7; 2. McRae 1'27"9; 3. Auriol et Kankkunen 1'28"; 5. Burns 1'28"7; Gr.N Easson 1'32"7; F2 Rowe 1'33"6

ES.8 Silverstone 3 (6,99 km)
1. McRae 4'50"6; 2. Auriol 4'51"8; 3. Gronholm 4'53"; 4. Sainz 4'54"; 5. A.McRae et Thiry 4'54"5; Gr.N Stohl 5'09"; F2 Laukkanen 5'04"2

ES.9 Silverstone 4 (6,99 km)
1. Auriol 4'51"9; 2. Gronholm 4'52"5; 3. De Mevius 4'53"8; 4. Lundgaard 4'54"; 5. Kankkunen 4'54"4; Gr.N Stohl 5'07"2; F2 Laukkanen 5'00"9

ES.10 Towcester (3,23 km)
1. Auriol 2'16"7; 2. Burns 2'17"2; 3. Thiry 2'17"4; 4. De Mevius 2'17"6; 5. A.McRae 2'17"8; Gr.N Stohl 2'26"7; F2 Kytoletho 2'28"8

ES.11 Donington 1 (6,30 km)
1. McRae et A.McRae 3'49"3; 3. De Mevius 3'49"7; 4. Sainz 3'49"9; 5. Lindholm 3'50"9; Gr.N Easson 4'05"1; F2 Eriksson 4'03"3

ES.12 Donington 2 (3,91 km)
1. A.McRae 3'44"4; 2. Auriol 3'44"8; 3. Sainz 3'45"7; 4. McRae 3'46"; 5. Rovanpera 3'46"6; Gr.N West 3'55"3; F2 Laukkanen 3'58"6

ES.13 Cheltenham 2 (1,61 km)
1. Burns et Thiry 1'22"6; 3. Kankkunen 1'22"9; 4. Sainz 1'23"; 5.A.McRae et Lindholm 1'23"4; Gr.N Arai et Easson 1'27"9; F2 Wearden 1'29"7

ES.14 Radnor (23,85 km)
1. Burns 11'58"7; 2. McRae 11'59"6; 3. Auriol 12'12"6; 4. A.McRae 12'17"1; 5. Kankkunen 12'20"6; Gr.N Stohl 13'18"8; F2 Laukkanen 13'17"1

ES.15 Myherin 1 (16,86 km)
1. Burns 9'51"5; 2. McRae 9'51"8; 3. Auriol 9'54"7; 4. Sainz 9'59"8; 5. A.McRae 10'02"9; Gr.N Stohl 10'55"5; F2 Rowe 11'02"

ES.16 Tywi (19,88 km)
1. Burns 12'18"1; 2. Auriol 12'19"8; 3. Sainz 12'24"6; 4. A.McRae 12'25"7; 5. McRae 12'36"7; Gr.N Higgins 13'21"8; F2 Gardemeister 13'38"7

ES.17 Esgair Dafydd (8,70 km)
1.McRae 5'24"; 2. Sainz 5'29"4; 3. Burns 5'31"3; 4. Kankkunen 5'35"9; 5. Thiry 5'39"9; Gr.N Stohl 6'02"8; F2 Laukkanen 6'01"7

ES.18 Crychan (21,99 km)
1. McRae 13'04"5; 2. Burns 13'10"9; 3. Sainz 13'17"2; 4. A.McRae 13'19"7; 5. Auriol 13'21"5; Gr.N Higgins 14'30"7; F2 Laukkanen 14'35"

ES.19 Cefn (9,15 km)
1. McRae 5'37"7; 2. Burns 5'41"2; 3. Sainz 5'43"9; 4. A.McRae 5'46"1; 5. Kankkunen 5'46"6; Gr.N Stohl 6'15"9; F2 Laukkanen 6'20"1

ES.20 Sweet Lamb (25,70 km)
1. Burns 16'35"4; 2. A.McRae 16'48"9; 3. Kankkunen 16'58"9; 4. Thiry 17'11"7; 5. De Mevius 17'12"1; Gr.N Higgins 18'10"4; F2 Laukkanen 18'23"9

ES.21 Myherin 2 (16,86 km)
1. Burns 10'24"7; 2. Kankkunen 10'32"4; 3. A.McRae 10'35"2; 4. De Mevius 10'45"2; 5. Thiry 10'47"9; Gr.N Stohl 11'25"6; F2 Gardemeister 11'37"7

ES.22 St.Gwynno (13,80 km)
1. Burns 8'05"6; 2. Dodd 8'12"9; 3. Thiry 8'19"9; 4. Stohl 8'20"5; 5. Walfridsson 8'21"8; F2 Kytolehto 8'24"1

ES.23 Tyle (10,65 km)
1.Burns 6'20"3; 2. Kankkunen 6'24"2; 3. Sainz 6'28"1; 4. De Mevius 6'35"5; 5. Thiry 6'36"1; Gr.N Stohl 6'54"1; F2 Gardemeister 7'12"7

ES.24 Rhondda (36,29 km)
1.Burns 20'45"3; 2. Thiry 21'09"4; 3. Kankkunen 21'15"4; 4. Lindholm 21'27"4; 5. Sainz 21'30"4; Gr.N Higgins 22'21"2; F2 Laukkanen 22'31"

ES.25 Resolfen (44,60 km)
1. Burns 25'30"5; 2. Kankkunen 26'02"9; 3. De Mevius 26'16"1; 4. Thiry 26'19"1; 5. Lindholm 26'24"5; Gr.N Stohl 27'15";
F2 Laukkanen 27'12"2

ES.26 Rheola (24,90 km)
1. Burns 13'59"9; 2. Kankkunen 14'07"4; 3. Thiry 14'08"; 4. Lindholm 14'13"5; 5. De Mevius 14'17"6; Gr.N Stohl 15'03"9; F2 Laukkanen 15'07"8

ES.27 Argoed (9,04 km)
1. Burns 5'38"9; 2. De Mevius 5'46"6; 3. Kankkunen 5'48"3; 4. Rovanpera 5'48"9; 5. Thiry 5'49"6; Gr.N Higgins 6'06"3; F2 Gardemeister 6'14"7

ES.28 Margam (16,83 km)
1. Burns 16'28"9; 2. Kankkunen 16'44"7; 3. Thiry 16'53"7; 4. De Mevius 16'55"9; 5. Lindholm 17'13"2; Gr.N Stohl 17'50"5; F2 Gardemeister 18'12"2

RESULTS AND RETIREMENTS

	Driver/Co-Driver	Car	N°	Gr	Total Time
1	Richard Burns - Robert Reid	Mitsubishi Carisma GT	2	A	3h50m30s.6
2	Juha Kankkunen - Juha Repo	Ford Escort WRC	7	A	3h54m17s1
3	Bruno Thiry - Stéphane Prévot	Ford Escort WRC	8	A	3h55m58s1
4	Grégoire de Mevius - Jean-Marc	Fortin Subaru Impreza	16	A	3h58m25s4
5	Sebastian Lindholm - Jukka Aho	Ford Escort WRC	24	A	3h58m46s2
6	Harri Rovanpera - Risto Pietilainen	Seat Cordoba WRC	9	A	4h01m03s9
7	Armin Schwarz - Manfred Hiemer	Ford Escort WRC	14	A	4h02m47s3
8	Krzysztof Holowczyc - Maciej Wislawski	Subaru Impreza	17	A	4h03m37s3
9	Markko Martin - Toomas Kitsing	Toyota Celica GT-Four	33	A	4h07m41s6
10	Manfred Stohl - Peter Muller	Mitsubishi Lancer Ev.5	53	N	4h09m37s8
ES.5	Tommi Makinen - Risto Manisenmaki	Mitsubishi Lancer Ev.	5	A	Accident
ES.5	Mark Higgins - Philip Mills	Nissan Almera Kit Car	23	A	Engine
ES.11	Marcus Gronholm - Timo Rautiainen	Toyota Corolla WRC	11	A	Engine fire
ES.14	Ari Vatanen - Fabrizia Pons	Subaru Impreza WRC	12	A	Engine
ES.16	Kenneth Eriksson - Staffan Parmander	Hyundai Coupé Kit Car	20	A	Accident
ES.18	Gwyndaf Evans - Howard Davies	Seat Cordoba WRC	10	A	Gearbox
ES.19	Colin McRae - Nicky Grist	Subaru Impreza WRC	3	A	Engine
ES.20	Dider Auriol - Denis Giraudet	Toyota Corolla WRC	6	A	Clutch
ES.22	Alister McRae - David Senior	Subaru Impreza WRC	4	A	Accident
ES.22	Gilles Panizzi - Hervé Panizzi	Subaru Impreza	21	N	Gearbox
ES.28	Carlos Sainz - Luis Moya	Toyota Corolla WRC	5	A	Engine

GOSSIP

• PANIZZI

The Panizzi brothers' first attempt at the rally of Great Britain ended on the first stage of the final leg with gearbox problems, after Gilles Panizzi had already complained about gearbox problems on the second day. Until that point, they had done remarkably well at the wheel of a Group N Subaru, prepared by Cilti Sport, with backing from Fruite. They were running 22nd overall and 5th in Group N.

• TWO LITRES

The Rally of Great Britain handed Seat its third consecutive world title in the two litre category, where they beat Peugeot and VW.

• PODIUM

By an incredible coincidence, the end of rally podium was an exact replica of next year's Subaru's driver line-up. Richard Burns found himself standing between Juha Kankkunen and Bruno Thiry.

• VATANEN

Ari Vatanen's 100th appearance on a world championship rally came to a sticky end. In special stage 14, the first of the second leg, the Subaru's engine cut out as he spun at a hairpin and the Finn was unable to get going again. He was twelfth overall at the time and was using a sequential gearbox with joystick on his Impreza WRC for the first time.

• THIRY

"Comparing my Escort with the other leading cars is like having a beauty contest between the Queen of England and Demi Moore." Despite Thiry's cutting wit on the subject of his car, he still managed to bring the old lady onto the podium behind Kankkunen to bring the Escort's thirty year career to an honourable close.

• DE MEVIUS

Gregoire de Mevius had a good run at the wheel of his private Impreza, finishing an excellent fourth after a tough battle with Finland's Lindholm. In 1999, de Mevius will be part of the factory Nissan team, trying to win the two litre championship at the wheel of an Almera Kit-Car. The other one will be entrusted to the Finn, Gardemeister.

PREVIOUS WINNERS

1974	Makinen - Liddon FORD ESCORT RS 1600
1975	Makinen - Liddon FORD ESCORT RS
1976	Clark - Pegg FORD ESCORT RS
1977	Waldegaard - Thorszelius FORD ESCORT RS
1978	Mikkola - Hertz Ford Escort RS
1979	Mikkola - Hertz Ford Escort RS
1980	Toivonen - White Talbot Sunbeam Lotus
1981	Mikkola - Hertz Audi Quattro
1982	Mikkola - Hertz Audi Quattro
1983	Blomqvist - Cederberg Audi Quattro
1984	Vatanen - Harryman Peugeot 205 T16
1985	Toivonen - Wilson Lancia Delta S4
1986	Salonen - Harjanne Peugeot 205 T16
1987	Kankkunen - Piironen Lancia Delta HF
1988	Alen - Kivimaki Lancia Delta Integrale
1989	Airikkala - McNamee Mitsubishi Galant VR4
1990	Sainz - Moya Toyota Celica GT-Four
1991	Kankkunen - Piironen Lancia Delta Integrale
1992	Sainz - Moya Toyota Celica Turbo 4WD
1993	Kankkunen - Piironen Toyota Celica Turbo 4WD
1994	McRae - Ringer Subaru Impreza
1995	McRae - Ringer Subaru Impreza
1996	Schwarz - Giraudet Toyota Celica GT-Four
1997	McRae - Grist Subaru Impreza WRC

EVENT LEADERS

ES.1: McRae et A.McRae
ES.2 - ES.15: McRae
ES.16: Burns
ES.17 - ES.19: McRae
ES.20 - ES.28: Burns

BEST PERFORMANCES

	1	2	3	4	5	6
Burns	1	4	3	1	-	-
McRae	10	2	1	1	1	-
A.McRae	3	1	1	3	3	-
Auriol	2	5	3	-	2	2
Sainz	1	1	5	4	2	4
Thiry	1	1	4	2	6	-
Kankkunen	-	5	5	2	3	5
De Mevius	-	1	3	5	2	2
Lindholm	-	-	-	2	4	4

CHAMPIONSHIP CLASSIFICATIONS

Pilotes :
1. Tommi Makinen 58
2. Carlos Sainz 56
3. ColinMcRae 45
4. Juha Kankkunen 39
5. Didier Auriol 34

Constructeurs :
1. Mitsubishi 91
2. Toyota 85
3. Subaru 65
4. Ford 53

Groupe N :
1. Gustavo Trelles 94
2. Manfred Stohl 71
3. Climent 37

Deux Litres :
1. Seat 81
2. Peugeot 69
3. VW 49

Team's Cup :
1. Scuderia Grifone 70
2. Toyota Saudi Arabia 36
3. Uruguay en Carrera 30

1998 World Championship for Drivers

	DRIVERS	Monte-Carlo	Swedish	Safari	Portugal	Catalunya	France	Argentina	Greece	New Zealand	Finland	Italy	Australia	Great Britain	TOTAL
1.	Tommi MAKINEN	0	10	0	0	4	0	10	0	4	10	10	10	0	58
2.	Carlos SAINZ	10	6	0	6	0	0	8	3	10	6	3	6	0	56
3.	Colin McRAE	4	0	0	10	0	10	2	10	2	0	4	3	0	45
4.	Juha KANKKUNEN	6	4	6	0	0	0	4	4	3	4	0	2	6	39
5.	Didier AURIOL	0	1	3	0	10	1	0	6	6	3	0	4	0	34
6.	Richard BURNS	2	0	10	3	3	0	3	0	0	2	0	0	10	33
7.	Piero LIATTI	3	0	0	1	0	4	1	1	1	0	6	0	0	17
8.	Freddy LOIX	0	0	0	4	6	0	0	2	0	0	0	1	0	13
9.	Bruno THIRY	1	0	0	0	0	2	0	0	0	0	1	0	4	8
10.	François DELECOUR	0	0	0	0	0	6	0	0	0	0	0	0	0	6
11.	Ari VATANEN	0	0	4	2	0	0	0	0	0	0	0	0	0	6
12.	Gilles PANIZZI	0	0	0	0	1	3	0	0	0	0	2	0	0	6
13.	Kenneth ERIKSSON	0	3	0	0	0	0	0	0	0	0	0	0	0	3
	Grégoire DE MEVIUS	0	0	0	0	0	0	0	0	0	0	0	0	3	3
15.	Harri ROVANPERA	0	0	2	0	0	0	0	0	0	0	0	0	1	3
16.	Philippe BUGALSKI	0	0	0	0	2	0	0	0	0	0	0	0	0	2
	Marcus GRONHOLM	0	2	0	0	0	0	0	0	0	0	0	0	0	2
	Sebastian LINDHOLM	0	0	0	0	0	0	0	0	0	0	0	0	2	2
19.	Thomas RADSTROM	0	0	0	0	0	0	0	0	0	1	0	0	0	1
	Raimund BAUMSCHLAGER	0	0	1	0	0	0	0	0	0	0	0	0	0	1

1998 World Championship for Manufacturers

	MANUFACTURERS	Monte-Carlo	Swedish	Safari	Portugal	Catalunya	France	Argentina	Greece	New Zealand	Finland	Italy	Australia	Great Britain	TOTAL
1.	MITSUBISHI	2	10	10	3	7	0	13	0	4	12	10	10	10	91
2.	TOYOTA	10	6	3	6	6	1	6	9	16	9	3	10	0	85
3.	SUBARU	7	3	0	11	0	14	3	11	3	0	10	3	0	65
4.	FORD	7	4	10	2	0	2	4	4	3	4	1	2	10	53
5.	SEAT	0	0	0	0	0	0	0	0	0	0	0	0	1	1

REGULATIONS: DRIVERS' CHAMPIONSHIP: All results count. 1st 10 point, 2nd 6 point, 3rd 4 points, 4th 3 points, 5th 2 points, 6th 1 point
MANUFACTURERS' CHAMPIONSHIP: To be eligible, the constructors who have registered with FIA, must take part in all the events with a minimum of two cars. The first two cars score the points according to their finishing position. All results are taken into consideration. Points scale is the same as for the drivers.

1998 Production Car Championship for Drivers (Group N)

	DRIVERS	Monte-Carlo	Swedish	Safari	Portugal	Catalunya	France	Argentina	Greece	New Zealand	Finland	Italy	Australia	Great Britain	TOTAL
1.	Gustavo TRELLES	0	0	0	13	13	8	13	13	8	13	5	8	(0)	94
2.	Manfred STOHL	13	0	8	8	8	13	0	0	5	0	(0)	3	13	71
3.	Luis CLIMENT	8	0	13	3	0	0	0	5	0	8	0	0	(0)	37
4.	Michael GUEST	0	0	0	0	0	0	0	0	19	0	0	13	(0)	26
5.	Hamed AL-WAHAIBI	0	0	0	1	0	0	8	8	2	0	0	(0)	5	24
6.	Jorge RECALDE	0	0	0	0	0	0	0	0	0	0	0	5	(0)	5
	Paul BAILEY	0	0	5	0	0	0	0	0	0	0	0	0	0	5
	Gabriel MENDEZ	0	0	0	0	5	0	0	0	0	0	0	0	(0)	5
	Marcos LIGATO	0	0	0	0	0	0	5	0	0	0	0	0	(0)	5
	Roberto SANCHEZ	0	0	0	2	3	0	0	0	0	0	0	0	(0)	5

REGULATIONS: The classification is based on the total number of rallies minus one. At least one rally outside Europe has to be entered. Points scored as follows: 1st 10, 2nd 6, 3rd 4, 4th 3, 5th 2, 6th 1. The points are added with those scored in the different capacity classes (up to 1300cc; 1301 - 2000cc, over 2000cc) on the following scale: 1st 3 points, 2nd 2 points, 3rd 1 point. Class points are only attributed to drivers finishing in the top six of the production car classification.

1998 Manufacturers Rally World Cup for 2 litres cars

MANUFACTURERS	Monte-Carlo	Swedish	Safari	Portugal	Catalunya	France	Argentina	Greece	New Zealand	Finland	Italy	Australia	Great Britain	TOTAL
1. SEAT	(4)	10	10	6	(3)	(0)	10	16	16	6	(0)	(6)	7	81
2. PEUGEOT	16	0	0	10	10	16	3	(0)	(0)	(0)	14	(0)	(0)	69
3. VOLKSWAGEN	(0)	3	10	4	(0)	(0)	6	(0)	3	12	(1)	10	2	51
4. RENAULT	(0)	2	(0)	(0)	(0)	1	5	3	1	(0)	2	2	10	26
5. HYUNDAI	0	0	5	3	0	0	(0)	(0)	4	(0)	(0)	5	(0)	17

REGULATIONS: In order to score points, the constructor must take part in at least 10 rallies of which two must be outside Europe. The 8 best results count for the final classification. The two best placed cars score points. Scale of points: as for the drivers.

1998 FIA Team Cup

TEAMS	Monte-Carlo	Swedish	Safari	Portugal	Catalunya	France	Argentina	Greece	New Zealand	Finland	Italy	Australia	Great Britain	TOTAL
1. H. F. GRIFONE	(0)	10	(0)	10	10	(0)	(0)	10	10	10	10	(0)	(0)	70
2. TOYOTA SAUDI ARABIA	0	0	0	(0)	(0)	10	(0)	(0)	(0)	6	(0)	10	10	36
3. URUGUAY EN CARRERA	0	0	(0)	4	6	4	10	(0)	6	(0)	(0)	(0)	(0)	30
4. SAWFISH RACING	0	0	10	0	(0)	(0)	6	(0)	4	(0)	(0)	(0)	6	26
5. TOYOTA TEAM TURKEY	0	0	0	6	(0)	6	(0)	6	(0)	(0)	(0)	6	(0)	24

REGULATIONS: To be eligible to score points each team must take part in 7 Cup rallies with at least one outside Europe, with a maximum of 2 cars (Group A or Group N) per team. Only the best placed car can score points according to its position relative to the other cup competitors, on the same scale of points as the FIA world rally championship.

➥ **The rally of Indonesia, initially registered in the FIA 1998 World Rally Championship was eventually cancelled for political reasons.**

World Championship for Manufacturers

1973	Alpine-Renault	1986	Peugeot
1974	Lancia	1987	Lancia
1975	Lancia	1988	Lancia
1976	Lancia	1989	Lancia
1977	Fiat	1990	Lancia
1978	Fiat	1991	Lancia
1979	Ford	1992	Lancia
1980	Fiat	1993	Toyota
1981	Talbot	1994	Toyota
1982	Audi	1995	Subaru
1983	Lancia	1996	Subaru
1984	Audi	1997	Subaru
1985	Peugeot	1998	Mitsubishi

World Championship for Drivers

1977	Sandro Munari (I)	1988	Miki Biasion (I)
1978	Markku Alen (SF)	1989	Miki Biasion (I)
1979	Bjorn Waldegaard (S)	1990	Carlos Sainz (E)
1980	Walter Rohrl (D)	1991	Juha Kankkunen (SF)
1981	Ari Vatanen (SF)	1992	Carlos Sainz (E)
1982	Walter Rohrl (D)	1993	Juha Kankkunen (SF)
1983	Hannu Mikkola (SF)	1994	Didier Auriol (F)
1984	Stig Blomqvist (S)	1995	Colin McRae (GB)
1985	Timo Salonen (SF)	1996	Tommi Makinen (SF)
1986	Juha Kankkunen (SF)	1997	Tommi Makinen (SF)
1987	Juha Kankkunen (SF)	1998	Tommi Makinen (SF)

1977-1978 : FIA Cup for drivers

Group N Cup Winners

1987	Alex Fiorio (I)	1993	Alex Fassina (I)
1988	Pascal Gaban (B)	1994	Jesus Puras (E)
1989	Alain Oreille (F)	1995	Rui Madeira (P)
1990	Alain Oreille (F)	1996	Gustavo Trelles (ROU)
1991	Grégoire de Mevius (B)	1997	Gustavo Trelles (ROU)
1992	Grégoire de Mevius (B)	1998	Gustavo Trelles (ROU)

Manufacturers of 2-Litre Cars Cup Winners

1993	General Motors Europe
1994	Skoda
1997	Seat
1998	Seat

World Championship for Manufacturers 2-Litre

1995	Peugeot
1996	Seat

National
Championships

Five drivers and five strong points: Jean-Joseph was undeniably the revelation of the championship. Bugalski did not have an easy time, but he gave his all to get back in the hunt for the title. Champeau and Mercier put on a great show just behind the big guns and Magaud was often the quickest man on the stages.

Jean-Joseph makes a name for himself

RIGHT TO THE BITTER END, THE FIGHT WAS UNDECIDED between the last of the Citroen men, Philippe Bugalski and the solitary Subaru privateer, Simon Jean-Joseph. "Bug" was left for dead early in the season but found the wherewithal to fight his way back into the game.

The game was not exactly evenly matched. In one corner, the Citroen factory, which is not in the habit of bean or people counting. The boss Guy Frequelin does not like getting down to business without full logistical back-up, with two factory built Xsara kit cars. These were in the very safe hands of Philippe Bugalski and Patrick Magaud. In the other corner, a small team, Cilti Sport, based at Saint-Vincent de Barbeyrargues near Montpelier, run by Paul Bernard, a former rhythm 'n blues singer and a French satellite for Prodrive. It runs a Subaru for its best customer, Simon Jean-Joseph. It has all the signs of a pro-am match with a chance that David might slay Goliath.

Nevertheless, Citroen kicked off the championship in a state of doubt, if that is what you would call wondering which of your crews, Bugalski-Chiaroni or Magaud-Perin will win it. But when the bad weather arrived, even though most events are run in summer, it moves the goal posts a bit as two wheel drive kit cars are not the ideal form of locomotion when the grip is less than perfect. It happened quite often that Bug would charge off into the lead, racking up the seconds, only to lose it all in one wet stage. It was enough to get angry about. Furthermore, the wheel of misfortune spun towards the Red army and its lead solidier. Philippe Bugalski was forced to retire on no less than three occasions. But above all, Simon Jean-Joseph, until recently considered something of daddy's little rich kid from a good Martinique family, demonstrated there was plenty of talent under that right foot, that he was capable of going quickly when he had to and he was also very reliable. Before the Touquet rally, round seven of the championship, the Citroen men had furrowed brows. Le Touquet is almost guaranteed to be a case of rain and no umbrella and fields of beet at the side of the roads. No surprise there. Jean-Joseph inflicted a third defeat on Citroen. Worse still, Frequelin, calculator in hand, as only the best eight results count out of ten rallies, was forced to sacrifice Magaud, so that Bugalski, slightly better placed in the championship, could save second place. Saved by the skin of his teeth, Bug now faced one heck of a challenge. He would have to win the three final events, if Jean-Joseph was to finish second on all three occasions. Not an easy task. The first appointment was in Antibes and although it might be in the south, the rain appeared as usual. The last stage was a demon. Bug takes it by 0.4 seconds. "I could see his tracks," Jean-Joseph said. "He was not using any more of the road than me." A minor detail - if the timing had been to the nearest second, as had long been the case, and the times had been rounded up, then the result would have been reversed. Strange that!

Second obstacle was the Cevennes rally. Big surprise, it didn't rain! Everything was looking good for Bug. All the more so as Jean-Joseph got it wrong and hit a barrier hard enough to stay there.

The third and final challenge was the Var rally. Frequelin did not bother entering a third Xsara as a diversionary tactic. It was to be a sporting contest and Jean-Joseph was already a winner before the start. He had won everyone's respect.

Classification before the Var rally.
1. Bugalski (Citroen)   231 pts
    Jean-Joseph (Subaru)   231 pts
3. Magaud (Citroen)   155 pts
4. M. Champeau (Renault)   91 pts
5. Rousselot (Renault)   89 pts

Once their own championship was out of the way, the main players were out in force for the Rally of Great Britain. The champion, Martin Rowe, Mark Higgins, his predecessor and Alister McRae did not get very far. However, Tapio Laukkanen was not too far from the top ten. One novelty was the Vauxhall Astra Kit Car, which proved quite competitive in the hands of Jarmo Kytolehto.

Rowe gets it right

ALISTER MCRAE TRIED EVERYTHING IN AN OUTDATED GOLF, Gwyndaff Evans and his Seat were in their element on the loose and led almost to the finish, but in the end it was the steady Martin Rowe who walked off with the title in his Renault Megane.

There are distant memories of an English team manager who succeeded in winning in France, a man with a grey beard for a smile by the name of David Richards. This time, events went the other way around with the French team, Auto Meca proving to be dominant across the Channel. For ten years now, Auto Meca has enjoyed a special relationship with Renault, expanding the role to developing as well as assembling the cars according to team boss Jean-Paul Januel. There was plenty of success with Sylvain Polo, Serge Jordan and Philippe Bugalski, but this time the English language was an essential item in the workshop. Martin Rowe actually comes from the Isle of Man, that little offshore banking paradise, constantly hidden in the fog, yet something of a motor sport island. Former champion Higgins is also a native of these parts and Nigel Mansell was a famous temporary resident. Proof

enough that on this little rocky outcrop in the Irish Sea, you do not have to travel on two wheels to enjoy your sport. The Tourist Trophy is still the main event on the island, when riders rocket through narrow streets, over pot holes, past pubs protected with straw bales and beer drinking fans. Higgins' father is actually an official on the TT. Coincidentally to all this, the Manxmen host the final round of the 1998 championship and while Evans scores no points, local lad Rowe takes an emphatic win.

There were seven events on the calendar, reserved exclusively for two litre cars. If the truth be known there were only five rallies as the Pirelli and Scottish were run in two legs. Another novelty was the mix of tarmac and gravel with some stages practiced and others not.

Rowe put a marker down immediately, winning the Welsh after the

young McRae was let down on the second day by his usually trusty Golf. Alister lost precious points there, as a no-score in such a short championship was pretty much a disaster.

On the Pirelli rally, run through Kielder Forest - what a shame the RAC did not use it this year- Rowe won the first part while Evans and Seat won the second.

Alister McRae fought back in Scotland on his home turf to win by just a second from Rowe and Evans who each one a leg.

In Ulster there were no wins to share and to Evans went the spoils in a clear cut race with little suspense. After that, as we said earlier, Evans failed to score on the Manx and Rowe won thanks to his Megane feeling much more at home on tarmac.

But was Rowe the best man? Autosport magazine, which naturally followed the championship very closely, reckons the driving honours pretty much follow the championship order: Rowe ahead of Evans but Laukkanen apparently deserved to be placed ahead of McRae as far as its writers were concerned. McRae's cause was not helped by an ageing Golf, which pushed him over the ragged edge on occasion - must be something to do with having a brother called Colin. Finland's Laukkanen deserves the plaudits for being quickest on the most stages, but he too has to learn when to be patient.

Classification:
1. Rowe (Renault)   164 pts
2. Evans (Seat)   153 pts
3. A McRae (Volkswagen)   133 pts
4. Laukkanen (Renault)   127 pts
5. Wearden (Honda)   102 pts

Paradoxically, although he took the title, Aghini did not have the honour of winning the most rallies, settling for a single victory at Lama. But, the master of his craft was happy to leave his main rivals, Dallavilla, Cunico and Navarra to squabble among themselves. Talk about leaving it to the last minute!

Hats off to Aghini

THE FORMER SANREMO WINNER, at the wheel of a Toyota WRC knew exactly how to exploit the rivalry between Navarra and Dallavilla, who although both in Subarus were driving for different teams.

No point in crying over what might have been. Andrea Aghini should have been contesting the world championship. He could have been an Italian driver in the Munari mould (7 world championship wins) or a Biasion (17 wins,) something this rally crazy country is still waiting for, as Piero Liatti, stuck on one win (1997 Monte Carlo) is yet to do it. Andrea Aghini had been so brilliant in the 1992 Sanremo that his team leader, Juha Kankkunen in second place, had not wanted to take the win which team orders were about to hand him. Then there was his 1993 Monte performance, when he set the first fastest time on the legendary Turini stage, ahead of all the gnarled old veterans who shook his hand and slapped him on the back as they welcomed him into the brotherhood of driving aces. Then Lancia retired and Aghini returned home to be called on occasionally by a team looking for a tarmac specialist to end the season. However, "Ago" did not give up driving and without sulking or cursing the rotten hand he had been dealt, he turned his attention to the Italian championship; a great series, perhaps the most competitive in Europe and therefore on the face of the planet. Just about anything goes, as in the world championship, with WRC four wheel drive machines from last year as well as two litre kit cars. Only some minor details are different. For example, Aghini has a Corolla which shares its silhouette with those factory cars used by Auriol or Sainz in the world championship, but the electrics are completely different. This has no real effect on what is a good series. The whingers will say it is expensive, but it must be worth doing as it attracts such a strong field of privateers, of which there are many in Italy; a tradition that goes back a long way.

But a championship is only as good as its competitors and this one certainly came up to the mark. No fewer than five drivers had the pleasure of being crowned, their heads still sweating from the effort of victory. Navarra (Subaru) kicked off the season at Clocco; Cunico (Ford) responded on the next round; Dallavilla (Subaru) picked up the win at Piamcavallo; Aghini (Toyota) woke up in San Marino followed shortly by Medeghini (Ford.) This rounded off the half season and any one of the five could win the title! One at a time, Medeghini at Libourne, Cunico at Lama and Dallavilla at Alpi Orientali tried to break away. But with all this five sided in-fighting there were bound to be a few incidents and alarums. This left Navarra with his one win and regular place finishes looking the most likely winner, with just two rounds to go. On the Messina rally, he knew a third place was all he needed but, locked in a duel with Dallavilla in a very competitive Subaru, he forgot the future while thinking of the present and threw it away in a ditch. His only chance was to leave the opposition a long way behind on the Sanremo, hoping that a few world championship regulars might get between him and his two rivals, Aghini and Dallavilla. But Navarra failed in his objective, leaving Aghini to pick up the title.

In the two litre class, Paolo Andreucci won pretty much as he pleased.

Classification:
1. Aghini (Toyota)	107	pts
2. Dallavilla (Subaru)	100	pts
3. Navarra (Subaru)	98.5	pts
4. Cunico (Ford)	92	pts
5. Medeghini (Ford)	79	pts

It is the not a French championship, but it certainly looks like one. In both Spain and Portugal, the PSA group was dominant with Puras' Xsara untroubled by Climent's Megane and Lopes 306 dealing easily with the Corolla of Campos.

It's a French thing...

A GOOD DOUBLE WIN FOR THE FRENCH constructors on the roads and tracks of the Iberian peninsula. Thanks to Jesus Puras, Citroen won easily in Spain, while Adruzilo Lopes did the job for Peugeot in Portugal.

His first name is Jesus, but perhaps he could be re-baptised and simply called God. Because Puras often believed he was alone on earth as he helped himself to the fruits of success, sharing them with no man. In Tenerife, he was out in front in his old ZX. In Cantabria, he got his hands on a Xsara, avoided the walls and won again. Llanes? Orense? Aviles? Asturias? Still Puras and we had only just reached the halfway point of the season. Jesus Puras was already the Spanish champion. He did not have it entirely his own way however. On the first event, the Corte Ingles, there was a stranger in town by the name of Gilles Panizzi and it looked like an interesting fight between the 306 and the ZX. But Puras had a puncture right at the start, giving Panizzi the chance to pull away and keep an eye on the Spaniard's crazy chase during which he made up a minute. It was not enough. No joy

either in Catalunya and the world championship round. Naturally Puras is out to impress, but his Citroen breaks too early. The same problem hit him on the non-championship Sanremo rally. Not one to mince his words, Puras had a right go at Frequelin and Citroen France who made him use a Velizy-prepared Xsara when he had wanted to use the Spanish-built car which had never failed him. Puras did not win in the Sierra Moreno either, because the event was cancelled, as the organisers had not settled their bill with the federation. Neither did he win in Vigo, as this too was scrubbed a few hours before it was due to start as oil had been spread liberally over the stages by some disgruntled local drivers whose licences were not quite correct. He allowed Manuel Muniente and his 306 to win in Corogne and Salou and Luis Climent took a win with his Maxi Megane at Lugo, simply because Puras had not been entered.

The evidence is clear for all to see: Puras is a large fish in a small pond in Spain. He is one of those quick tempered Latins, most at home on tarmac. It is only his difficult and egocentric nature which seems to come between him and an international career. With a world Group N title in 1994 and the two litre world championship wrapped up with Seat in 1996, he should have gone further. At 35 he is not quite yet too old for that to happen.

In Portugal, it was Peugeot rather than Citroen that did the winning, offering the PSA group a nice double header in the Iberian peninsula. Adruzilo Lopes and his 306 Maxi had a relatively easy time,

mainly thanks to the superiority of the chassis on tarmac. Nevertheless, he had to wait until the end of the championship to be sure of the title, as he was threatened by Miguel Campos. His Mitsubishi Carisma acquired sufficient points to dominate in Group N. Lopes took the lead in the penultimate round, the Algarve, which in a strange break with tradition was run on asphalt. He then closed the book in the final event, the Dao Lafoes rally. It was still open, but he made sure of things by setting fastest times on all twelve stages. Lopes won more rallies than anyone else; five victories split four to one, tarmac to loose. That's what you call a job well done.

SPAIN
Classification:
(before the Madrid rally:)

1. Puras (Citroen)	1416	pts
2. Climent (Renault)	1146	pts
3. J. Azcona (Citroen)	1015	pts
4. Muniente (Peugeot)	932	pts
5. Vallejo (Citroen)	904	pts

PORTUGAL
Classification:

1. Lopes (Peugeot)	1439.5	pts
2. Campos (Mitsubishi)	1270.5	pts
3. Macedo (Renault)	1201	pts
4. Azeredo (Renault)	1136.5	pts
5. Peres (Peugeot)	1125	pts

DRIVERS WHO HAVE WON WORLD CHAMPIONSHIP RALLIES FROM 1973 TO 1998

DRIVER	NO. of wins	RALLIES
Andrea Aghini (I)	1	1992 I
Pentti Airikkala (SF)	1	1989 GB
Markku Alen (SF)	20	1975 P 1976 SF 1977 P **1978** P-SF-I 1979 SF 1980 SF 1981 P 1983 F-I 1984 F 1986 I-USA 1987 P-GR-SF 1988 S-SF-GB
Alain Ambrosino (F)	1	1988 CI
Ove Andersson (S)	1	1975 EAK
Jean-Claude Andruet (F)	3	1973 MC 1974 F 1977 I
Didier Auriol (F)	18	1988 F 1989 F 1990 MC-F-I 1991 I 1992 MC-F-GR-RA-SF-AUS 1993 MC **1994** F-RA-I 1995 F 1998 E
Fulvio Bacchelli (I)	1	1977 NZ
Bernard Béguin (F)	1	1987 F
Miki Biasion (I)	17	1986 RA 1987 MC-RA-I **1988** P-EAK-GR-USA-I **1989** MC-P-EAK-GR-I 1990 P-RA 1993 GR
Stig Blomqvist (S)	11	1973 S 1977 S 1979 S 1982 S-I 1983 GB **1984** S-GR-NZ-RA-CI
Walter Boyce (CDN)	1	1973 USA
Richard Burns (GB)	2	1998 GB
Ingvar Carlsson (S)	2	1989 S-NZ
Roger Clark (GB)	1	1976 GB
Gianfranco Cunico (I)	1	1993 I
Bernard Darniche (F)	7	1973 MA 1975 F 1977 F 1978 F 1979 MC-F 1981 F
François Delecour (F)	4	1993 P-F-E 1994 MC
Ian Duncan (EAK)	1	1994 EAK
Per Eklund (S)	1	1976 S
Mikael Ericsson (S)	2	1989 RA-SF
Kenneth Eriksson (S)	6	1987 CI 1991 S 1995 S-AUS 1997 S-NZ
Tony Fassina (I)	1	1979 I
Guy Fréquelin (F)	1	1981 RA
Sepp Haider (A)	1	1988 NZ
Kyosti Hamalainen (SF)	1	1977 SF
Mats Jonsson (S)	2	1992 S 1993 S
Harry Kallstom (S)	1	1976 GR
Juha Kankkunen (SF)	21	1985 EAK-CI **1986** S-GR-NZ **1987** USA-GB 1989 AUS 1990 AUS **1991** EAK-GR-SF-AUS-GB 1992 P **1993** EAK-RA-SF-AUS-GB 1994 P
Anders Kullang (S)	1	1980 S
Piero Liatti (I)	1	1997 MC
Colin McRae (GB)	16	1993 NZ 1994 NZ-GB **1995** NZ-GB 1996 GR-I-E 1997 EAK-F-I-AUS-GB 1998 P-F-GR
Timo Makinen (SF)	4	1973 SF-GB 1974 GB 1975 GB
Tommi Makinen (SF)	15	1994 SF **1996** S-EAK-RA-SF-AUS 1997 P-E-RA-SF **1998** S-RA-SF-I-AUS
Shekhar Mehta (EAK)	5	1973 EAK 1979 EAK 1980 EAK 1981 EAK 1982 EAK
Hannu Mikkola (SF)	18	1974 SF 1975 MA-SF 1978 GB 1979 P-NZ-GB-CI 1981 S-GB 1982 SF-GB **1983** S-P-RA-SF 1984 P 1987 EAK
Joaquim Moutinho (P)	1	1986 P
Michèle Mouton (F)	4	1981 I 1982 P-GR-BR
Sandro Munari (I)	7	1974 I-CDN 1975 MC 1976 MC-P-F **1977** MC
Jean-Pierre Nicolas	5	1973 F 1976 MA 1978 MC-EAK-CI
Alain Oreille (F)	1	1989 CI
Rafaelle Pinto (P)	1	1974 P
Jean Ragnotti (F)	3	1981 MC 1982 F 1985 F
Jorge Recalde (RA)	1	1988 RA
Walter Röhrl (D)	14	1975 GR 1978 GR-CDN **1980** MC-P-RA-I **1982** MC-CI 1983 MC-GR-NZ 1984 MC 1985 I
Bruno Saby (F)	2	1986 F 1988 MC-NZ
Carlos Sainz (E)	22	**1990** GR-NZ-SF-GB 1991 MC-P-F-NZ-RA **1992** EAK-NZ-E-GB 1994 GR 1995 MC-P-E 1996 RI 1997 GR-RI 1998 MC-NZ
Timo Salonen (SF)	11	1977 CDN 1980 NZ 1981 CI **1985** P-GR-NZ-RA-SF 1986 SF-GB 1987 S
Armin Schwarz (D)	1	1991 E
Kenjiro Shinozuka (J)	2	1991 CI 1992 CI
Joginder Singh (EAK)	2	1974 EAK 1976 EAK
Patrick Tauziac (F)	1	1990 CI
Jean-Luc ThÈrier (F)	5	1973 P-GR-I 1974 USA 1980 F
Henri Toivonen (SF)	3	1980 GB 1985 GB 1986 MC
Ari Vatanen (SF)	10	1980 GR **1981** GR-BR-SF 1983 EAK 1984 SF-I-GB 1985 MC-S
Bjorn Waldegaard (S)	16	1975 S-I 1976 I 1977 EAK-GR-GB 1978 S **1979** GR-CDN 1980 CI 1982 NZ 1983 CI 1984 EAK 1986 EAK-CI 1990 EAK
Achim Warmbold (D)	2	1973 PL-A
Franz Wittmann (A)	1	1987 NZ

A: Austria - AUS: Australia - BR: Brazil - CDN: Canada - CI: Ivory Coast - E: Spain - EAK : Kenya - F: France - GB: Great Britain - GR: Greece - I: Italy - MA: Marocco - MC: Monte-Carlo - NZ: New Zealand - P: Portugal - PL: Poland - RA: Argentina - RI: Indonesia - S: Sweden - SF: Finland - USA : United States of America